From Politics
to Piety

7.27

From Politics
to Piety

THE EMERGENCE
OF PHARISAIC JUDAISM

Jacob Neusner

Brown University
Providence, Rhode Island

Prentice-Hall, Inc., *Englewood Cliffs, New Jersey*

1037

ISBN: P 0–13–331439–1
       C 0–13–331447–2

Library of Congress Catalog Card Number: 72–3822

Printed in the United States of America

10 9 8 7 6 5 4 3 2 1

PRENTICE-HALL INTERNATIONAL, INC., *London*
PRENTICE-HALL OF AUSTRALIA, PTY. LTD., *Sydney*
PRENTICE-HALL OF CANADA, LTD., *Toronto*
PRENTICE-HALL OF INDIA PRIVATE LIMITED, *New Delhi*
PRENTICE-HALL OF JAPAN, INC., *Tokyo*

ACKNOWLEDGMENTS

The author is indebted to the following for permission to reprint copyrighted material:

The Jewish Theological Seminary of America for permission to reprint Morton Smith, "Palestinian Judaism in the First Century," *Israel: Its Role in Civilization,* ed., Moshe Davis. pp. 75–76, 78–81. © 1956 by The Jewish Theological Seminary of America.

Schocken Books, Inc., for permission to reprint Elias Rickerman, *The Maccabees,* pp. 157, 162, 174, and 163–165. © 1962 by Schocken Books, Inc.

Division of Christian Education of the National Council of Churches of Christ in the United States of America for permission to reprint translations of New Testament scriptures from *The Oxford Annotated Bible with Apocrypha. Revised Standard Version.* © 1946 by Division of Christian Education of the National Council of the Churches of Christ in the United States of America.

The President and Fellows of Harvard College for permission to reprint passages from *Josephus, with an English Translation by H. St. J. Thackeray. I. The Life. II. The Jewish War, Books I–III. Josephus with an English Translation by Ralph Marcus. VII. Jewish Antiquities, Books XII–XIV. Josephus with an English Translation by Ralph Marcus. VIII. Jewish Antiquities, Books XV–XVII. Josephus with an English Translation by Louis H. Feldman. IX. Jewish Antiquities, Books XVIII–XX.* [Copyright IX only.] © 1965 by the President and Fellows of Harvard College.

Yale University Press for permission to reprint *The Fathers According to Rabbi Nathan*, translated from the Hebrew by Judah Goldin, pp. 35–37. © 1955 by Yale University Press.

The cover illustrations are taken from Karl H. Kraeling, "The Synagogue at Dura," in *The Excavation at Dura Europa*, copyribht 1956 by Yale University Press. The illustrations are used courtesy of Dura Europas Publications, Yale University, New Haven, Conn. These illustrations may also be found in Erwin R. Goodenough, *Jewish Symbols in the Greco-Roman Period*, Vol. XI, "Symbolism in the Dura Synagogue." Bollingen Series XXXVII, Copyright © 1964 by Bollingen Foundation. Published by Bollingen Foundation and Princeton University Press.

for
Yochanan and Yocheved Muffs

Abbreviations

1 QS   Manual of Discipline

1 QSa   Appendix to 1 QS

b.   Babylonian Talmud

Ber.   Berakhot (Talmudic Laws on Blessings)

B.Q.   Bava Qamma ("First Gate," Civil Law)

Deut.   Deuteronomy

Ed.   'Eduyyot (Testimonies)

Eruv.   'Eruvin (Talmudic Laws of Sabbath Limits)

Git.   Gittin (Talmudic Laws of Divorce)

Hag.   Ḥagigah (Talmudic Laws of the Festal Sacrifice)

Jn.   John

Lev.   Leviticus

Lk.   Luke

M.   Mishnah (Code of Oral Torah Issued by Judah the Patriarch, *ca.* 200 A.D.)

Men.   Menaḥot (Talmudic Laws on the Cultic Meal Offerings)

Mk. Mark

Mt. Matthew

Num. Numbers

Par. Parah (Talmudic Laws of the Red Heifer Sacrifice)

Pes. Pesaḥim (Talmudic Laws of the Paschal Sacrifice)

Ps. Psalms

Qid. Qiddushin (Talmudic Laws of Betrothals)

Qoh. Qohelet (Ecclesiastes)

Shab. Shabbat (Talmudic Tractate of Sabbath Laws)

Shev. Shevi'it (Talmudic Laws on the Seventh Year)

Sot. Soṭah (Laws on Suspected Adulteress)

Suk. Sukkah (Laws of Tabernacles)

Ta. Ta'anit (Laws of Fasts)

Ter. Terumot (Laws of Heave Offerings)

Tos. Tosefta (Supplement to the Mishnah, Issued about 250 A.D.)

Uqs. 'Uqṣin (Laws of the Uncleanness of Stalks)

Yev. Yevamot (Laws of Levirate Marriage)

Chronology

The analysis that follows takes for granted knowledge of a number of important historical facts:

1. A Jewish dynasty, the Maccabees, ruled Palestine from *ca.* 165 to *ca.* 60 B.C.

2. The Romans supported King Herod, who took over from the last of the Maccabees, for nearly the whole of the rest of the first century B.C., and ruled directly thereafter.

3. In 66 A.D. the Jews revolted against Rome.

4. In 70 A.D. Rome retook Jerusalem, and the sanctuary there, the Temple, was destroyed.

5. In the aftermath of the war, the surviving Pharisees, led first by Yohanan ben Zakkai, then by the patriarch, Gamaliel II, founded in Yavneh, a quasi-political academy in which the powers of self-government left by Romans in Jewish hands were vested. The academy lasted from 70 to *ca.* 125 A.D.

6. In 132–135 a second revolt against Rome, led by the messiah-general, Bar Kokhba, produced greater disaster than the first.

7. Afterward, a new rabbinical academy-government was founded at Usha, in Galilee. The patriarch was Simeon b. Gamaliel, who ruled from *ca.* 140 to *ca.* 170 A.D., and was succeeded by his son, Judah.

The following dates are important for the understanding of our work:

166 B.C.	Revolt of Mattathias, founder of Maccabean dynasty
165–63 B.C.	Maccabees rule Jewish Palestine
142 B.C.	Simon Maccabee establishes independence
134–104 B.C.	Reign of John Hyrcanus
104–76 B.C.	Reign of Alexander Jannaeus, who fights Pharisees
76–67 B.C.	Reign of Alexandra Salome, who favors Pharisees
63 B.C.	Pompey takes Jerusalem for Rome, end of Maccabean rule
37–4 B.C.	Reign of Herod
ca. 30 B.C.–10 A.D.	Hillel and Shammai
ca. 1–70 A.D.	Houses of Shammai and Hillel
ca. 10–40 A.D.	Gamaliel I
ca. 30–66 A.D.	Simeon b. Gamaliel I
37 A.D.	Josephus born
ca. 50–90 A.D.	The Gospels written
66 A.D.	Revolt against Rome
70 A.D.	Jerusalem falls, Temple destroyed by Romans
70 A.D.	Yohanan b. Zakkai founds academy at Yavneh, with his disciples Eliezer b. Hyrcanus and Joshua b. Hananiah
ca. 75 A.D.	Josephus publishes *Jewish War*
ca. 80 A.D.	Gamaliel II heads academy at Yavneh, establishes his dynasty as patriarchal head of rabbinical government, and achieves Roman recognition as head of the Jewish community
ca. 90–135 A.D.	Aqiba dominates rabbinical movement
93 A.D.	Josephus publishes *Jewish Antiquities*
ca. 100 A.D.	Josephus writes the *Life*
ca. 125 A.D.	End of Yavneh academy, fall of Gamaliel II
132–135 A.D.	Bar Kokhba War
ca. 140 A.D.	Simeon b. Gamaliel II, son of Gamaliel II of Yavneh, reestablishes academy and patriarchal government at Usha
ca. 170–210 A.D.	Dominance of Simeon's son, Judah the Patriarch
ca. 200 A.D.	Promulgation of Mishnah
ca. 250 A.D.	Publication of Tosefta, supplementary traditions to Mishnah

ca. 400–450 A.D. Publication of the Palestinian Talmud, consisting of the Mishnah of Judah the Patriarch, and the *Gemara,* the record of the discussions on that Mishnah in the rabbinical academies of Palestine

ca. 500–600 A.D. Publication of the Babylonian Talmud, consisting of the Mishnah and *Gemara,* the record discussions on the Mishnah and other traditions of law and theology evolved in the rabbinical academies of Babylonia

Contents

Preface   xix

1
The Problem of the
Historical Pharisees_____1

The Sources   1

In the Aftermath
of Disaster   2

Theology   3

Polemics   4

Modern Scholarship   5

Who Were
the Pharisees?   7

2
Hillel _____ 13

Hillel's Importance   13

Hillel as Legislator   14

Hillel's Wise Sayings   19

The Legend
of Hillel's Rise to Power   23

Hillel Descends
from David   35

Hillel and Shammai   35

The Historical Hillel   41

3
Josephus's Pharisees:
"The Real Administrators
of the State" _____ 45

Josephus   45

The Pharisees of War   48

The Pharisees of Antiquities   54

The Pharisees
as Politicians   64

4
The Gospels' Pharisees:
"Brood of Vipers" _____ 67

Survey of the Gospels' Traditions
about the Pharisees   67

The Pharisees
and Ritual Purity   78

5
The Rabbinical Traditions
about the Pharisees _____ 81

An Overview   81

Pharisaic Law   82

The Missing Traditions   90

Attestations   92

Conclusion   95

6
Traditions of Yavneh
(70–125 A.D.) _____ 97

Yavneh   97

The Houses
of Shammai and Hillel   100

Some Yavnean Traditions   103

The Yavnean Stratum   121

7
Traditions of Usha
(140–170 A.D.) _____ 123

Usha   123

Some Ushan Traditions   124

The Ushan Stratum   134

After Usha: The Circle
of Judah the Patriarch (*ca.* 170–210 A.D.)   138

* 8
The Pharisees
in History _____ 143

Suggestions
for Further Reading _____ 155

Glossary _____ 157

Index of Biblical
and Talmudic Passages _____ 161

General Index _____ 165

Preface

While every history of ancient Judaism and Christianity gives a detailed picture of the Pharisees, none systematically and critically analyzes the traits and tendencies of the discrete sources combined to form such an account. Consequently, we have many theories but few facts, sophisticated theologies but uncritical, naive histories of Pharisaism which yield heated arguments unillumined by disciplined, reasoned understanding. Progress in the study of the growth of Pharisaic Judaism before 70 A.D. will depend upon accumulation of detailed knowledge and a determined effort to cease theorizing about the age. We must honestly attempt to understand not only what was going on in the first century, but also—and most crucially—*how* and *whether* we know anything at all about what was going on. "Theories and arguments should follow in the wake of laborious study, not guide it in their determining ways, however alluring these may look among the thickets and brush that cover the ground."[1]

Here you are invited to share the painful task of assessing difficult sources and criticizing the nature of extant information about the Pharisees before 70 A.D. At the outset, you may learn more than you wanted to know about the Pharisees, but the real reward of your labor ought to be mature

---

[1] G.R. Elton, in his review of F. Smith Fussner, *Tudor History and the Historians,* in *History and Theory,* 10, 2 (1971), p. 258.

skepticism about the nature of historical knowledge. "History is a skeptical, not a devotional study."[2] The concrete experience of practical skepticism is all I have to offer.

The price of that experience of historical method is a less coherent picture than we might like. The three sources of Pharisaism—Josephus, the Gospels, and the Talmudic traditions about pre-70 "rabbis," all of them shaped after 70 A.D.—cannot be moulded into a single continuous narrative. The picture drawn by the later rabbis, given in Chapters Two and Five through Seven, is not to be integrated into those composed, respectively, by Josephus and the Gospel writers. Each is treated by itself. Only at the end is an effort made to compose a cogent account, and this is limited to a few plausible generalities.

Since Hillel is the best-known of the pre-70 Pharisees, and predominates in the rabbinical traditions about the Pharisees before 70 A.D., we begin by asking what we know about the historical Hillel. As a contemporary of Jesus and the figure of comparable importance in Pharisaic Judaism, Hillel dominates the rabbinical traditions about the Pharisees before 70. The standard methods of historical criticism produce a completely negative result; the historical Hillel is virtually unavailable to us. By the normal canons of historical inquiry, we can say nothing at all about him. That does not mean the historical Pharisees have left no useful records, but rather that the available records have not been properly studied. The right questions have not been asked. Pertinent materials external to rabbinical literature—Josephus and the Gospels—have not been properly exploited.

Then, we shall review Josephus's references to the Pharisees. These consist primarily of a number of stories about the Pharisees as a political party in the time of the Maccabees, ca. 160–60 B.C. We shall compare what Josephus says about the Pharisees in his *War*, published ca. 75 A.D., with what he says 20 years later, in *Antiquities*. The main difference between the two accounts is the allegation, frequently repeated in the latter, that the Pharisees ran Jewish Palestine. Naturally, we wonder how Josephus discovered in 95 A.D. what he had not known in 75, and in seeking the answer we shall have to investigate the events of Josephus's life and times after 75, rather than those of early Maccabean times. Our inquiry will lead us to consider the later history of the Jews, after the Temple was destroyed in 70 A.D., in quest of the historical facts of the period while the Temple was still standing.

Third, we shall consider the stories and sayings concerning the Pharisees in the New Testament. Setting aside materials pertinent primarily to the inner life of the Church, on such themes as relations between Jesus and the Pharisees, the Pharisees and the trial and death of Jesus, and Paul's attitude

[2] *Ibid.*

to them, we shall find that beyond the polemic, the New Testament a few valuable facts about Pharisaic Judaism. It stresses the sorts of laws Pharisaic Judaism thought it important to keep, but it does not reveal detailed knowledge of what their observation meant.

Fourth, at greatest length, we shall examine some rabbinical traditions about the Pharisees, for these constitute the largest corpus of information. These traditions occur in documents edited between *ca.* 200 A.D. and *ca.* 600 A.D.: The Mishnah, or code of the Oral Torah, promulgated by Judah the Patriarch in *ca.* 200 A.D., the Tosefta, a collection of supplementary traditions pertinent to the Mishnah but excluded from it, compiled in *ca.* 250 A.D., the Palestinian Talmud's *Gemara,* or commentary on the Mishnah, deriving from *ca.* 400–450 A.D., and the Babylonian Talmud's *Gemara,* redacted, or edited, in *ca.* 500–600 A.D.

We shall first review the substance of the laws attributed to the Pharisees before 70 A.D., since it will quickly become evident that the legal agenda we should expect to find on the basis of the Gospels' descriptions of the Pharisees is precisely what we do find when we examine laws attributed to pre-70 Pharisees in the literature of their rabbinical successors. Then we shall ask: How can we isolate traditions from earlier times from those first known later on? Here I shall propose a theory of attestation and spell out its consequences in the subsequent chapters.

Having determined a time sequence in the formation of the rabbinical traditions about the Pharisees, we shall next examine the earliest stratum of traditions, that redacted at Yavneh between *ca.* 70 and *ca.* 125 A.D. Yavneh was the site of the academy founded by Yohanan b. Zakkai in the aftermath of the destruction of Jerusalem. The earliest effort to put into final form important traditions about the Pharisees was made there. Next we turn to the following important stratum, that of the Ushan academy, *ca.* 140–170 A.D., founded after the disastrous Bar Kokhba War, fought between *ca.* 132 and 135 A.D. Both major academies were created after, and in consequence of, major calamities, and in both cases the traditions of the Pharisees received considerable attention.

The analysis of rabbinical traditions about the pre-70 Pharisees concentrates on their form and structure; apart from legal materials, the themes of which I think reliably represent the laws of the historical Pharisees, we do not pay much attention to their content, such as religious ideals, moral teachings, and theological insights. For our purposes the most interesting problems are methodological and historical: how to recover accurate knowledge about what the Pharisaic sect really was like. While the ideas of the sect would be of interest, we must first ask whether we are merely reading anachronistic representations of those ideals by later authorities. Just as we are unable to say much about the theology of Pharisaic Judaism, so we shall quickly find that the wise sayings of Hillel, the stories of his rise to power, the history of Pharisaism composed at Usha, and similar, important elements of the rabbinical tradition, all tell us a great deal more about first and second century rabbinical Judaism, the politics of the academies, and the problems of the rabbis, than they do about the historical Pharisees before 70 A.D.

No source is historically useless. The problem is always to determine just what it is good for—what place, period, or master it accurately por-trays.

While the Pharisees have been and are much maligned, I am not in-terested in composing an apology for them. Apologetics, which is an honor-able part of the theological enterprise, has no place in the work of historians. But even if it did, the substance of the anti-Pharisaic polemic is such that historical inquiry can do little to verify or refute it. The New Testament portrays the Pharisees as a "brood of vipers," hypocrites, men who cared for externals but not for the spirit. I cannot find among sources now available to us evidence that will tell us whether the Pharisees were really hypocrites or actually sincere; whether they were a brood of vipers or a nest of doves; and whether they cared for the heart as much as for the belly. If we had diaries, we might reasonably assess whether a man said one thing to the world and another to himself—assuming he told the truth to his diary. But we do not have diaries, let alone other sorts of information about what people really thought. Since we cannot truly know whether the Pharisees were hypocrites or sincere, we might as well not wonder about it.

The problems before us are sufficiently complex to occupy our energies. They derive not from the apologetic enterprise but from historical inquiry. We want to know, first, whether and how we know anything at all, and second, the historical status of our knowledge—a middle range of issues, between naive credulousness or gullibility on one side, and the indifference to historical inquiry exhibited by friendly or hostile polemicists on the other.

Chapters Two and Five through Seven draw upon parts of my *The Rabbinic Traditions about the Pharises before 70 A.D. I. The Masters. II. The Houses. III. Conclusions* (Leiden: E.J. Brill, 1971). Chapter Eight is based upon my *Life of Yohanan ben Zakkai*, 2nd ed. (Leiden: E.J. Brill, 1969), and *Development of a Legend: Studies on the Traditions Concern-ing Yohanan ben Zakkai* (Leiden: E.J. Brill, 1970). My cordial thanks go to Professor John Wilson, Princeton University, Professor John Reeder, Brown University, and, especially, Mr. George Coy, my friend and editor at Prentice-Hall, for their sage editorial comments. My colleague and friend, Professor Horst R. Moehring, provided invaluable guidance on the Pharisees in Josephus and in the New Testament. I could not have undertaken this book without his assistance, which he has given generously. I profited from the counsel of Professors John Strugnell, Harvard University, Wayne A. Meeks, Yale University, and my teacher, Morton Smith, Columbia University. Professors W. Sibley Towner and Brevard S. Childs, Yale University gave important assistance in my studies on the *Rabbinic Traditions*. Mrs. Pat Vigneau, Professor David Goodblatt, and Mr. William Scott Green, all of Brown University, read the manuscript and helped clarify it. None of these friends bears the onus for errors of fact or judgment.

This work was completed during my tenure as a Fellow of the American Council of Learned Societies, which coincided with a sabbatical leave at Brown University. I am grateful for this support for my research. In addition, Brown University paid the costs of typing the manuscript and preparing the indexes, as well as numerous other research expenses. I appreciate my University's continuing, generous support for my research.

The dedication, to Professor Yochanan Muffs, Jewish Theological Seminary, and Mrs. Yocheved Muffs, Anti-Defamation League of B'nai B'rith, is a token of affection for old and beloved friends on the occasion of their second wedding anniversary.

Providence, Rhode Island   Jacob Neusner

1

The Problem of the
Historical Pharisees

The Sources

What do we know about the Pharisees before the destruction of Jerusalem in 70 A.D.? More important, how do we know anything about them at all?

Our task is to make critical use of three separate bodies of information: first, the historical narratives of Josephus, a Jewish historian who, between 75 and *ca.* 100 A.D., wrote the history of the Jews from the beginnings to the destruction of Jerusalem, including the war against Rome which had led to the destruction; second, biographical traditions about, and sayings attributed to, Jesus, assembled in the nascent Christian community between *ca.* 50 and *ca.* 90 A.D.; third, the laws and sayings attributed to pre-70 Pharisees by their successors and heirs, the rabbis of late first and second century Palestine.[1]

These separate sources are quite different in character. The first is a systematic, coherent historical narrative. The second is a well-edited col-

---

[1] A full account of the rabbinical materials is given in my *The Rabbinic Traditions about the Pharisees before 70 I. The Masters. II. The Houses. III. Conclusions* (Leiden: E. J. Brill, 1971). For pericopae in which Pharisees and Sadducees are juxtaposed, see Ellis Rivkin, "Defining the Pharisees: The Tannaitic Sources," *Hebrew Union College Annual,* 1970, pp. 205–49.

lection of stories and sayings. The third consists chiefly of laws, arranged by legal categories in codes and commentaries on those codes. Moreover, the purposes of the authors or compilers of the respective collections differ from one another.

Josephus was engaged in explaining to the Jewish world of his day that Rome was not at fault for the destruction of the Temple, and in telling the Roman world that the Jewish people had been misled, and therefore not to be held responsible for the terrible war.

The interest of the Gospels is not in the history of the Jewish people, but in the life and teachings of Jesus, to which that history supplies background.

The rabbinical legislators show no keen interest in narrative, biographical, or historical problems, but take as their task the promulgation of laws for the government and administration of the Jewish community.

The historical question we bring to the sources would have been remote and incomprehensible to all three, for we want to know what really happened. How accurate are our sources? Our measure of accuracy is historical reality. To what historical situation does a story testify? What apologetic or polemical purposes are reflected in the narrative? What is the history of a saying or story? Whose interest does it serve? What case does it help to make? We thus begin with a skepticism that does not characterize the ancient sources, and we are not perturbed by fundamentally negative results.

Much that we are told about the Pharisees reflects the situation, interests, and viewpoint of the teller, not of the historical Pharisees. The historical enterprise therefore promises modest results, for all we know about the historical Pharisees consists in what three interested parties have to tell us, which is in turn shaped by their beliefs and concerns. But that is always the difficulty in the study of the history of religious movements and leaders around whose teachings later controversies tend to focus, and to whose authority later disputes are referred. The study of the historical Pharisees therefore serves to illustrate a commonplace methodological difficulty. Consideration of these sometimes difficult sources may provide useful experience in analyzing other historical-religious sources as well.

In the Aftermath
of Disaster

The single most important event in the history of Judaism from the destruction of the Temple by the Babylonians in 586 B.C. to the conquest of Palestine by the Arabs in *ca.* 640 A.D. was the destruction of the Second Temple by the Romans in 70 A.D.

It was decisive not only because the political basis of Jewish community life had rested on the Temple government, but also because the religious life of the people had centered on the sacrificial cult. To be sure, small groups tended to refocus their life away from, and in opposition to, the Temple. But for the mass, the Temple represented the nexus between heaven and earth. God had revealed his will in the Torah—the revelation to Moses at Sinai—which contained numerous cultic laws. Those laws were kept in the Temple, where the daily sacrifices and the exact sacrificial technology represented a primary means by which Israel served their father in heaven. Destruction of the Second Temple therefore provided the point of contention for all parties who, in the aftermath, claimed to tell the Jews the meaning of the recent unhappy events and the way in which they now should live.

All of the several sources concerning pre-70 Pharisaic Judaism were shaped in response to the crisis of 70 A.D. With the Temple in ruins it was important to preserve and, especially, to interpret, the record of what had gone before. Josephus tells the story of the people and the great war. The Gospels record the climactic moment in Israel's supernatural life. The rabbis describe the party to which they traced their origin, and through which they claimed to reach back to the authority of Moses at Sinai. The issue in all three cases was: What is the meaning of the decisive history just passed?

To Josephus the answer is that Israel's welfare depends upon obedience to the laws of the Torah as expounded by the Pharisees and upon peaceful relationships with Rome.

The Gospels claim that, with the coming of the Messiah, the Temple ceased to enjoy its former importance, and those who had had charge of Israel's life—chief among them the priests, scribes, and Pharisees—were shown through their disbelief to have ignored the hour of their salvation. Their unbelief is explained in part by the Pharisees' hypocrisy and self-seeking.

The rabbis contend that the continuity of the Mosaic Torah is unbroken. Destruction of the Temple, while lamentable, does not mean Israel has lost all means of service to the Creator. The way of the Pharisees leads, without break, back to Sinai and forward to the rabbinical circle reforming at Yavneh. The Oral Torah revealed by Moses and handed on from prophet to scribe, sage, and rabbi remains in the hands of Israel. The legal record of pre-70 Pharisaism requires careful preservation because it remains wholly in effect.

Theology

The theological side to Pharisaic Judaism before 70 A.D., however, is not easily accessible, for the pre-70 beliefs, ideas, and values have been taken over and revised by the rabbinical masters after that time. We therefore cannot reliably claim that an idea first known to us in a later rabbinical document, from the third century and afterward, was originally both known and understood in the same way. George Foot Moore[2] accurately portrays the religion of the rabbis responsible for the documents he used in the composition of his picture. It would be more aptly titled "the Judaism of the rabbis of the late second and third centuries, more or less." That title is not meant to detract from the grandeur of Moore's achievement, but it ought to indicate exactly *whose* "Judaism" is under discussion.

For pre-70 Pharisaic Judaism, our sources of information tell little of theological interest. A number of books in the Apocrypha and Pseudepigrapha of the Old Testament are attributed to Pharisaic writers, but none of these documents positively identifies its author as a Pharisee. Secure attribution of a work can only be made when an absolutely peculiar characteristic of the possible author can be shown to be an essential element in the structure of the whole work. No reliance can be placed on elements which appear in only one or another episode, or which appear in several episodes but are secondary and detachable details. These may be accretions. Above all, motifs which are not certainly peculiar to one sect cannot prove that sect was the source. No available assignment of an apocryphal or pseudepigraphical book to a Pharisaic author can pass these tests. Most such attributions were made by scholars who thought that all pre-70 Palestinian Jews were either Sadducees, Pharisees, Essenes, members of the "Fourth Philosophy," or Zealots, and therefore felt obliged to attribute all supposedly pre-70 Palestinian Jewish works to one of these four groups. That supposition is untenable. I have therefore omitted all reference to apocryphal and pseudepigraphical literature. Perhaps when scholarly progress in the study of that literature permits, we may expand our conceptions about pre-70 Pharisaism.

But for now, the only reliable information derives from Josephus, the Gospels, and rabbinical literature, beginning with the Mishnah, the lawcode of Judah the Patriarch. As is clear, none of these gives an accurate account of Pharisaic theology before 70. Josephus concentrates on political questions, and the theological teachings to which he does allude are primarily of a general philosophical character. The Gospels have no interest in Pharisaic theology, and rabbinical attributions of theological sayings to the Pharisaic masters before 70, which are not likely to be reliable, constitute little more than a collection of sage comments, commonplaces of practical wisdom.

Polemics

The historical task is made still more complicated by the long history of abuse to which the Pharisees have been subjected in Western civilization. The New Testament's negative picture was widely reproduced in Christian

[2] George Foot Moore, *Judaism in the First Centuries of the Christian Era. The Age of the Tannaim* (Cambridge: Harvard University Press, 1927).

preaching, writing, and scholarship. To the present day one will find the Pharisees described in exactly the polemical spirit of the Gospels, as if the synoptic writers had intended to write an objective, critical history, not a highly partisan caricature. "Pharisee" became a synonym for hypocrite, and "pharisaic" for formalism or self-righteousness. Thus these definitions:[3]

> *Pharisaic:* Resembling the Pharisees in being strict in doctrine and ritual, without the spirit of piety; laying stress upon the outward show of religion and morality, and assuming superiority on that account; hypocritical; formal; self-righteous.
>
> *Pharisaism:* The character and spirit of the Pharisees; hypocrisy; formalism; self-righteousness.
>
> *Pharisee:* One of an ancient Jewish sect distinguished by their strict observance of the traditional and written law, and by their pretensions to superior sanctity. A person of this disposition; a self-righteous person; a formalist; a hypocrite.

Lexicography in the service of an anti-Judaic Christian theology thus accurately reproduces the polemic of the Gospels.

These definitions of Pharisee and Pharisaic are part of the cultural background of the West, an aspect of the anti-Semitism nurtured by Christian theology of a certain sort. They cannot be allowed to influence the issues of our inquiry. We want to get behind these cultural artifacts, which are unrelated to the historical task.

Naturally, on the Jewish side, a contrary polemic was not lacking. Since rabbinical traditions contain numerous stories and sayings attributed to Pharisaic masters of the period before 70 A.D., it was easy for Jewish scholarship to demonstrate not only the theological animus, but also the historical incompetence of those Christian scholars of ancient and modern times who ignored important parts of the Pharisaic record. Hillel, a near-contemporary of Jesus, and the most important figure in pre-70 Pharisaism according to the rabbinical traditions, is credited with the aphorism, "What is hateful to yourself, do not do to your neighbor. That is the entire Torah. All the rest is commentary. Now go forth and learn." He is also made to say, "If I am not for myself, who will be for me? But when I am for myself, what am I? And if not now, when?" These and similar sayings are routinely cited as evidence that Pharisees were not hypocrites, formalists, or self-righteous men.

Modern Scholarship

Religious and theological disputes have seriously impeded the study of pre-70 Pharisaism. The history of modern scholarship on the Pharisees

---

[3] *Shorter Oxford English Dictionary* (3rd rev. ed.; Oxford: Clarendon Press, 1955), pp. 1485–86.

begins in the early nineteenth century, when Talmudists with university training encountered the anti-Pharisaic, anti-Judaic, and frequently anti-Semitic attitudes of Christian scholars in universities, who carried out polemical tasks of Christian theology in the guise of writing academic history. The Jewish historians then undertook the defense.

Two polemical themes recur in their writings. First, the Christians' account of the Pharisees ignores rabbinic sources, and is therefore incomplete. The Christian scholars do not know the rabbinical literature, therefore whatever they say may be discounted because of their "ignorance." Second, the Pharisees were the very opposite of what Christians say about them.

The former polemic produced the Christian response that the rabbinical materials are not reliable because they are "late" or "tendentious" (as if the Gospels were not!). Many Christian scholars drew back from using rabbinic materials, or relied on what they presumed to be accurate secondary accounts, because they were intimidated by the claims of the Jewish opposition as to the difficulty of proper understanding, and because they had slight opportunity to study the materials with knowledgeable scholars of Judaism.

The latter polemic—to prove the Pharisees the opposite of what had been said of them—was all too successful. When Christian scholars became persuaded that the earlier Christian view had been incorrect, they took up the polemic in favor of the Pharisees. They relied on Jewish scholarship, and retained its uncritical attitude toward the Talmudic materials. Consequently, sources on both sides were more often cited as facts than analyzed as problems. We commonly find a source cited without attention to how it is supposed to prove the "fact" it purportedly contains. Systematic and disciplined analysis of texts is rare, allusion to unexamined texts commonplace.

Reservations about the method and results of previous scholars should not be taken as evidence that their work is utterly worthless. But all previous studies of the Pharisees are seriously inadequate because, in general, the historical question has been asked too quickly and answered uncritically. The fault lies in the false presumption that nearly all sources, appearing in any sort of document, early, late, or medieval, contain accurate historical information about the men and events of which they speak.

Historians are further to be blamed for allowing the theologians to set the issue: Were the Pharisees really hypocrites? The issues concerning the nineteenth-century Jewish scholars were: What shall we say in response to the Christian theological critique of Pharisaism? How shall we disprove the allegations of the Christians' holy books? On the Christian side, there were few "historians" worthy of the name, for most served the Church and not the cause of accurate and unbiased historical knowledge. Since the Christian theological scholars established the agenda, the Jewish scholars can hardly be condemned for responding to it, especially when contemporary anti-Semitism was both expressed and aided by the Christian scholarly assessment of Pharisaism. In fact, the European Jewish scholars turn out to have been fighting for the lives of the Jews of their own day and place. They lost that fight.

The history of scholarship on the Pharisees thus cannot be divorced from the history of Judaism and of Christianity in the nineteenth and twentieth centuries, from the sociology of the Jews in Europe and the U.S., and from the interrelationships between the two religious traditions. It is not our intention to describe the course of those complex and interrelated histories. Rather, we shall consider the three important sources of information on pre-70 Pharisaism to see what can be learned from each.

Our first problem is of method, our second, of historical result. The historical-critical approach followed here is revolutionary only in its application to the study of Pharisaism. In the study of nearly all other aspects of the history and culture of antiquity—whether in Classics, or History, or Biblical, or Ancient Near Eastern studies—one attitude predominates: You do not take at face value what a source purports to reveal. You ask, *Cui bono?* Whose interest is served by a story, a law, or a saying? What is the bias, the polemical intent of an author? These things must be taken into account in assessing the historical usefulness of every source. Our task thus is not to invent or to elucidate problems of historical method. It is merely to close the culture gap of approximately two centuries, between the critical study of nearly all other aspects of religious history in antiquity and the uncritical treatment of the problem of the Pharisees.

Who Were the Pharisees?

At the outset of our inquiry it is best that we seek perspective on the Pharisaic sect in its own setting. Josephus tells us that "more than 6,000 Pharisees" refused to take an oath of loyalty to Herod:

> There was also a group of Jews priding itself on its adherence to ancestral custom and claiming to observe the laws of which the Deity approves, and by these men, called Pharisees, the women of the court [of Herod] were ruled. These men were able to help the king greatly because of their foresight, and yet they were obviously intent upon combating and injuring him. At last when the whole Jewish people affirmed by an oath that it would be loyal to Caesar and to the king's government, these men, over six thousand in number, refused to take this oath, and when the king punished them with a fine, Pheroras' wife paid the fine for them. In return for her friendliness they foretold— for they were believed to have foreknowledge of things through God's appearances to them—that by God's decree Herod's throne would be

taken from him, both from himself and his descendants, and the royal power would fall to her and Pherora and to any children that they might have....[4]

What was the position of these 6,000 Pharisees in relationship to the mass of the Jewish population?

Morton Smith, the great historian of antiquity, points out that the man who was a Pharisee was not primarily a Pharisee all the time. He presumably played many roles in society. Gamaliel is described in Acts 5:34 as a Pharisee in the council of the Temple. Was he appointed to the council because he was a Pharisee, and thus represented the party or sect there? Or was he a Pharisee who also happened for some other reason, perhaps social distinction or political and economic power, to be appointed in the Temple? Was he then a Temple councillor who also happened to be a Pharisee? What was the meaning of "being a Pharisee" in the lives of various sorts of people? It seems most likely that to be a Pharisee was not a profession, but an avocation.

Pharisaism was, in terms of ancient civilization, a sect within the "philosophy" of Judaism. Smith stresses:

> ...Judaism to the ancient world was a philosophy. That world had no general term for *religion*. It could speak of a particular system of rites (a cult or an initiation), or a particular set of beliefs (doctrines or opinions), or a legal code, or a body of national customs or traditions; but for the peculiar synthesis of all these which we call a "religion," the one Hellenistic word which came closest was "philosophy." So when Judaism first took shape and became conscious of itself and its own peculiarity in the Hellenized world of the later Persian Empire, it described itself with the Hellenic term meaning the wisdom of its people (Deut. 4:6). To the success of this concept within Judaism the long roll call of the wisdom literature bears witness. Further, the claim was accepted by the surrounding world. To those who admired Judaism it was "the cult of wisdom" (for so we should translate the word "philosophy" which they used to describe it), and to those who disliked it was "atheism," which is simply the other side of the coin, the regular term of abuse applied to philosophy by its opponents.[5]

The Pharisees claimed to be authoritative because they taught a philosophy that derived from Moses at Sinai. They therefore preserved a "chain of tradition" reaching back from their own day to the authority of remote antiquity. Their piety was centered on the revelation of Moses. Smith says:

4 Josephus, *Jewish Antiquities* 17:41–4, trans. Ralph Marcus (Cambridge: Harvard University Press, 1963), pp. 391, 393.

5 Morton Smith, "Palestinian Judaism in the First Century," in *Israel: Its Role in Civilization*, ed. Moshe Davis (New York: Harper Row, Publishers, 1956), pp. 67–81.

It is...not surprising that Jews living, as Palestinian Jews did, in the Greco-Roman world, and thinking of their religion as the practice of wisdom, should think of the groups in their society which were distinguished by peculiar theories and practices as different schools of the national philosophy.

Their claim to authority was put in the form of a chain of successors by whom the true philosophy had been handed down. Elias Bickerman...[6] has demonstrated the parallel between this list [below, p. 104] and the list alleged by the philosophic schools, and has remarked that the Greek and Pharisaic lists differed from those of the priestly "philosophies" of the barbarians in being lists of teachers, not of ancestors. He also mentions, apropos of the "houses" of Hillel and Shammai, the fact that "house of so-and-so" is a regular form of reference to a philosophic school founded by so-and-so; and he showed that both the Greek and the Jewish philosophic schools justified their peculiar teachings by claiming accurate tradition from an authoritative master.[7]

Thus Palestinian Judaism overall, and the Pharisaic sect in particular, are to be seen as Jewish modes of a common, international cultural "style" known as Hellenism. To see Palestinian Judaism outside of its context within world civilization is to misinterpret the meaning of its accomplishments. The Jews were not an isolated or provincial people, and their "philosophy" was not incomprehensible, at least in form, to the rest of civilized mankind. The Jews, on the contrary, responded to the challenge of Hellenism by shaping a uniquely Jewish form of that common culture. Nor was this merely in generalities. The Pharisees, for one, exhibited numerous traits familiar to Hellenistic culture, as Smith points out:

Not only was the theory of the Pharisaic school that of a school of Greek philosophy, but so were its practices. Its teachers taught without pay, like philosophers; they attached to themselves particular disciples who followed them around and served them, like philosophers; they looked to gifts for support, like philosophers; they were exempt from taxation, like philosophers; they were distinguished in the street by their walk, speech, and peculiar clothing, like philosophers; they practiced and praised asceticism, like philosophers; and finally—what is, after all the meat of the matter—they discussed the questions philosophers discussed and reached the conclusions philosophers reached.

Here there is no need to argue the matter, for Professor Wolfson, in his...classic study of Philo,[8] has demonstrated at length the pos-

---

6 Elias Bickerman, "La Chaine de la tradition pharisienne," *Revue biblique,* 59, 1952, pp. 44–54.

7 Smith, "Palestinian Judaism in the First Century," pp. 79–80.

8 Harry A. Wolfson, *Philo* (Cambridge: Harvard University Press, 1948), 2 vol.

sibility of paralleling a philosophic system point by point from the opinions of the Rabbis. Now one, or two, or two dozen parallels might be dismissed as coincidental: all men, by virtue of mere humanity, are similar and life presents them with similar problems; it is not surprising, therefore, that they should often and independently reach the same answers.

But parallels of terminology are another matter, and here we come...to Professor Lieberman's demonstration that some of the most important terms of Rabbinic Biblical exegesis have been borrowed from the Greek.[9] This is basic.... The existence of such borrowings can be explained only by a period of profound Hellenization, and once the existence of such a period has been hypothecated it is plausible to attribute to it also the astounding series of parallels which Professor Wolfson has shown to exist between the content of philosophic and Rabbinic thought.

In sum, then, the discoveries and research of the past twenty-five years have left us with a picture of Palestinian Judaism in the first century far different from that conceived by earlier students of the period. We now see a Judaism which had behind it a long period of thoroughgoing Hellenization—Hellenization modified, but not thrown off, by the revival of nationalism and nationalistic and antiquarian interest in native tradition and classic language (an interest itself typically Hellenistic). As the Greek language had permeated the whole country, so Greek thought, in one way or another, had affected the court and the commons, the Temple...the school and the synagogue.

If there was any such thing, then, as an "orthodox Judaism," it must have been that which is now almost unknown to us, the religion of the average "people of the land." But the different parts of the country were so different, such gulfs of feeling and practice separated Idumea, Judea, Caesarea, and Galilee, that even on this level there was probably no more agreement between them than between any one of them and a similar area in the Diaspora. And in addition to the local differences, the country swarmed with special sects, each devoted to its own tradition. Some of these, the followings of particular prophets, may have been spontaneous revivals of Israelite religion as simple as anything in Judges. But even what little we know of these prophets suggests that some of them, at least, taught a complex theology. As for the major philosophic sects—the Pharisees, Sadducees, and Essenes—the largest and ultimately the most influential of them, the Pharisees, numbered only about 6,000, had no real hold either on the government or on the masses of the people, and was, as were the others, profoundly Hellenized.

---

9 Saul Lieberman, *Greek in Jewish Palestine* (New York: Jewish Theological Seminary of America, 1942); *Hellenism in Jewish Palestine* (New York: Jewish Theological Seminary of America, 1950).

This period of Palestinian Jewish history, then, is the successor to one marked by great receptivity to outside influences. It is itself characterized by original developments of those influences. These developments, by their variety, vigor, and eventual significance, made this small country during this brief period the seedbed of the subsequent religious history of the Western world.[10]

We learn from Smith's characterization that the Pharisees were a small group within Palestinian Judaism, a philosophical school with a particular set of beliefs and religious practices. They claimed the right to rule all the Jews by virtue of their possessing the "Oral Torah" of Moses, that is, the body of traditions not written in Scriptures, but revealed to Moses at Mount Sinai along with the written Torah. They referred to a list of masters extending back to Moses, whom they later called "our rabbi." In their own setting, however, the Pharisees were much like any other Hellenistic philosophical school or sect.

Their importance in later times derives from two facts. First, they play a large role in the Gospels' accounts of the life of Jesus. Second, they produced the rabbinical masters who, after 70 A.D., defined the law and doctrine that became normative for the Judaic tradition. Judaism as it is now known begins with the Pharisees of the two centuries before the destruction of Jerusalem and the Temple in 70 A.D.

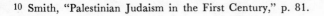

10 Smith, "Palestinian Judaism in the First Century," p. 81.

2

Hillel

Hillel's Importance

Hillel's name predominates in the rabbinical traditions about the Pharisees. Indeed, the greater part of those traditions deal with him, the party of his followers, called the House of Hillel, and of their opponents within Pharisaism, Shammai and the House of Shammai.

Hillel was a near-contemporary of Jesus. The dates commonly assigned to him are *ca.* 50 B.C. to *ca.* 10 A.D. Some of his teachings, moreover, are in spirit and even in exact wording close to the teachings of Jesus. Such a well-known saying as the Golden Rule is attributed to Hillel in negative form: "What is hateful to yourself do not do to your neighbor. That is the entire Torah. All the rest is commentary. Now go forth and learn." That saying went from country to country and from culture to culture, always being attributed to the leading sage or wise man of the place. It is a virtually universal teaching of wisdom, and its attribution to Hillel tells us that he was regarded as the supreme authority within the Pharisaic movement.

Part of the reason for Hillel's predominance is that his followers took over the leadership of Pharisaic Judaism from the followers of Shammai. After 70 A.D. at Yavneh, adherents of the House of Hillel were in charge of the formation of traditions about pre-70 times, just as they controlled the legal decisions of their own place and time.

Another part of the reason ought to be the historical importance of Hillel in his own day. Hillel evidently transformed the Pharisees from a political party to a table-fellowship sect. Josephus's stories about the Pharisees before Hillel's time consistently persent the group as a political force. Both the Gospels' and the Talmudic traditions about the Pharisees after his time portray them as a religious sect characterized by stress on careful tithing and maintenance of the cultic purity laws outside of the Temple, in their own homes. Since these pictures surround Hillel chronologically, and since he is the most important figure in the rabbinical tradition, it may well be that he transformed Pharisaism from a political party to a circle of pious sectarians.

But the rabbinical traditions about Hillel do not describe that "revolution"; it is merely our supposition that an important change took place in his time. His responsibility for it is a further conjecture.

Hillel as Legislator

To be sure, Hillel is represented as a legislator who not only interpreted existing statutes, but made new and important changes in the law. His most important ordinance follows. The Scriptural rule is that the advent of the Seventh Year in the septennial cycle carries with it remission of all debts. In consequence, people would not lend money to those in need, for fear they would not get it back. Hillel accommodated the law to the conditions of everyday life by creating a legal way out of the remission of debts by the Seventh Year. If the lender deposited a certificate, called the *prozbul,* in which the court took over the debts and preserved them from being annulled in the Seventh Year, then the debts would remain valid. Hence people could supply necessary small loans. The Scriptures refer to individuals ("Whatever of yours that is with your brother") but do not refer to property in the hands of the court ("Yours, not the court's").

> A. *Whatever of yours that is with your brother your hand should release* (Deut. 15:3)—but not he who gives his mortgages to the court.
> B. On this basis, they said
> C. Hillel ordained the *prozbul.*
> D. On account of the order of the world.
> E. That he saw the people, that they held back from lending to one another and transgressed what is written in the Torah.
> F. He arose and ordained the *prozbul.*
> G. And this is the formula of the *prozbul*: "I give to you, so-and-so and so-and-so, the judges in such-and-such place, every debt which I have, that I may collect it whenever I like," and the judges seal below, or the witnesses.[1]

[1] Sifré Deut. 113.

First comes the anonymous exegesis on which the *prozbul,* the document circumventing remission of debts in the Seventh Year, allegedly is based: debts in the hands of a court are not released by the advent of the sabbatical year. The rest of the pericope seems to depend upon the exegesis. In fact parts C-D and E-F do not.

Part B suggests that Hillel ordained the *prozbul* on the basis of the Scriptural exegesis, while part E gives another, different, reason, not based upon scriptural exegesis at all, but upon a wordplay on *order/ordain* in verbal and nominative forms. Part C is a simple, stock phrase report of the whole matter. It could have stood with either part D or part B, but parts B and D make one another redundant.

The "historical event," part E, on which the *prozbul* is based poses a problem, for the same conditions that provoked the *prozbul* in Hillel's time surely pertained for many centuries. How can one explain why in *just* Hillel's time the people discovered the "evil impulse" described in Deut. 15:9–10? Part E actually is a "historical" paraphrase of Deut. 15:9–10:

> Take heed lest there be a base thought in your heart and you say, "The Seventh Year, the year of release is near," and your eye be hostile to your poor brother and you give him nothing.... You shall give to him freely...because for this the Lord your God will bless you.... For the poor will never cease out of the land.

The absence of an explicit reference to this Scripture is striking (it *is* quoted in later versions), but the foregoing story about not lending before the year of release takes the place of the Scripture's description of this same "event." The story thus serves as an exegesis, through historical narrative, of Deut. 15:9–10.

Part F then repeats part C, adding the words *arose and* to supply a connection with part E, and thus to preserve the fictitious historical framework. Part G is tacked on; the story is complete without it. Part G could as well have followed part A. We do not know what Hillel said; part G ignores him, and part F satisfactorily completes his story. Including the formula is superfluous here, but makes good sense following part A. Presumably the anonymous exegesis consisted of part A + G, to which various Hillel-materials are attached, first by assigning the exegesis to Hillel (parts B-C), then by making up a story (parts E-F).

Part B introduces the story: *On this basis,* referring to the exegesis, therefore tying the following to it, Hillel ordained the *prozbul.* The intrusion of *they said* makes no sense. We are not told *who* said. It is a stock introduction to a new story or clause. Actually it ties to the opening of part E, *they said that he saw,* or to part C, *they said that Hillel.* But part D and part E cannot be joined.

Two different stories therefore have been put together. One is parts

A + B, C + G:

> (But not he who gives)
> On this basis (omit: *they said*)
> Hillel ordained the *prozbul*
> (And this is the formula)

The other is parts A + C, D, E, F + G:

> (But not he who gives)
> Hillel ordained
> On account of the order of the world
> (omit: *that*) He saw the people, that they held back
> He arose and ordained

The version of parts A + B, C + G is the simplest statement of matters. Parts D, E, F, introduce a "historical" provocation for the matter, ignoring the exegesis and reporting an "event" to take its place. The two versions actually did circulate separately.

The viewpoint of the former version is that Hillel's action was based upon sound exegesis of Scripture, and did not represent modification of the law merely to accommodate the law to historical circumstances. Rather, the law always had been what Hillel now said, but it was Hillel who recognized that fact and acted upon it. Hillel's greatness is in recovering the tradition, not in inventing new laws to meet the needs of the time.

The contrary tendency ignores the exegesis. Hillel *did* change the law to accommodate it to the needs of the day. The decree was "for the order of the world" and had no exegetical basis in Mosaic law. The specific problem that provoked changing the law therefore has to be spelled out. Others who choose to issue ordinances are similarly justified as circumstances require.

Not only did the two stories circulate separately, but the clumsy means by which they are amalgamated, e.g., the repetition of the "reason" for the decree and the use of *that* both where it fits and where it does not fit, suggest that completed versions already existed before the pericope was put together.

We have no firm basis on which to formulate a theory of events. Perhaps Hillel actually made such a decree for the reasons specified, and the fact that he could do so underlines his immense power and prestige within Pharisaism. But that decree would not have affected the great numbers of Palestinian Jews who were not Pharisees. Debtors, moreover, were here given a good motive to dislike Pharisees, who now rendered their debts into a perpetual burden.

This leads to the possibility that the *prozbul* existed before Hillel's day. He served as a convenient name on which to hang Pharisaic acceptance of it, despite contravening Scriptural law. But then the debtors' interest would become problematical. On one hand, the debts are now allowed to pile up and be carried forward. On the other hand, the theory of the *prozbul* for Pharisaic consumption is that it loosens credit. But both theories presuppose the law was widely observed, and debts forgiven according to Deuteronomic law. Evidence of actual practice here become decisive; I know no evidence of what people actually did.[2]

While historical considerations lead to an impasse, form-critical ones do not. The story represents the effort, first, to attribute the anonymous exegetical justification of the *prozbul* to Hillel, and then to combine both views of ordinances—a compromise between those who held that one may legislate to meet the needs of the day and those who held that legislation always depended upon Scriptural exegesis. The latter believed exegesis was possible for all needed legislation. The former may have thought otherwise, or, more likely, had no sufficiently rich exegetical tradition that permitted them to rely upon Scriptural exegesis for important matters.

It was Aqiba and his associates at Yavneh who so enriched the exegetical tradition of the rabbis that they could find whatever they wanted in Scripture. Earlier, before *ca.* 90 A.D., those who had to issue decrees without the Aqiban method thought it reasonable merely because the times obviously required it, for example, Yavneans, from Yohanan b. Zakkai's time to Aqiba's. Their view of matters is consistently represented in stories of Yohanan's own decrees: Yohanan did what the times required, with or without Scriptural proof. It was natural to shape Hillelite materials in the same framework, even where it distorted the materials. It seems likely that the first viewpoint would appropriately derive from circles influenced by Aqiban exegetical innovations, the second from circles in which those innovations were either unknown or unacceptable. The second might be the older of the two, but it is no more credible, from a historical viewpoint, on that account.

Here is another account of legislation instituted by Hillel, concerning a situation parallel to that dealt with by Hillel's *prozbul*. The Scriptures held that, just as the Seventh Year brought about remission of debts, so the

---

[2] That is not to suggest the Sabbatical Year's remission of debts was ignored. On the contrary, we have good evidence that it was taken into account in the making of loans. For example, Pierre Benoit, J.T. Milik, *et al.,* eds., *Discoveries in the Judaean Desert* (London: Oxford University Press, 1961), II, pp. 100–104, Document no. 18, contains an Aramaic acknowledgment of a debt, published by J.T. Milik. The acknowledgment, dated in the second year of Nero, that is, 55–56, is issued by the lender, who states that the borrower has declared before him that he borrowed a sum of money. Repayment is due on a certain date. "If not, one fifth plus the full loan is to be repaid, even if it is the year of release." The document is signed by the lender and three witnesses. What is striking is that this document is nothing like the *prozbul* attributed to Hillel. So the year of release *was* taken into account (we can hardly say it was *observed*), but the measures by which its effects were annulled have nothing whatever to do with those assigned to Hillel.

Jubilee Year, coming at the end of seven septennates, or 49 years, likewise led to the return to the original owner of property sold in the interval. But if the original owner did not, in the first year after the sale, redeem (re-purchase) the property, then the Jubilee Year would not lead to its return. Hence it was important for the new purchaser to retain possession of the property through the first year. Again, the social circumstances of the day mitigated against the biblical law's effectiveness, for the purchaser took measures to avoid restoring the property to the hand of the original owner. Hillel therefore ruled that the Temple might serve as recipient of the funds. Once the original owner had given the money to Temple authorities, he had completed the requirements of the law and returned to his status as full owner of the property. The machinations of the purchaser would then not avail.

> [If a man sells a dwelling house in a walled city, he may redeem it within a whole year after its sale; for a full year he shall have the right of redemption. If it is not redeemed within a full year, then the house that is in the walled city shall be made sure] in perpetuity [to him who brought it throughout his generations; it shall not be released in the jubilee (Lev. 25:29–30)]...to include one who gives a gift.
>
> B. At first he [the purchaser] would hide on the day on which the twelve months [were completed] so that it [the house] should be permanently sold to him.
>
> C. Hillel the Elder ordained that he [the seller] should assign his coins [for redemption of the property] to the [Temple] fund, and he [the original seller then] would break down the door and enter. Whenever the other [purchaser] wishes, he may come and take his money.[3]

The Scripture is merely cited. Parts B-C are independent of the foregoing and do not allude to it. Hillel's ordinance pertains to the sale only, as is clear in part C. The connection to Lev. 25:30 is merely in theme.

The phrase beginning *Hillel the Elder ordained* certainly could not have been transmitted apart from the description of the situation necessitating the ordinance.

The assumption is that a problem "at first" presented itself in Hillel's time. We are not told when purchasers began to prevent redemptions. The difficulty of redeeming land must have become apparent long before Hillel came from Babylonia. It is incredible that for 500 or 1,000 years, purchasers were able to get away with violation of the intent of Scriptural rules, so that only Hillel was able to stop the practice.

This imposes a considerable demand on one's imagination. The historical facts, moreover, hardly support the allegation that Hillel or any Pharisee would have been able to make adjustments in so important a matter as

---

[3] Sifra Behar 4.8.

transfer of real property. The further assumption that the Temple authorities participated in the process hardly demands much attention. I doubt that any decree of a Pharisaic master would have won not only the compliance, but the active participation, of the Temple authorities. So the whole story is probably a fabrication.

Perhaps the Pharisees handed on, or the later rabbis independently knew about, the tradition of how the effects of Lev. 25:29–30 were coped with. Long ago it was worked out that a man could deposit his funds with the appropriate public authority and reacquire his property. Then the rabbis attached the tradition to the name of Hillel, giving it both the form and substance we know today.

Another possibility is that the law never was enforced at all. No one could redeem property once it was sold. But rabbis *assumed* that the laws of Scripture were enforced. They thereupon invented the story of Hillel's ordinance to solve the fabricated problem of what to do if the purchaser will not accept one's money. The theory assumed legal weight when the rabbis came in time actually to govern the life of the Jewish community. They may have felt the need to explain how the well-known law of Lev. 25:29–30 had been enforced and would again be enforced when the Temple was rebuilt. I know of no evidence that people ever actually carried out this law or that its application constituted a difficult problem. Not much is to be gained by spinning out theories based on rabbinical traditions about application of laws in Temple times. Since the Pharisees as a sect did not control the government and the Temple, they could not do what the tradition said Hillel had done. Then why invent such a tradition? What provoked concern for the law in the first place? The requirements of the exegesis of Scriptures seem the likeliest provocation.

Hillel's Wise Sayings

To Hillel are attributed numerous wise sayings, many more than to all other Pharisaic masters put together. The most famous is the Golden Rule (p. 13). Others are as follows:

> Hillel says, "Be of the disciples of Aaron, loving peace, and pursuing peace, loving mankind, and bringing them near to the Torah."
> He used to say, "A name made great is a name destroyed, and he that increases not decreases, and he that learns not is worthy of death, and he that makes worldly use of the crown perishes."
> He used to say, "If I am not for myself who is for me? and being for mine own self, what am I? And if not now, when?"[4]

---

[4] M. Avot 1:12–14.

[*With flaming fire at his right hand* (Deut. 33:3)]:

Just as fire makes a mark on the flesh of whoever touches it, so whoever makes profit in matters of Torah loses his life.

For so would Hillel say, "*And he who uses the crown shall perish. . . .*"[5]

A. Hillel said, "(1.) Do not separate from the congregation; and (2.) do not trust yourself until the day of your death; and (3.) do not judge your fellow until you come to his place; and (4.) do not say a thing which cannot be heard, for it will be heard in the end; and (5.) say not, 'When I have leisure I will study.' Perhaps you will not have leisure."

B. He used to say, "(6.) A brutish man dreads not sin; and (7.) an ignorant man cannot be saintly; and (8.) the bashful man cannot learn; and (9.) the impatient man cannot teach; and (10.) he that engages overmuch in trade cannot become wise; and (11.) where there are no men, strive to be a man."

C. Also he once saw one skull floating on the face of the water. He said to it, (12.) "*Because you drowned they drowned you, and at the last they that drowned you shall be drowned.*"

D. He used to say, (13.) "The more [= He who multiplies] flesh, the more worms; (14.) the more possessions, the more care; (15.) the more women, the more witchcraft; (16.) the more slave-women, the more thieving; (17.) the more Torah, the more life; (18.) the more schooling, the more wisdom; (19.) the more counsel, the more understanding; (20.) the more righteousness, the more peace. (21.) If a man has gained a good name he has gained [it] for himself; (22.) if he has gained for himself words of Torah, he has gained for himself life in the world to come."[6]

The italicized logia are in Aramaic, the rest in Hebrew. The pericope is a collection of moral sayings, in the simplest structure. The various clauses are joined by *and, he used to say,* or, in the case of part C, *also.* A "historical" narrative setting is invented for the saying about the skull.

The 23 separate sayings are not all of the same kind. The first five are separate, unrelated logia, with *and* merely a connecting word; where the thematic connection is obvious, as in the antonymic parts later on, no *and* is supplied. Part B contains five related, evenly balanced sayings, and then an independent logion (no. 11). Part C, as noted, is a separate logion which is given a narrative setting. Part D returns to the model of part B, in which 13–16 are balanced. pairs of negative characteristics, 17–20 positive ones, as follows:

---

[5] Midrash Tannaim ed. David Hoffmann, p. 211.
[6] M. Avot 2:5–7.

flesh/worms	Torah/life
possessions/care	schooling/wisdom
women/witchcraft	counsel/understanding
women/lewdness	
	righteousness/peace
slave women/thieving	

Then come 21 and 22 the contrast between the good name for oneself and the words of Torah for life in the world to come.

It is difficult to imagine parts D and B as composites of separate sayings. They are clearly arranged to make a single point through a set of discrete examples. Part C is a separate *narrative + logion,* and part A is a composite of logia. The likelihood is that once the form had been stated, it generated many new examples.

That such sayings circulated in Hillel's name before 200 A.D. is unlikely, since none is ever quoted, referred to, or attributed to him prior to the third century masters. This is prima facie evidence that the whole is late. But other such balanced syzygies of moral sayings occur in Hillel's name, perhaps accounting for the attribution to him of any that followed the same pattern, or generating new sayings according to the original formula.

The preceding pericope obviously is a composite. Parts B, C, and D represent substantial developments into rather sophisticated forms—the first and the last are balanced images, the middle a story. None can be regarded as primitive. The sayings in part A, famous in their own right, presumably were popular proverbs assigned to Hillel.

> A. R. Sadoq says, "Keep not aloof from the congregation, and do not make yourself like those who seek to influence the judges. Make them [words of Torah] not a crown wherewith to magnify yourself or a spade wherewith to dig."
> B. And thus Hillel used to say, *"He that makes worldly use of the crown shall perish."*
> C. Thus you may learn that he that makes profit out of words of Torah takes his life from the world.[7]

Hillel's *worldly use* saying now serves as a gloss on the saying of R. Sadoq, a later master in Jerusalem and early Yavneh. It circulated as an independent logion. The italicized words are in Aramaic. The Hebrew subscription (part C) supplies a commentary.

Citation of Hillel's saying as a gloss on R. Sadoq's proves nothing about the antiquity of the former. An editor, shaping the whole, might well have drawn the Hillel-saying from available materials. R. Sadoq need not have heard it. If he had, he presumably would have cited it, or alluded to its

---

7 M. Avot 4:5.

striking image, in the name of Hillel. He refers to a crown, hence the editor brought together two *crown*-sayings originally circulating independently of one another.

> Hillel the Elder says:
> 1. "Do not be seen naked; do not be seen clothed.
> 2. "Do not be seen standing; and do not be seen sitting.
> 3. "Do not be seen laughing, and do not be seen weeping, for it is said, *There is a time to laugh and a time to weep, a time to embrace and a time to refrain from embracing* (Qoh. 3:4–5)."[8]
> Hillel the Elder says:
> 4. "When they are gathering, scatter, and when they are scattering, gather.
> 5. "When you see that the Torah is beloved of all Israel and all rejoice in it, you scatter it abroad, as it is said, *Some scatter and gain more* (Prov. 11:24).
> 6. "When you see the Torah is forgotten in Israel and not everyone pays attention to it, you gather it in, as it is said, *A time to work for the Lord* (Ps. 119:126)."[9]

Tos. Ber. 2:21 is a set of matched amplifications of the teaching not to separate oneself from the community. One should not do what the community at large is not doing, and vice versa, one should not refrain from doing what the community at large is doing. But study of Torah is an exception.

The meaning of Tos. Ber. 6:24 is that when the disciples come together to appreciate and review teachings of Torah, they should "scatter," that is, teach widely. But when teachings are lost and people forget the Torah, then they should engage in independent study, without trying to educate the masses. The saying thus applies the foregoing rules to study of Torah: One should not do the opposite of what the community is doing, but, in regard to Torah, one cannot waste Torah traditions on a heedless audience or stop his own study because others are not interested. So the two sayings form a coherent, antonymic pair. But they do not circulate as a pair, and are never brought into relationship.

Both sets of logia obviously are highly developed, indeed are even supplied with appropriate proof texts. The three examples of Tos. Ber. 2:21 are matched by the three of Tos. Ber. 6:24, though any one of the three might have stood by itself and made its own point. I do not think we are dealing with six independent logia, but rather with two sets.

---

8 Tos. Ber. 2:21.
9 Tos. Ber. 6:24.

The Legend
of Hillel's Rise to Power

The most complex set of Hillel traditions deals with his rise to power. He came from Babylonia as an obscure immigrant, but, miraculously, his learning was recognized, and he was made *Nasi,* or patriarch. We shall consider the whole repertoire of versions of this story, first the Tosefta's, then the Palestinian Talmud's, and finally the Babylonian Talmud's, noting how the first and simplest example is later embellished according to various tendencies.

A. One time the fourteenth [of Nisan, the eve of Passover] fell on the Sabbath.

They asked Hillel the Elder, "Does the *Pesah* [Passover-offering] override the Sabbath? [That is, is the Passover-sacrifice offered on the Sabbath?]"

He said to them, "And do we have only one *Pesah* in the year which overrides the Sabbath? We have many more than three hundred *Pesahs* in the year, and they override the Sabbath."

[The meaning is that many sacrifices override the Sabbath. During the year hundreds of sacrifices are offered on that day, including the two daily burnt offerings and the two additional sacrifices of every Sabbath, besides extra sacrifices offered on the Sabbath which occurs in the middle of the week of Passover and the week of Tabernacles. Hillel, however, dissimulates, for the question is not, Does one make a sacrifice on the Sabbath? Everyone knows one does so. The issue is, Do we make this particular offering, in connection with the Passover, on that day? When Hillel replies that "many *Pesahs* override the Sabbath," he thus says the Passover offering is no different from the normal cultic offerings carried out through the year.]

B. The whole courtyard collected against him.

He said to them, "The continual offering is a community sacrifice, and the *Pesah* is a community sacrifice. Just as the continual offering, a community sacrifice, overrides the Sabbath, so the *Pesah* is a community sacrifice and overrides the Sabbath.

[This reply is more to the point, for now Hillel explicitly states that he regards the Passover sacrifice as no different from the continual offering. The two have in common the fact that the community is responsible for supplying them. Hence they will have in common other traits as well.]

C. "Another matter: It is said concerning the continual offering: *In its season* (Num. 28:2), and it is said with reference to the *Pesah:*

In its season (Num. 9:2). Just as the continual offering, concerning which *In its season* is said, overrides the Sabbath, so the *Pesah*, concerning which *In its season* is said, overrides the Sabbath."

[The comparison to the continual offering is developed, now in relationship to Scriptures. Scriptures use the same language with reference to both the Passover offering and the continual offering. This shows the two are comparable and will be subject to the same rules.]

>D. "And furthermore [it is a] *qal vehomer* [argument *a fortiori*]: Although the continual offering, which does not produce the [severe] liability of *cutting off*, overrides the Sabbath, the *Pesah*, which *does* produce the liability of *cutting off*—is it not logical that it should override the Sabbath?
>E. "And further, I have received from my masters [the tradition] that the *Pesah* overrides the Sabbath, and not [merely] the first *Pesah* but the second, and not [merely] the community *Pesah* but the individual *Pesah* [as well]."

[Hillel now claims that the foregoing arguments do not matter, for he has a tradition from his masters, who are not specified, that the Passover sacrifice is to be offered on the Sabbath. The question then rises, If so, what should people do who, not knowing the law, did not make proper preparations to make the offering?]

>F. They said to him, "What will be the rule for the people who on the Sabbath did not bring knives and *Pesah*-offerings to the sanctuary?"
>G. He said to them, "Leave them alone. The holy spirit is upon them. If they are not prophets, they are disciples of the prophets."
>H. What did Israel [the Jews] do in that hour? He whose *Pesah* was a lamb hid it in its wool; if it was a kid, he tied it between its horns; so they brought knives and *Pesahs* to the sanctuary and slew their *Pesah*-sacrifices.
>I. On that very day they appointed Hillel as *Nasi,* and he would teach to them concerning the laws of the Pesah.[10]

The pericope is transparently composite, a collection of loosely related traditions on Hillel's dispute with "them," and his consequent elevation to the position of *Nasi*. The dispute supplies a dramatic, narrative setting for exegeses which could have stood separately, anonymously, and without such a setting. The stories of Hillel's rise to power thus were joined with exegeses of *Pesah* and the Sabbath.

---

[10] Tos. Pisha 4:13.

Part A introduces the whole matter and is complete in itself: Hillel was asked and thereupon supplied a complete and final answer. The following arguments are attached to it by the *whole courtyard* supposedly disagreeing with him, but saying nothing in response to his repertoire. Later on "they" would be named, still later "they" would demolish his arguments.

The arguments are as follows:

A. Many *Pesahs* override the Sabbath;

B. Community sacrifices such as the Passover offering override the Sabbath;

C. *Its season* applies both to continual offering and to *Pesah,* thus both override Sabbath;

D. *Qal vehomer* [argument a fortiori];

E. I have a *tradition* from my masters.

Nothing is said about who the masters are. This would be added later on.

In part F the response is given: Everyone forthwith agrees. Part F could as well have followed part A (or any of the subsequent arguments), but is held back until the whole repertoire is completed.

Part G is a still further, separate element, in which a probably well-known apothegm ("If they are not prophets...") is attributed to Hillel, followed by part H, an illustration of the prophetic heritage. The people can be relied on, because they do have access to the holy spirit, or at least automatically do the right thing.

Then comes part I, *on that very day.* The House of Hillel persistently appealed to the holy spirit and other supernatural informants in deciding questions of law. But no claim of supernatural revelation was asserted in Hillel's behalf. On the contrary, his failure to receive the holy spirit had to be explained away.

Distinguishing the exegetical from the narrative elements, we find the following:

Narrative	Exegetical
A. One time	A. Many *Pesahs* everride
B. Joined issue [or E.]	B. Community sacrifices
F. What to do?	C. *In its season*
G. Holy spirit	D. *Qal vehomer*
H. What did people do?	E. Tradition
I. They made him *Nasi*	

We see, therefore, that, except for A or E, but not both, the exegetical and dispute materials are independent of the narrative framework; all, including A and E, are inserted without much, if any, reference to the narrative details. We can reconstruct the event without referring to the exegetical argumentation. The composite pericope gives every evidence of coming at the end of a long process of development. The problem of the *Pesah* comes before the arguments. The story of the rise to power is developed in its own terms. Then the two are combined.

As to the historical framework, we are told that for generations no one had known what to do when the eve of Passover, the fourteenth of Nisan, fell on the Sabbath, until Hillel came along and told them. Yet this contradicts part E and parts G-H, in which we are told, "You *can* rely on what the people normally do and do not have to depend upon exegetical investigation, except for *post facto* justification for accepted practice." Later on this anomaly is explained, with reference to part E.

This state of affairs is tied to the foregoing by the explanation that Hillel himself had approved referring to popular practice, saying that the people are under the holy spirit. Since other sayings concerning Hillel (p. 129) allege he alone of his generation was worthy of receiving the holy spirit, but the generation in which he lived was of such poor character that the holy spirit was withheld in their day even from Hillel, the pericope must be set apart from other sorts of Hillel traditions. But I cannot suggest who would have wanted to allege in Hillel's name that the holy spirit is upon Israel, or what polemic was involved in so stating.

Part A contradicts parts F-G, for part A alleges no one knew what to do until Hillel came, and parts F-G claim everyone knew precisely what to do, but Hillel was able either to provide adequate exegetical authority or to cite masters. But no one else in Jerusalem had heard anything from those same masters on this subject.

Shemaiah and Abtalion, supposedly his teachers, are not mentioned, probably because at the outset it would have been incredible that only Hillel knew their teaching about a matter of Temple procedure that must have arisen several times in their lifetimes alone. But later they are inserted as a gloss on "my masters." The anomaly then has to be explained: "You were too lazy to study with Shemaiah and Abtalion. That is why you did not know their traditions."

The little narrative in part H is a separate story, without any real connection to the rest except *in that hour*, which, like *one time* and *on that very day*, is a convenient joining formula for the historical-narrative framework. These considerations require further division of the narrative framework into part A and parts F, G, and H; part I is still a third element in the narrative.

The anonymity of the pericope, the clumsy joining of its composite elements into a single, unitary account, and the historical dubiety of the story that Hillel's arguments were accepted by Temple authorities and he was therefore made patriarch or *Nasi* over the Temple all point to a relatively late date for the story as a whole. I do not see how anyone could have made it up or put it together while the Temple was standing, for at that point no one could have believed it. My guess is that available exegetical elements were claimed for Hillel after the narrative parts were put together; then Hillel's name could be supplied for *any* exegesis proving that the *Pesah* offering overrides the Sabbath. The arguments could have been worked out at the same period, then attached to the story of Hillel's rise to power, once the issue of the *Pesah* was established as the primary theme of that story.

The obvious division in the narrative is between the elements that say Hillel became *Nasi* because of the excellence of his exegetical ingenuity, and those that say he became *Nasi* because he had a tradition from his masters. But here that distinction does not seem to be important. In the Palestinian and Babylonian Talmudic versions, it is developed into a major polemic. No one dramatically underlines that Hillel was ignored until he could quote his masters, for part E is pretty much equivalent to the foregoing. Hence the real contrast is between the allegation that people do know what to do and do not require rabbinical instruction, but merely rabbinical confirmation for what they already do, and the thesis that until Hillel's exegeses, no one, even his masters, knew what to do at all. I am not sure who would have wanted to advance the former theory, but since it seems to me to claim less for Hillel, I imagine it would not have come from the patriarchal circles, who would have preferred the view that Hillel was superior even to his masters, Shemaiah and Abtalion. It seems unlikely to me that any of this contains a shred of historically usable information.

The next version, which occurs in the Palestinian Talmud, first introduces the names of Hillel's opposition. They now are the "Elders of Bathyra." The Bathyrans were Babylonian Jewish immigrants who came at the time of Herod and were settled in frontier regions, northeast of the Sea of Galilee, to protect the border. They founded the town of Bathyra, whence the name. Herod put some of them into the Temple hierarchy. They next turn up at Yavneh, where they are represented as opposing Yohanan b. Zakkai's right to make liturgical decisions formerly vested in the Temple. At the end of the second century, Judah the Patriarch alludes to the Bathyrans giving up their office to his ancestor Hillel. This means that the story which we are about to consider was known, in substantially its present form, by Judah's time. The version just considered, which ignores the Bathyrans, has to come well before Judah the Patriarch. Numerous other glosses embellish the earlier account; the elements of Tos. Pisha are re-arranged in various ways.

A. This law was lost from the Elders of Bathyra.

B. One time the fourteenth [of Nisan] turned out to coincide with the Sabbath, and they did not know whether the *Pesah* [Passover offering] overrides the Sabbath or not.

They said, "There is here a certain Babylonian, and Hillel is his name, who studied with Shemaiah and Abtalion. [He] knows whether the *Pesah* overrides the Sabbath or not. Perhaps there will be profit from him."

They sent and called him.

C. They said to him, "Have you ever heard, when the fourteenth [of Nisan] coincides with the Sabbath, whether it overrides the Sabbath or not?"

D. He said to them, "And do we have only one *Pesah* alone that overrides the Sabbath in the whole year? And do not many *Pesahs* override the Sabbath in the whole year?"

E. (Some Tannaim teach a hundred, and some Tannaim teach two hundred, and some Tannaim teach three hundred.

He who said one hundred [refers to] continual offerings.

He who said two hundred [refers to] continual offerings and Sabbath additional-offerings.

He who said three hundred [refers to] continual offerings, Sabbath addition-offerings, [and those] of festivals, and of New Moons, and of seasons.)

E'. They said to him, "We have already said that there is with you profit."

F. He began expounding for them by means of arguments based on *heqqesh*, *qal vehomer* and *gezerah shavah*:

G. "*Heqqesh:* Since the continual offering is a community sacrifice and the *Pesah* is a community sacrifice, just as the continual offering, a community sacrifice, overrides [the] Sabbath, so the *Pesah*, a community sacrifice, overrides the Sabbath.

H. "*Qal vehomer:* If the continual offering, [improperly] doing which does not produce the liability of cutting off, overrides the Sabbath, the *Pesah*, [improperly] doing which *does* produce the liability of cutting off, all the more so should override the Sabbath.

I. "*Gezerah shavah:* Concerning the continual offering, *In its season* is said (Num. 28:2), and concerning the *Pesah*, *In its season* is said (Num. 9:3). Just as the continual offering, concerning which is said *In its season* overrides the Sabbath, so the *Pesah*, concerning which *In its season* is said, overrides the Sabbath."

J. They said to him, "We have already said, 'There is no profit [benefit] from the Babylonian.'

K. "As to the *heqqesh* which you said, there is a reply: No—for if you say so concerning the continual offering, there is a limit to the continual offering, but can you say so concerning the *Pesah*, which has no limit? [The two are different, and the same rule therefore cannot apply.]

L. "The *qal vehomer* which you stated has a reply: No—if you say so concerning the continual offering, which is the most sacred, will you say so of the *Pesah*, which is of lesser sanctity? [So the argument collapses.]

M. "As to the *gezerah shavah* that you said: A man may not reason a *gezerah shavah* on his own [but must cite it from tradition]. . . ."

N. Even though he sat and expounded for them all day, they did not accept [it] from him, until he said to them, "May [evil] come upon me! Thus have I heard from Shemaiah and Abtalion!"

When they heard this from him, they arose and appointed him *Nasi* over them.

O. When they had appointed him *Nasi* over them, he began to criticize them, saying, "Who caused you to need this Babylonian? Is it not because you did not serve the two great men of the world, Shemaiah and Abtalion, who were sitting with you?"

P. Since he criticized them, the law was forgotten by him.

Q. They said to him, "What shall we do for the people who did not bring their knives?"

R. He said to them, "This law have I heard, but I have forgotten [it]. But leave Israel [alone]. If they are not prophets, they are disciples of prophets."

S. Forthwith, whoever had a lamb as his *Pesah* would hide it [knife] in its wool; [if] it was a kid he would tie the knife between its horns. So their *Pesahs* turned out to be bringing their knives with them.

T. When he saw the deed, he remembered the law.

U. He said, "Thus have I heard from Shemaiah and Abtalion."[11]

The pericope before us is a veritable repertoire of traditions on Hillel and the Temple—but apart from the superscription, part A, the Bathyrans are completely forgotten. That detail must have been added last. Linking Hillel to the fall of the Bathyrans certainly comes after the formation, around Hillel's discipleship of Shemaiah and Abtalion, of the bulk of the materials on his rise to power. The essential story is contained in the following parts:

B. No one knew what to do when Passover, the fourteenth of Nisan, coincided with the Sabbath, so "a certain Babylonian" is called, because of his discipleship of Shemaiah and Abtalion.

C. He is asked the question.

D. He says the answer is obvious: Many *pesahs* override the Sabbath!

E'. They accept his explanation.

At this point, the story could have ended; nothing is required to complete the picture. We do not have to be told about the immediate abdication (N) of the Bathyrans. That "event" is no issue.

Part E is certainly a late gloss on part D; Tos. Pisha has already corrected the language of *many* to read *three hundred,* which I assume is a scribal improvement of an otherwise older version.

Then comes a new and different repertoire of materials: Hillel's proofs. We have no reason to attribute them to Hillel himself. They are additional

11 y. Pes. 6:1.

"proofs" anyone might have supplied for the same proposition, an exercise in exegetical logic independent of the historical setting:

F. Superscription for the whole.
G. *Heqqesh.*
H. *Qal vehomer.*
I. *Gezerah shavah.*
K. Refutation of *heqqesh.*
L. Refutation of *qal vehomer.*
M. Refutation of *gezerah shavah.*

After part I comes a revision of part E', this time in negative form. Having accepted his proof, "they" now reject it! Part J certainly marks the end of a separate and complete version. Parts K, L, and M explain the rejection of proofs attributed to Hillel.

Part N is a separate element in the story, joined to the foregoing by "even though he sat and expounded." The point is that he has a tradition from his teachers, Shemaiah and Abtalion, on which basis he is made *Nasi.* This now concludes Hillel's proofs and artificially links them to the "historical" account.

Afterward comes another, separate story concerning Hillel's gloating at the fall of the Bathyrans. It underlines the importance of serving Shemaiah and Abtalion, and in fact represents a secondary development of part N: Hillel came of office only because he had studied with Shemaiah and Abtalion; the Bathyrans lost office only because they had not paid them adequate attention.

Part P is a connecting element, leading into a third story referring to what to do for the people who had not brought their knives. Obviously, Hillel knew the answer—that is the point of the foregoing. But since the narrator intends to tell how the people are really prophets, he makes Hillel forget what he had learned, because of a moral lapse! This allows the famous logion to be stated by Hillel: "Leave Israel alone. If they are not prophets. . . ." The saying is then illustrated by the behavior of the people. The theme of part P is recovered in parts T-U ("he remembered the law"). Then comes the phrase: *Thus have I heard. . . .*

The foregoing analysis leads to division of the whole pericope into the following separate parts:

I. Parts B, C, D, E': Hillel solves the problem, all agree.
II. Parts F-M + N: Repertoire of exegetical proofs, all refuted. Part N may have been contributed by the final editorial hand, tying the whole to part A—but in doing so, the editor has repeated part U.
III. Parts O-P: Hillel underlines the fault of the opposition, but is supernaturally punished on that account.

IV. Parts Q-S, with subscription T-U: The people knew what to do all along, because they are disciples of prophets. Hillel thereupon says their practice conformed to the law.

Let us now reconsider the picture presented by each of the four elements.

I. B, C, D, E': No one knew the law. Hillel, who had studied with Shemaiah and Abtalion, was listened to on that account. He said the answer was obvious, and the others forthwith agreed.

The tendency of the first story is to stress that Hillel knew the law, *but* was recognized only because of his discipleship of Shemaiah and Abtalion. However, as soon as he stated the law, *without* referring to and quoting his masters, everyone exclaimed in agreement.

II. F, G, H, I, J, K, L, M, N: Hillel tried every logical-exegetical device, without success. Finally he said the tradition comes from Shemaiah-Abtalion, and the opposition thereupon abdicated and made him *Nasi*.

The tendency of the first story is underlined. Now Hillel's knowledge is of no consequence; all that matters is the ability to cite Shamaiah and Abtalion. But once he could do so, the opposition not merely agrees, but abdicates office and places Hillel in it instead! So Hillel owes his power to his discipleship, not to his logic. Discipleship is the key to authority, while mere ability to reason makes no difference.

III. O-P: When Hillel became *Nasi*, he behaved so obnoxiously that heaven punished him by depriving him of what had made him *Nasi* to begin with: knowledge of the traditions of Shemaiah and Abtalion.

The story follows the same tendency as the foregoing.

IV. Q, R, S, T, U: Hillel did not know the law. He observed what people did and was reminded that the people were following the correct procedures as enunciated by Shemaiah and Abtalion.

The four stories make much the same point through the reworking of various materials. Hillel's importance depends upon Shemaiah and Abtalion. Without knowing *their* traditions, he would not have been recognized and would not have persuaded the opposition.

The redactor of the stories stands outside of the Hillelite circle and, of course, comes well after its predominance was an established fact. Everyone knows who "the certain Babylonian" is, and is well aware of his rise to power.

The real question is, why did the redactor of the whole, as well as those responsible for the formation of the several parts, choose to emphasize

Hillel's utter subordination to his masters, a theme virtually absent in the earlier version? Whatever the brilliance of one's logic, possessing accurate traditions from a recognized master is decisive. Who would have wanted to say so, and to whom? No story about Hillel in power can have failed to reflect the importance of the later patriarchate, and the importance to the patriarchate, from *ca.* 150 A.D. onward, of Hillel stories.

Is a patriarchal interest at hand? I do not see any. The patriarch would not necessarily have objected to all elements of the portrayal of Hillel; his rise to power is represented as creditable.

But an obvious antipatriarchal tendency appears in division III, and somewhat more subtly in division IV: the *Nasi* may be punished by Heaven for harassing the rest of the sages. Hillel was no better than others. Since everyone knew what he knew, all he could contribute was the attribution to Shemaiah and Abtalion. Divisions I-II consistently portray Hillel as important because of his masters, but we need not hear an echo that the *Nasi* had better listen to his masters, since no one openly accused the *Nasi* of "ignorance." So the story has been developed into a polemic in favor of discipleship. The patriarch thus is warned that the collegium of the rabbinical masters is decisive in the formation of the law.

The latest version of the story is as follows:

A. Our rabbis taught: This law was hidden from the sons of Bathyra.

B. On one occasion, the fourteenth [of Nisan] coincided with the Sabbath. They forgot and did not know whether the Passover overrides the Sabbath or not.

They said, "Is there any man who knows whether *Pesah* overrides the Sabbath or not?"

They said to them, "There is a certain man who has come up from Babylonia, and Hillel the Babylonian is his name, who served the two greatest men of the time, and he knows whether or not the Passover overrides the Sabbath."

[Thereupon] they sent and called him. They said to him, "Do you know whether the Passover overrides the Sabbath or not?"

He said to them, "Have we then only one Passover during the year which overrides the Sabbath? Do we not have many more than two hundred Passovers during the year which override the Sabbath!"

C. They said to him, "How do you know it?"

He said to them, *"In its appointed time* is stated in connection with the Passover, and *In its appointed time* is stated in connection with the continual offering; just as *In its appointed time* which is said in connection with the continual offering overrides the Sabbath, so *In its appointed time* which is said in connection with the Passover overrides the Sabbath.

D. "Moreover, it is a *qal vehomer*: If the continual offering [the omission of] which is not punished by cutting off, overrides the Sabbath, the Passover, [neglect of] which *is* punished by cutting off—is it not logical that it should override the Sabbath!"

E. They immediately set him at their head and appointed him *Nasi* over them, and the whole day he was sitting and expounding on the laws of Passover.

F. He began rebuking them with words.

He said to them, "Who caused it for you that I should come up from Babylonia to be *Nasi* over you? It was the laziness that was in you, because you did not serve the two great men of the generation, Shemaiah and Abtalion."

G. They said to him, "Rabbi, what if a man forgot and did not bring a knife on the eve of the Sabbath?"

He said to them, "I have heard this law but have forgotten it. But leave it to Israel. If they are not prophets, yet they are the disciples of prophets!"

On the morrow, he whose Passover was a lamb stuck it [the knife] in its wool; he whose Passover was a goat stuck it between its horns.

He saw the deed and remembered the law and and said, "Thus have I received the tradition from the mouth of Shemaiah and Abtalion."

H. An [anonymous] Master said, *"In its appointed season* is stated in connection with the Passover, and *In its appointed time* is stated in connection with the continual offering: just as *In its appointed time* which is said in connection with the continual offering overrides the Sabbath, so *In its appointed time* which is said in connection with the Passover overrides the Sabbath."

I. *And how do we know that the continual offering itself overrides the Sabbath? Shall we say, because "In its appointed time" is written in connection with it? Then the Passover too, surely, "In its appointed time" is written in connection with it? Hence [you must say that] "In its appointed time" has no significance for him [Hillel]; then here too, "In its appointed time" should have no significance for him?* [Italics =Aramaic]

Rather Scripture says, *This is the burnt-offering of every Sabbath, beside the continual burnt-offering* (Num. 28:10); *whence it follows that the continual burnt-offering [tamid] is offered on the Sabbath.*

J. The Master said: "Moreover, it follows *qal vehomer*: if the continual offering [the omission of] which is not punished by 'cutting off' overrides the Sabbath; then the Passover, [neglect of] which is punished by 'cutting off'—is it not logical that it overrides the Sabbath!"

[But] *this can be refuted*: as to the continual offering, that is because it is constantly and entirely [burnt].

He first told them the qal vehomer argument, but they refuted it; [so] then he told them the gezerah shavah. But since he had received the tradition of a gezerah shavah, what was the need of an a minori argument?

Rather he spoke to them on their ground: "It is well that you do not learn a gezerah shavah, because a man cannot argue [by] a *gezerah shavah* of his own accord. But [an inference] *qal vehomer,* which a man *can* argue of his own accord, *you should have argued!"*

Said they to him, "It is a fallacious qal vehomer argument."

K. The Master said, "On the morrow, he whose Passover was a lamb stuck in its wool; [he whose Passover was] a goat stuck it between its horns."

But he performed work with sacred animals? [They did] as [did] Hillel.

L. For it was taught: It was related of Hillel: As long as he lived, no man ever committed trespass through his burnt-offering. But he brought it unconsecrated to the Temple Court, consecrated it, laid his hand upon it, and slaughtered it. . . . [This is further discussed.]

M. Rav Judah [d. 297 A.D.] said in Rav's [d. 247 A.D.] name: "Whoever is boastful, if he is a sage, his wisdom departs from him; if he is a prophet, his prophecy departs from him." If he is a Sage, his wisdom departs from him: [we learn this] from Hillel.

For the Master said, "He began rebuking them with words, and [then] he said to them, 'I have heard this law but have forgotten it.' "[12]

We have a firm *terminus ante quem* for parts F-G, in part M: Rav Judah, d. 297. The attribution to Rav could move the date back by about 50 years. Parts F-G are a secondary development of the brief pericope given in the summary of F-G in part M: He began to rebuke them, and then forgot his learning. This has been attached to the Passover story, and the law Hillel forgot is made the issue. The practice of the common folk thereupon is added as well, but is not integral to the brief pericope. It now is a story openly hostile to patriarchs who harass the sages.

Part A begins with a standard superscription. The Palestinian Talmudic story is followed through part B, then part C begins with a new connecting phrase, *How do you know it?* This is missing in the Palestinian version, which has the assembled throng without qualm accept Hillel's first argument, y. Pes. part E′. The connector is an improvement, for it explains why all the subsequent exegetical proofs are introduced.

Then comes the *gezerah shavah,* part C, the *qal vehomer,* part D, but the other materials are dropped, particularly the *heqqesh,* y. Pes. parts G and K. The Babylonian version now makes Hillel *Nasi,* and that ends the story. The further story of how he forgot his learning follows in the same sequence as in the Palestinian version, but with the omission of parts K, L, and M of the Palestinian version, in which Hillel's several proofs are refuted by "the assembled throng." This whole assemblage is added afterward, in the Babylonian parts H, I, and J. It is no longer integral to the historical event,

12 b. Pes. 66a–b.

but now serves as an anonymous commentary on the purported arguments. Parts F-G are not much different from y. Pes. parts O-T.

Part K introduces a new pericope. In Hillel's time people brought their sacrifices in an ordinary (profane) state, and only after they reached the Temple did they declare them sacrifices. This prevented the sin of performing work with sacred animals. The tendency is to show how excellent was Hillel's governance of the cult. The passage gives in historical form what could well have been a legal logion, as follows: Hillel says, *One does not lay on hands until....*

Now we have *two hundred pesahs* in part B, and the several Tannaitic versions and glosses in y. Pes. are dropped.

Hillel Descends from David

In the following pericope, the ancestry of Hillel is traced to David. It was a convention of the political life of the Jews that King David of biblical times would stand behind anyone who claimed to exercise legitimate authority over Israel. We find, for example, that the Maccabees, Jesus, the patriarch of Palestine, the exilarch, ruler of the Jewish community of Babylonia, and even King Herod all claimed to descend from David. In Hillel's case, the claim is given as follows:

> R. Levi said, "A scroll of genealogies did they find in Jerusalem, and written in it was, 'Hillel from David....' "[13]

Levi, a contemporary of Judah the Patriarch, makes the first reference to the Davidic origins of Hillel. Since the patriarch claimed to descend from Hillel as well as from David, it was of course important to find such a scroll. The first evidences of the patriarchal claim to Davidic ancestry come with Judah the Patriarch at the end of the second century. The tradition of Levi comes at the earliest in the third century. Hillel's Davidic origins play no role in stories about his rise to power, nor does the theme occur elsewhere in Hillel materials. It is a late allegation in response to the political-theological needs of the patriarch, but its absence from other stories does not prove that they are earlier, merely different.

Hillel and Shammai

In the beginning were the House of Shammai and the House of Hillel, presumably dating from *ca.* 10 A.D. to 70 A.D. Afterward came the traditions

[13] y. Ta. 4:2.

about Shammai and Hillel themselves. That is to say, the earliest well-attested traditions about pre-70 times, emanating from the academy of Yavneh after 70, deal with the legal traditions attributed to these two groups within Pharisaism. Only much later, after the Bar Kokhba War, do we find attestations for stories about the founders of the Houses.

The relationships between the Houses of Shammai and Hillel thus produced stories about the relationship between the founding fathers, Shammai and Hillel. While the materials concerning the houses are fair and balanced, and give equal respect to the opinions of each side, the stories about the founding fathers do not. On the contrary, the Hillelites, responsible for the entire corpus of Hillel-Shammai stories, consistently represent Shammai unfavorably. Three examples of this tendency follow.

> A. When one vintages the grapes for the vat—
> Shammai says, "It [the juice] is made fit [to become unclean]."
> Hillel says "It is not made fit [to become unclean]."
> B. Said Hillel to Shammai, "Why do they vintage [grapes] in purity, and do not gather [olives] in purity?"
> C. "If you anger me," he replied, "I will decree uncleanness also in the case of olive-gathering."
> D. A sword did they plant in the school.
> They said, "He who enters, let him enter, but he who departs, let him not depart!"
> E. And on that day Hillel was submissive and sat before Shammai, like one of the disciples.
> E'. And it was as grievous to Israel as the day on which the [golden] calf was made.[14]

Part A certainly stands apart from the following fable and is complete in itself. It seems reasonable that the materials of part A, in which Shammai enjoys full parity with Hillel, come early. The subject matter—uncleanness— is congruent to such an early venue. Parts B, C, D, and E are later augmentations of the tradition in part A. In parts B-C, Hillel appears as subordinate to Shammai. He points out an inconsistency in Shammai's argument, to which Shammai replies that the decree can easily be made consistent, and more stringent: "I will decree." Shammai is represented as able to issue such a decree, and thereupon silence Hillel.

Part D is curious. We are asked to believe someone set up a sword in the schoolhouse to keep everyone (= Shammai's majority) inside. Hillel therefore was forced to submit to Shammai's judgment. The allegation that Shammai's rulings were effected by force is egregious. Other materials allege that the numbers of the House of Shammai exceeded those of the House of Hillel, resulting in the adoption of Shammaite rulings, but nowhere else

14 b. Shab. 17a.

do we hear of the use of weapons. If Shammai enjoyed a majority inside, why the sword? Would it not have sufficed to take a vote? Is it a Hillelite assertion that only force kept the Shammaite majority in line? We do not know the Shammaites' view of matters, but we may take it for granted that parts D and E preserve that of the Hillelites. The stock phrase in the subscription, part E, conforms to the spirit of the foregoing narrative, though it is not integral to it.

The authenticity of the legal tradition seems to me highly probable. The credibility of the accompanying narrative—explaining on the part of Hillelites that the only way Shammaite opinions prevailed was by force of arms, that Shammai silenced Hillel and his logic with an effective threat, that Hillel was outnumbered, that all those who would come would be likely to agree with the Shammaites, and that Hillel was reduced to the status of a disciple—meant to explain in a most unflattering manner the fact that Shammai's opinion once did prevail, is negligible. It is difficult to estimate when such assertions would have proved important; I can think of no point at which they would have been irrelevant or incredible. Presumably a later, rather than an earlier, date would be preferable, however, for after the Shammaite party had lost any substantive influence in the rabbinical movement, it would have been easier to explain their earlier preponderance as a matter of force rather than of the logical appeal of their arguments. But this cannot be a decisive argument.

Another example of the denigration of Shammai is as follows:

A. Our rabbis taught:
A man should always be gentle like Hillel, and not impatient like Shammai.
B. It once happened that two men made a wager with each other, saying, "He who goes and makes Hillel angry shall receive four hundred *zuz*."
Said one, "I will anger him."
That day was the Sabbath eve, and Hillel was washing his head. He went, passed by the door of his house, and called out, "Is Hillel here? Is Hillel here?"
Thereupon he robed and went out to him, saying, "My son, what do you seek?"
"I have a question to ask," said he.
"Ask, my son," he said to him.
He asked, "Why are heads of the Babylonians round?"
"My son, you have asked a great question," he said. "Because they have no skillful midwives."
He departed, tarried a while, returned, and said, "Is Hillel here? Is Hillel here?"
He robed and went out to him, saying, "My son, what do you seek?"

"I have a question to ask," said he.

"Ask, my son," he said.

He asked, "Why are the eyes of the Palmyreans bleared?"

"My son, you have asked a great question," said he. "Because they live in sandy places."

He departed, tarried a while, returned, and said, "Is Hillel here? Is Hillel here?"

He robed and went out to him, saying, "My son, what do you seek?"

"I have a question to ask," said he.

"Ask, my son," he said.

He asked, "Why are the feet of the Africans wide?"

"My son, you have asked a great question," said he. "Because they live in watery marshes."

"I have many questions to ask," said he, "but fear that you may become angry."

Thereupon he robed, sat before him and said, "Ask all the questions you have to ask."

"Are you the Hillel whom they call the *Nasi* of Israel?"

"Yes," he said.

"If that is you," he said, "may there not be many like you in Israel."

"Why, my son?" said he.

"Because I have lost four hundred *zuz* through you," complained he.

"Be careful of your moods," he answered.

"Hillel is worth it that you should lose four hundred *zuz* and yet another four hundred *zuz* through him, yet Hillel shall not lose his temper."

C. Our rabbis taught:

A certain heathen once came before Shammai and asked him, "How many Torahs have you?"

"Two," he replied, "The Written Torah and the Oral Torah."

"I believe you with respect to the Written Torah, but not with respect to the Oral Torah. Make me a proselyte on condition that you teach me the Written Torah [only]."

He scolded and repulsed him in anger.

[When] he went before Hillel, he accepted him as a proselyte.

On the first day he taught him, *Alef, bet, gimmel, delet* [= A, B, C, D]; the following day he reversed [them] to him.

"But yesterday you did not teach them to me thus," he said.

"Must you not rely upon me? Then rely upon me with respect to the Oral [Torah] too."

D. On another occasion it happened that a certain heathen came before Shammai and said to him, "Make me a proselyte, on condition that you teach me the whole Torah while I stand on one foot."

Thereupon he repulsed him with the builder's cubit which was in his hand.

[When] he went before Hillel, he converted him.

He said to him, "What is hateful to you, do not to your neighbor. That is the whole Torah, while the rest is the commentary thereof; go and learn [it]."

E. On another occasion it happened that a certain heathen was passing behind a school and heard the voice of a scribe reciting, "And these are the garments which they shall make: a breastplate, and an ephod."

Said he, "For whom are these?"

"For the High Priest," they said.

Then said that heathen to himself, "I will go and become a proselyte, that I may be appointed a High Priest."

So he went before Shammai and said to him, "Make me a proselyte on condition that you appoint me a High Priest."

But he repulsed him with the builder's cubit which was in his hand.

He then went before Hillel. He made him a proselyte.

Said he to him, "Can any man be made a king but he who knows the arts of government? Go and study the arts of government!"

He went and read. When he came to *And the stranger that cometh nigh shall be put to death,* he asked him, "To whom does this verse apply?"

"Even to David, King of Israel," was the answer.

Thereupon that proselyte reasoned within himself *a fortiori* [*qal vehomer*]: "If Israel, who are called sons of the Omnipresent, and whom in His love for them He designated *Israel is my son, my first born* (Ex. 4:22), yet it is written of them, *And the stranger that cometh nigh shall be put to death*—how much more so a mere proselyte, who comes with his staff and wallet!"

Then he went before Shammai and said to him, "Am I then eligible to be a High Priest? Is it not written in the Torah, *And the stranger that cometh nigh shall be put to death?*"

He went before Hillel and said to him, "O gentle Hillel: blessings rest on your head for bringing me under the wings of the *Shekhinah* [divine Presence]!"

F. Some time later the three met in one place. Said they, "Shammai's impatience sought to drive us from the world, but Hillel's gentleness brought us under the wings of the *Shekhinah*."[15]

We have four separate stories, united with a superscription (part A) and subscription (part E). The stories as a group are in graceful Hebrew style. They certainly could have been told separately, but have been collected to make a single point, given at the end: Hillel was patient, Shammai querulous. The editor of the whole pericope has carefully supplied the moral of the stories.

[15] b. Shab. 30b–31a.

Part C could have ended with the phrase noting that Hillel made him a proselyte, the intention of which is repeated in parts D and E. The alphabet story is a separate element, but relates closely to the preceding story. Parts D and E likewise seem unitary accounts from a single hand. Part F reverts to the superscription, now spelling out what the patience of Hillel had meant.

The four stories of course reflect the Hillelite viewpoint, but we have no idea which Hillelites—early or late, patriarchal or rabbinical, Palestinian or Babylonian. I discern only a few stock phrases, such as "Hillel is worth," "Be gentle like Hillel *and* not impatient like Shammai." But extended, detailed, smooth stories such as these are not built upon such brief stock phrases; they merely draw upon them at critical turning points or climaxes in the original narrative. Another well-known saying is the Aramaic *What is hateful...*, around which the second act of part D is built.

In the following, virtues of Shammai are turned into criticism:

> A. It was taught: They said concerning Shammai the Elder [that] all his days he would eat in honor of the Sabbath.
> He found a handsome animal and said, "Let this be for the Sabbath." [If afterwards] he found one more handsome, he put aside the second [for the Sabbath] and ate the first.
> B. But Hillel the Elder had a different trait. All his deeds [were] for the sake of heaven, as it is said: *Blessed be the Lord, day by day* (Ps. 68:20).
> C. It was likewise taught: The House of Shammai say, "From the first day of the week [prepare] for your Sabbath."
> And the House of Hillel say, *"Blessed be the Lord, day by day"* (Ps. 68:20).

Here Shammai's good deed becomes a vice. Part A certainly stood separately. By itself it is a story of how the virtuous Shammai kept the Sabbath, always setting aside the best things he could for that purpose. But the addition of part B shows Hillel to be superior—his religiosity did not await the occasion of the Sabbath.

Part C then gives us what must be the beginning of the matter, a dispute between the Houses, which has been rendered into stories about the founding masters by the foregoing narratives. That seems important, for the House of Shammai's story about Shammai is no less creditable than the House of Hillel's story about Hillel. If this is so, the literary history is not difficult to recover:

I. Original teaching of the masters:
  1. Shammai: *Sabbath*
  2. Hillel: *Always be grateful*
II. The Houses:
  1. Shammai's House: *Prepare for the Sabbath all week long.*
  2. Hillel's House: *Be grateful every day.*

III. The stories:
    1. Shammai: They said concerning Shammai the Elder....
    2. Hillel the Elder: All his deeds were for the sake of heaven....

To this point, the traditions were independent of one another and did not contrast Hillel favorably against Shammai. Then, at stage IV, the contrast is drawn:

IV. The stories brought together:
But Hillel the Elder had a different trait.

The Historical Hillel

Our analysis of stories about Hillel repeatedly brings us to the rabbinical academies and patriarchal politics of the period after 70 A.D. When we are able to locate a master who knows a Hillel story, and who may therefore supply us with a date as to the *terminus ante quem* of such a story, he usually is an authority at Usha, *ca.* 140, after the Bar Kokhba War, or even later. So we may claim that it is at Usha that Hillel as an individual, apart from the House that bears his name, becomes a central figure. His migration from Babylonia is taken for granted, and his rise to power is the subject of serious historical efforts. Some of his moral sayings and ordinances are first attested to at Usha. Part of the reason may be the renewed interest of the patriarchate, now under Simeon b. Gamaliel II, in discovering for itself more agreeable ancestors than the discredited Gamaliel II. In addition (for it was not a patriarchal venture alone), there was interest in recovering usable spiritual heroes from within Pharisaism itself, in place of Bar Kokhba and other messianic types.

The immense corpus of Hillel traditions exhibits one uniform quality: Unlike stories about Shammai, which are rarely friendly, no story is overtly hostile to Hillel. None was shaped by circles intending an unfavorable account of the man and his teachings. This is because the traditions were shaped by Hillelite heirs, both those who claimed to be his disciples, such as Yohanan b. Zakkai, and those, such as Gamaliel II, Simeon b. Gamaliel II, the House of Hillel, and especially, Judah the Patriarch, who claimed to be his descendants. Indeed, the whole corpus of Mishnaic literature was shaped by Hillelites.

Hillel pericopae served to supply points of origin for many legal and literary phenomena. Stories about Hillel as a model for virtue stand pretty much by themselves. Later masters made extensive use of the name of Hillel. From the destruction of the Temple onward, Hillel was everywhere claimed as the major authority—after Moses and Ezra—for the Oral Torah. Hillel could always be added to make stories more impressive. There was no limit to the claims made in his behalf as source of Torah traditions.

Despite the rich and impressive Hillel tradition, however, we can hardly conclude that with Hillel the rabbinic traditions about pre-70 Pharisees enter the pages of history. The traditions concerning Hillel do not lay a considerable claim to historical plausibility. They provide an accurate account only of what later generations thought important to say about, or in the name of, Hillel.

After 70 A.D. traditions about a man were shaped by his immediate disciples and discussed by people who actually knew him. Remarks about these traditions, made out of context in other settings, frequently provide attestation that a living tradition of what a master had said and done was shaped very soon after his death, and even during his lifetime. They often supply a *terminus ante quem*. That does not mean the master actually said and did what the disciples and later contemporaries claim, but it does mean we stand close to the master. Reduction of the sayings and traditions to formal logia, even to written notes, and later to published compilations (such as the Mishnah) further contributes to the historical interest of the later masters' traditions.

Hillel's materials, by contrast, do not exhibit the marks of similar, exact processes of nearly-contemporary editing and redaction, whether to oral form or to written documents. To Hillel are assigned neither masters nor disciples. He does not quote anyone, except in the context of a historical narrative, and then he does not repeat what "they" said to him, merely reports their law. No master of his day or before the Yavnean period ever quotes, or even knows about, him. He is supposed to be the leading master of his time, but no one ever says, "So have I received from Hillel."

On the face of it, therefore, both form and style of the Hillel corpus differ from later materials. If Hillel is the first Pharisee to emerge in the model of the later first century Pharisees and later rabbis, it is because the later rabbis adopted him and made him their own, not because he managed to transmit his sayings. The rabbis adopted him because of the later patriarchal claim to descend from him. It became interesting to tell stories about Hillel. Those who favored the patriarch would emphasize Hillel's merits; those who criticized the patriarch might stress that Hillel's virtue lay in his knowledge of Torah, not in his political role. Similarly, the House of Hillel's advocates in Yavneh and Usha had a strong motive to develop stories about the founder of their House. So the growth of the Hillel tradition was fostered by several distinct groups, and through their stories the several groups were able to address themselves to their own issues.

For the moment all we can say with certainty is that successive groups found it important to shape Hillel materials, and the conditions reflected in these materials are often not of actual historical realities (no Pharisee, even Hillel, ran the Temple), but rather the realities of life and fantasies of the shapers of the pericopae. The historical Hillel may stand behind some of the Hillel materials befqre us, but it will take much study before we can suggest concrete hypotheses about him.

The only firm conclusion is that Hillel was likely to have lived sometime before the destruction of the Temple and to have played an important part in the politics of the Pharisaic party. We may further hypothesize that traditions about his teachings on the festivals (Passover), on purity laws, and on legal theory (the ordinances) may go back to him. But the materials before us are so highly developed and sophisticated that we cannot recover anything like his own words.

We have now reached a methodological impasse. By isolating Hillel materials and asking some obvious questions about the historical usefulness of their contents and about the provenance of, and the interests reflected in, the telling of Hillel stories, we find ourselves in the middle decades of the second century A.D., rather than in the last decades of the first century B.C. Whether or not the rabbinical traditions about the Pharisees—the richest and most detailed account of the pre-70 sect—are useful for historical purposes, they obviously cannot be used as we have just now attempted without careful attention to relevant sources from other than rabbinical circles and without a systematic, disciplined effort to assign traditions to a particular stratum and to a particular circle.

First, however, let us ask ourselves, What has gone wrong? We have raised questions that presuppose that exact accounts of the way things happened are contained in the stories before us. We have assumed more accurate, detailed historical information than is in fact available. We wondered whether Hillel could really have issued the *prozbul* or whether he truly said the wise sayings attributed to him. But pressing such issues implies that the literary materials to which we bring them contain some firsthand information about Hillel. In other words, we have not strayed far from the fundamentalist reservation. We have concentrated our attention on the substance of sayings and the content of stories. If the sayings and stories came from reasonably reliable, contemporary observers, our questions would be legitimate. But with data first appearing in documents finally redacted 200 years after the events, it obviously will not serve the historical inquiry to investigate, at the very outset, detailed historical questions. The substance must stand aside in favor of the form; the issues of transmission and attestation must be faced.

We therefore begin again, this time with Josephus and his picture of the Pharisees, because he claims to have been a Pharisee and because he was familiar with Jerusalem before 70 A.D. We shall refrain from asking questions of detail, but shall seek some reasonably plausible generalities. We wonder not whether John Hyrcanus "really" said what he said to the Pharisees, but what overall picture of the Pharisees may emerge from Josephus's stories about him. In the Gospels we shall try to isolate the main outlines of the early Christian portrait of Pharisaism, but we shall not inquire whether Jesus "really" said that one should keep both purity laws and the rules of righteousness. When we return to the rabbinic traditions about the Pharisees, we shall look for the basic agenda, rather than for exact details, of Pharisaic law and theology. Considering the nature of the sources in our hands, we have no sound alternative.

3

Josephus's Pharisees:
"The Real Administrators
of the State"

Josephus

Why is Josephus a more credible historian than the rabbinical story-tellers whose work we have just examined? First, he himself claims to be a historian, writing an account of things that actually happened. Second, he lived in the period before 70 A.D. and participated in its most important events. Third, he wrote shortly after 70, and therefore his memory of events was still fresh. Finally, and most important, while we have to attempt to uncover the development of rabbinical stories, we may take for granted that the account of Josephus underwent no similarly extensive revision and re-working by later historians. Admittedly, there were some interpolations, but in the main we have pretty much what Josephus actually wrote. So the historian stands in direct relationship to his history. We know who he was, we are able to locate his particular biases, and his writings do not involve a century of revisions by other hands.

Author of the most important historical works on the Jews in antiquity, Josephus, the son of Matthias, was born to a priestly family in 37–8 A.D. In 66 A.D., when the great revolt against Rome broke out, he was sent from Jerusalem to lead the struggle in Galilee. With the fall of the town of Jotapata after a siege lasting 47 days, Josephus fell into the hands of the Romans. He prophesied that their commander, Vespasian, would become emperor, and when, two years later, Vespasian indeed was proclaimed emperor, he liberated Josephus. The Jewish general then served the Romans as interpreter during the siege of Jerusalem, and as historian of the war afterward. In 70 A.D., after the city had fallen and the Temple had been destroyed, Josephus was taken to Rome and enjoyed the patronage of the Flavian emperors, first Vespasian, then Titus. He died sometime after 100 A.D.

Four of his works, all written in Rome, come down from ancient times: *The Jewish War, Antiquities, Life,* and a treatise, *Against Apion.* The *War* was first written in Aramaic, an appeal to the Jews of the Parthian Empire not to blame Rome for the destruction of the Temple, which had been caused by the Jews' own misdeeds, and a defense of the Romans' administration of Palestine and conduct of the war. This was then translated into Greek, in a second edition, and published sometime between 75 and 79 A.D. Sixteen years later, in 93–94 A.D., he issued his *Antiquities,* a history of ancient Israel down to 70 A.D. The *Life* came still later, sometime after 100 A.D., as did *Against Apion.*[1]

Josephus claims in his autobiography that he himself was a Pharisee:

> At about the age of sixteen I determined to gain personal experience of the several sects into which our nation is divided. These, as I have frequently mentioned, are three in number—the first that of the Pharisees, the second that of the Sadducees, and the third that of the Essenes. I thought that, after a thorough investigation, I should be in a position to select the best. So I submitted myself to hard training and laborious exercises and passed through the three courses. Not content, however, with the experience thus gained, on hearing of one named Bannus, who dwelt in the wilderness, wearing only such clothing as trees provided, feeding on such things as grew of themselves, and using frequent ablutions of cold water, by day and night, for purity's sake, I became his devoted disciple. With him I lived for three years and, having accomplished my purpose, returned to the city. Being now in my nineteenth year I began to govern my life by the rules of the Pharisees, a sect having points of resemblance to that which the Greeks call the Stoic school.[2]

Josephus repeatedly tells us that ancient Judaism was divided into three sects—though we know of others—and here alleges he himself underwent the training imposed by each of them.

If this is true, the whole process of entering the three sects seems to have been compressed into a very brief period. He says he began to study them at the age of 16, then lived with Bannus for three years, and now he is 19.

---

[1] Josephus, *Life; Against Apion,* trans. H. St. J. Thackeray (Cambridge: Harvard University Press, 1926), pp. vii–xii.

[2] Josephus, *Life,* pp. 5–7, ls. 9–12.

He declares he chose to follow the Pharisaic rules. So the three years of apprenticeship with Bannus consumed the whole time devoted to the study of all the sects, and Bannus does not represent one of those sects. In all, Josephus does not suggest he studied Pharisaism, Essenism, and Sadduceism for a considerable period. Pharisees generally required a training period of 12 months, and the Essenes likewise imposed a long novitiate; we have no information about the Sadducees. So Josephus's evidence about the sects and his story of his own actions do not seem to correlate. He wants the reader to know that he knew what he was talking about, and that he was a Pharisee. But nothing else in the story of his *Life* tells us what being a Pharisee meant to Josephus. Like Luke's similar allegation in behalf of Paul (Acts 22:3; see Phil. 3:5), it is part of his credentials.

We do, however, gain a picture of how the Pharisees functioned from Josephus's story of his doings during the revolutionary period. On the eve of the war, Josephus says, he opposed sedition, and therefore feared for his life. He sought asylum in the Temple court. "When...the chieftains of the...brigands had been put to death, I ventured out of the Temple and once more consorted with the chief priests and the leading Pharisees."[3]

Later, during Josephus's time as commander of Galilee, his enemies in Galilee sent a mission to Jerusalem seeking his removal as commander. The emissaries went to Simeon the son of Gamaliel, whom we shall meet again:

> This Simeon was a native of Jerusalem, of a very illustrious family, and of the sect of the Pharisees, who have the reputation of being unrivalled experts in their country's laws. A man highly gifted with intelligence and judgment, he could by sheer genius retrieve an unfortunate situation in the affairs of state....[4]

Simeon received the embassy and agreed to remove Josephus from office. The administration then sent a deputation "comprising different classes of society but of equal standing in education. Two of them...were from the lower ranks and adherents of the Pharisees; the third...also a Pharisee, came from a priestly family; the youngest...was descended from high priests":

> Their instructions were to approach the Galileans and ascertain the reason for their devotion to me. If they attributed it to my being a native of Jerusalem, they were to reply that so were all four of them. If to my expert knowledge of their laws, they should retort that neither were they ignorant of the customs of their fathers. If again they asserted that their affection was due to my priestly office, they should answer that two of them were likewise priests.[5]

3 Josephus, *Life*, 21–2, pp. 9–11.
4 Ibid., 191–93, pp. 71–73.
5 Ibid., 197–98, p. 75.

The Pharisees are invariably represented as experts in the law, and of greater importance, as an important political party in charge of the conduct of the war, able to make or break commanders in the field. In Jerusalem they enjoyed the highest offices. Their leaders are men of political experience and great power.

But whether their offices and power came to them because they were Pharisees, or whether they were officers and men of power who happened also to be Pharisees, is not settled by Josephus's picture. The answer to that question depends upon what it meant to be a Pharisee in the last decades before destruction of the Temple. What was the character of the Pharisaic group? What were their beliefs and practices? Do these relate to the holding of public office, or are they irrelevant to politics? In other words, was one a Pharisee by profession, or was "being a Pharisee" an avocation, something that might be a distinguishing trait of a person whose public life focused upon matters other than those of concern to the party?

The Pharisees of War

Josephus's first work, the *War,* presents an entirely consistent picture: The Pharisees were a political party, active in the court affairs of the Maccabean state. To understand Josephus's account, we must review the history of the Maccabees.

The Maccabees founded an independent Jewish state in Palestine in 165 B.C., and ruled until 63 B.C., when the Romans conquered the country. They came to power as head of a Jewish revolt against Antiochus IV Epiphanes, King of Syria (including Palestine), by whose orders the Temple at Jerusalem had been desecrated and turned into a pagan sanctuary. Antiochus had further decreed that Jews no longer observe the commandments of the Mosaic revelation, the Torah. They could not circumcize their sons, sanctify the Sabbath, and worship one God alone. The animal Jews regarded as most repulsive, the pig, was offered as a sacrifice on local altars and in Jerusalem.

The biblical Book of Daniel, written during the period of persecution, tells us that a nameless seer felt the end of time was at hand. Only God's direct intervention could save Israel.

In the winter of 166 B.C., the king's agents came to Modin, near Lydda, and set up the pagan altar. When the first Jew came out to offer the sacrifice, Mattathias, a priest, killed him and the king's agent as well. Mattathias and his followers undertook a guerilla war against the Syrian-Greek rulers. Shortly thereafter, Mattathias died, and his son, Judah the Maccabee ("hammer") took over. Owing to his successes, the Syrian government rescinded the persecution of Judaism, and in 164 granted the Jews their former rights.

Judah ignored the decree, retook Jerusalem, purified the Temple, and fortified the city. After a protracted struggle, Judah succeeded in establishing himself and his family as the legitimate regime. When he died in 160 B.C., his brothers carried on the government and made the country independent. In 142 B.C., Simon, the last of the brothers, obtained Israel's complete freedom from tribute.[6] His son, John Hyrcanus, succeeded in 134. John's mother had been a war captive who later married the priest, Simon, though this was contrary to law, since captive women usually were ravished and therefore prohibited to the priesthood.

John "became a Hellenistic prince like his contemporaries and rivals."[7] Each prince strove to expand his frontiers. For his part, John conquered the coastal plain, and, later on, Galilee, Samaria, and Idumea (the biblical Edom). His son Alexander Jannaeus ruled from 104 to 76 B.C., with power extending from the Egyptian border to Mount Carmel, and from the Mediterranean to Trans-Jordan.

The Maccabean dynasty, having risen to prevent the assimilation of "the Torah" into Hellenism, now incorporated Hellenic culture into "the Torah." As Bickerman says,

> This accommodation of new elements to the Bible, this consideration for native tradition, characterizes the Hellenization carried through under the Maccabees.[8]

Bickerman observes that while the biblical prophets laid slight emphasis on study, but regarded prophetic admonitions and divine chastisement as leading to repentance, the Pharisees held that piety is attained through teaching. He states:

> But this is a Hellenic, one might say, a Platonic notion, that education could so transform the individual and the entire people that the nation would be capable of fulfilling the divine task set it.[9]

The Pharisees constituted a political party which sought, and for a time evidently won, domination of the political institutions of the Maccabean kingdom. In other words, however they might hope to *teach* people to conform to the Torah, they were prepared to coerce them to conform

6 Elias Bickerman, *The Maccabees. An Account of their History from the Beginnings to the Fall of the House of the Hasmoneans* (New York: Schocken Books, 1947), p. 147. This work has been republished as *From Ezra to the Last of the Maccabees: Foundations of Post-biblical Judaism* (New York: Schocken Books, 1962). Page references are to the 1962 edition.

7 Ibid., p. 78.

8 Ibid., p. 89.

9 Ibid., p. 162.

through the instruments of government. Bickerman says, "Early Pharisaism was a belligerent movement that knew how to hate."[10]

When Alexander Jannaeus died, his wife Alexandra Salome succeeded. Here is the point at which Josephus's Pharisees first enter the picture in *War,* because Alexandra Salome put the government in their hands. They thereupon executed Jannaeus's counselors, who had been their enemies, and exercised power with a high hand. The anti-Pharisaic opposition at this time was led by the queen's second son, Aristobulus. When the queen died in 67 B.C., Aristobulus won the throne. His brother, Hyrcanus, allied to Antipater the Idumean, father of Herod, besieged Aristobulus in the Temple of Jerusalem. The Roman general in the Near East, Pompey, intervened and supported Aristobulus, but he found reason to change his mind and preferred Hyrcanus. The Romans then took Jerusalem in the fall of 63, and the independent government of the Maccabean dynasty came to an end. A few years later, Herod was entrusted with the rule of Judea.[11]

Of the political role of the Pharisaic political party, Bickerman writes:

> ...Pharisaism had led to an estrangement of the people from the dynasty. Before Pompey at Damascus there appeared an embassy of Jews, who set forth to him that Rome had long been the protector of the Jews, who had thus enjoyed autonomy. Their head had been a High Priest, not a king. Their present Maccabean rulers, they declared, had enslaved the people and destroyed their ancestral constitution; they maintained their position only by terror and by the support of their soldiery....[12]

The Pharisaic position was that foreign domination was acceptable, so long as the Torah was the binding law on the Jews. Since the Pharisees also claimed that they themselves determined the substance of the Torah, this position constituted not merely a religious, but also a political claim. In effect they were saying, "We shall rule the country, in collaboration with whatever foreign power is willing to make possible our dominion over the inner life of Israel."

We may now understand what Josephus has to tell us in *War.* The Pharisees occur in three important passages. First, without being introduced or extensively described, but standing without a history, they suddenly make an appearance as the dominant power in the reign of Alexandra Salome. They are later alluded to in connection with the court affairs of Herod. Finally, in Josephus's long account of Jewish sectarianism, the Pharisees receive requisite attention.

---

[10] Bickerman, *From Ezra to the Last of the Maccabees,* p. 103.
[11] Ibid., p. 107.
[12] Ibid., p. 109.

THE PHARISEES
AND ALEXANDRA SALOME

Alexander bequeathed the kingdom to his wife Alexandra, being convinced that the Jews would bow to her authority as they would to no other, because by her utter lack of his brutality and by her opposition to his crimes she had won the affections of the populace. Nor was he mistaken in these expectations; for this frail woman firmly held the reins of government, thanks to her reputation for piety. She was, indeed, the very strictest observer of the national traditions and would deprive of office any offenders against the sacred laws. Of the two sons whom she had by Alexander, she appointed the elder, Hyrcanus, high priest, out of consideration alike for his age and his disposition, which was too lethargic to be troubled about public affairs; the younger, Aristobulus, as a hot-head, she confined to a private life.

Beside Alexandra, and growing as she grew, arose the Pharisees, a body of Jews with the reputation of excelling the rest of their nation in the observances of religion, and as exact exponents of the laws. To them, being herself intensely religious, she listened with too great deference; while they, gradually taking advantage of an ingenuous woman, became at length the real administrators of the state, at liberty to banish and to recall, to loose and to bind, whom they would. In short, the enjoyments of royal authority were theirs; its expenses and burdens fell to Alexandra. She proved, however, to be a wonderful administrator in larger affairs, and, by continual recruiting doubled her army, besides collecting a considerable body of foreign troops; so that she not only strengthened her own nation, but became a formidable foe to foreign potentates. But if she ruled the nation, the Pharisees ruled her.

Thus they put to death Diogenes, a distinguished man who had been a friend of Alexander, accusing him of having advised the king to crucify his eight hundred victims. They further urged Alexandra to make away with the others who had instigated Alexander to punish those men; and as she from superstitious motives always gave way, they proceeded to kill whomsoever they would. The most eminent of the citizens thus imperilled sought refuge with Aristobulus, who persuaded his mother to spare their lives in consideration of their rank, but, if she was not satisfied of their innocence, to expel them from the city. Their security being thus guaranteed, they dispersed about the country.[13]

The Pharisees are repeatedly represented by Josephus as "excelling" in religion and as teachers of the laws. But the substance of their religion and

---

[13] Josephus, *War*, trans. H. St. J. Thackeray (Cambridge: Harvard University Press, 1956), 1:107–14, pp. 53, 55.

of the laws they taught is not described. The party has no history. Josephus does not take for granted we know who they are, for he tells us they are "a body of Jews with the reputation of excelling the rest." But their beliefs, doctrines, and religious and social goals are ignored. Noted merely as a "body of Jews" (*syntagma ti Ioudaiōn*), they play upon the queen's religiosity, take advantage of her guillibility, and gradually assume real power. Moreover, they exercise that power to their own advantage, murdering their enemies—which tells us they have a sorry past to avenge in Maccabean politics.

A rebellion which took place under Alexander Jannaeus led to the crucifixion of 800 of the king's enemies: "Eight thousand of the hostile faction fled beyond the borders of Judaea."[14] In his story of the rebellion, Josephus does not name the "hostile faction," but we find reason to suppose the armed rebels of Alexander Jannaeus's time were Pharisees. Why did the Pharisees take arms in rebellion against Alexander Jannaeus? Were the philosophical issues on which they differed from the king and his supporters so heatedly argued that only war would settle the matter? Under Alexandra Salome, the Pharisees killed anyone they wanted, and eminent citizens took refuge with Aristobulus, the heir apparent. Why did the politics of the day lead to bloodshed? What made the Pharisees—supposedly a "school"— murder their opponents, just as some of them had earlier been murdered? Clearly, Josephus's story of what the Pharisees did exhibits a disparity from his account of what they believed. Belief in life after death ought not to have produced civil war.

IN HEROD'S COURT

> The king was furiously indignant, particularly at the wife of Pheroras, the principal object of Salome's charges. He, accordingly, assembled a council of his friends and relations and accused the wretched woman of numerous misdeeds, among others of insulting his own daughters, of subsidizing the Pharisees to oppose him, and of alienating his brother, after bewitching him with drugs.[15]

What is interesting in this reference is the view that the Pharisees, like any other political party, might be "subsidized" to support one party and oppose another.

A PHILOSOPHICAL SCHOOL

Josephus's first description of the philosophical schools is as follows:

> Of the two first-named schools, the Pharisees who are considered the most accurate interpreters of the laws, and hold the position of the

---

14 Josephus, *War*, 1:97, p. 49.
15 Ibid., 1:571, p. 271.

leading sect, attribute everything to Fate and to God; they hold that to act rightly or otherwise rests, indeed, for the most part with men, but that in each action Fate cooperates. Every soul, they maintain, is perishable, but the soul of the good alone passes into another body, while the souls of the wicked suffer eternal punishment.

The Sadducees, the second of the orders, do away with Fate altogether, and remove God beyond, not merely the commission, but the very sight, of evil. They maintain that man has the free choice of good or evil, and that it rests with each man's will whether he follows the one or the other. As for the persistence of the soul after death, penalties in the underworld, and rewards, they will have none of them.

The Pharisees are affectionate to each other and cultivate harmonious relations with the community. The Sadducees, on the contrary, are, even among themselves, rather boorish in their behavior, and in their intercourse with their peers are as rude as to aliens. Such is what I have to say on the Jewish philosophical schools.[16]

The foregoing account represents Josephus's Pharisees as of 75 A.D. We find no claim that the Pharisees are the most popular sect and have a massive public following, or that no one can effectively govern Palestine without their support. All we hear is their opinion on two issues, Fate, or providence, and punishment of the soul after death. The Sadducees are matched opposites, not believing in Fate or in life after death. The Essenes, who are described at far greater length (*War*, 2:119–161) hold that the soul is immortal, believe in reward and punishment after death, and can foretell the future. Josephus adds, "Such are the theological views of the Essenes concerning the soul, whereby they irresistibly attract all who have once tasted their philosophy" (later, as we have already seen, he claims that he himself was able to resist their philosophy and so joined the Pharisees). Here the Sadducees and Pharisees address themselves to identical issues, and take the two extreme positions. In context, the two parties are not very important; neither one receives a significant description. The Pharisees are seen not as a political party, but as a philosophical school. The phrase about their being "the most accurate interpreters of the laws" and "the leading sect" are all that link the Pharisees of the sectarian passage to the Pharisees of the history of Queen Alexandra Salome.

As to the doctrines attributed to the Pharisees, Bickerman points out that these mark the Pharisees as a Hellenistic sect:

In this way Maccabean Hellenism succeeded in parrying spiritual movements which might otherwise have destroyed traditional Judaism. For example, the Hellenistic world surrounding Judaism was caught up by a new revelation that solved the problem of evil on earth: retribution would come after death, when the wicked would be punished and

16 Ibid., 2:162–66, pp. 385–87.

the righteous rewarded and awakened to new life. Such notions are alien to the Bible, indeed in contradiction to it, for the Torah promises reward and punishment in this life. Hence the Sadducees rejected the new doctrine and ridiculed the Pharisaic teaching of resurrection. If they had been the only authoritative representatives of Judaism, Judaism would either have lagged behind the times or grown rigid. . . . The Pharisees. . .adopted the Hellenistic doctrine of resurrection, but subsumed it under the principles of the Torah. What to the pagans was an event dictated more or less by necessity appears among the Jews as the working of the free will of God. . . .[17]

What is Hellenistic in Pharisaic Judaism? It is the stress on tradition as the guide to the formation of social life and personal values. That tradition, not written down, endured in the life of the masters and was learned from their precept and example. The concept of a truth outside of Scriptures opened the way to the accomodation of new ideas and values within the structure of inherited symbols—holy words, holy deeds, holy doctrines. The "oral Torah" opened the Judaic tradition to the future. Those who defined and carried on the tradition felt confident that they might discover new truths in ancient Scriptures, thus preserving a welcoming attitude toward the world.

The Pharisees of Antiquities

In 95 A.D., 20 years after he wrote *War,* Josephus greatly expanded his picture, adding important details to familiar accounts and entirely new materials as well. To understand the additions, we must recall that at the same time he wrote *Antiquities,* Josephus was claiming he himself was a Pharisee.

Pharisees who survived the destruction of Jerusalem in 70 spent the next 20 years establishing themselves as the dominant group. Led by Yohanan ben Zakkai, they had created a Jewish administration at the coastal town of Yavneh. This administration assumed those powers of self-government left in Jewish hands by the Roman regime. By 90 A.D., the head of the Yavnean government, Gamaliel II, grandson of the Gamaliel mentioned as a Pharisee in the Temple council in Acts 5:34, and son of the Simeon ben Gamaliel alluded to in Josephus's *Life* as a leader of the Jerusalem government in 66 A.D., had negotiated with the Roman government for recognition as head of Palestinian Jewry. The basis for settlement was the Yavneans' agreement to oppose subversion of Roman rule in exchange for Roman support of the Yavneans' control over the Jews—the same

17 Bickerman, *From Ezra to the Last of the Maccabees,* pp. 94–97.

agreement offered to Pompey in 63 B.C. The Yavnean authorities, called rabbis—whence "rabbinical Judaism"—thus continued the Pharisaic political and foreign policies initiated at the end of Maccabean times. This time, however, the Pharisees met with no competition. The Herodian dynasty had long since passed from the scene. The Essenes were wiped out in the war. The Sadducees, who had controlled the country through their power in the Temple government, lost their power base with the destruction of the Temple and evidently ceased to constitute an important political force.

If one read only *War* without knowledge of the *Life*, one might suppose Josephus took most keen interest in the Essenes and certainly sympathized with their ascetic way of life. That surmise would receive support if we knew that he spent three years of his adolescence with Bannus, whose way of living corresponded in important ways to that of the Essenes, though Josephus does not call him an Essene. So one might expect that the great historian regarded the Essenes as the leading Jewish "philosophical school." But he does not. The Essenes of *War* are cut down to size; the Pharisees of *Antiquities* predominate. Josephus now says that the country cannot be governed without their cooperation, and that he himself is one of them. Josephus was in fact part of the pro-Roman priestly aristocracy before the war of 66–73. But nothing in his account suggests he was a Pharisee, as he later claimed in his autobiography.

A PHILOSOPHICAL SCHOOL

Antiquities has two "philosophical school" passages. The first is brief, interrupting the narrative of Josephus's account of Jonathan Maccabee's agreement with Rome of *ca.* 140 B.C. The second coincides, as in *War,* with the beginning of procuratorial government, in the beginning of the first century A.D. Josephus here alludes to a rebellion led by Judas, a Gaulanite, and Saddok, a Pharisee who started a "fourth school of philosophy" in addition to the three already known, namely, a school of people who sought the destruction of Roman rule. The passage thus corresponds in position and function to *War* 2:162–166. The first of the two accounts is as follows:

> Now at this time there were three schools of thought among the Jews, which held different opinions concerning human affairs; the first being that of the Pharisees, the second that of the Sadducees, and the third that of the Essenes. As for the Pharisees, they say that certain events are the work of Fate, but not all; as to other events, it depends upon ourselves whether they shall take place or not. The sect of Essenes, however, declares that Fate is mistress of all things, and that nothing befalls men unless it be in accordance with her decree. But the Sadducees do away with Fate, holding that there is no such thing and that human actions are not achieved in accordance with her decree,

but that all things lie within our own power, so that we ourselves are responsible for our well-being, while we suffer misfortune through our own thoughtlessness. Of these matters, however, I have given a more detailed account in the second book of the *Jewish History*.[18]

Fate, or providence, is thus the primary issue. The three "schools" take all possible positions: fate governs all; fate governs nothing; fate governs some things but not everything. The Pharisees enjoy the golden middle. In the *War* the Pharisees are given the same position, but there the issue of the immortality of the soul is also introduced.

The second "philosophical school" account is as follows:

> The Jews, from the most ancient times, had three philosophies pertaining to their traditions, that of the Essenes, that of the Sadducees, and, thirdly, that of the group called the Pharisees. To be sure, I have spoken about them in the second book of the *Jewish War*, but nevertheless I shall here too dwell on them for a moment.
>
> The Pharisees simplify their standard of living, making no concession to luxury. They follow the guidance of that which their doctrine has selected and transmitted as good, attaching the chief importance to the observance of those commandments which it has seen fit to dictate to them. They show respect and deference to their elders, nor do they rashly presume to contradict their proposals. Though they postulate that everything is brought about by fate, still they do not deprive the human will of the pursuit of what is in man's power, since it was God's good pleasure that there should be a fusion and that the will of man with his virtue and vice should be admitted to the council-chamber of fate. They believe that souls have power to survive death and that there are rewards and punishments under the earth for those who have led lives of virtue or vice: eternal imprisonment is the lot of evil souls, while the good souls receive an easy passage to a new life. Because of these views they are, as a matter of fact, extremely influential among the townsfolk; and all prayers and sacred rites of divine worship are performed according to their exposition. This is the great tribute that the inhabitants of the cities, by practising the highest ideals both in their way of living and in their discourse, have paid to the excellence of the Pharisees.
>
> The Sadducees hold that the soul perishes along with the body. They own no observance of any sort apart from the laws; in fact, they reckon it a virtue to dispute with the teachers of the path of wisdom that they pursue. There are but few men to whom this doctrine has been made known, but these are men of the highest standing. They accomplish practically nothing, however. For whenever they assume some office, though they submit unwillingly and perforce, yet submit

---

[18] Josephus, *Antiquities*, trans. R. Marcus (Cambridge: Harvard University Press, 1957), 13:171–73, pp. 311, 313.

they do to the formulas of the Pharisees, since otherwise the masses would not tolerate them.[19]

This considerable account adds to the Pharisees' virtues their simple style of living—the asceticism Josephus had admired—and deference to the elders; earlier he said the Sadducees were boorish. The issues of providence and life after death, last judgment, and reward and punishment for deeds done in this life are alluded to.

What is entirely new is the allegation that the townspeople follow only the Pharisees, and that the Temple is conducted according to their law. Of this we have formerly heard nothing. With the Temple in ruins for a quarter of a century and the old priesthood decimated and scattered, it was now possible to place the Pharisees in a position of power of which, in Temple times, they had scarcely dreamed. The Sadducees, moreover, are forced to do whatever the Pharisees tell them, for otherwise the people would ignore them—an even more extreme allegation. Later we shall hear that the followers of Shammai, the rival in Pharisaic politics to the predominant leader, Hillel, knew that "the law really follows Hillel," and therefore all their decisions were in accord with Hillelite doctrine. The allegation of Josephus is of the same order, and equally incredible.

THE PHARISEES
AND JOHN HYRCANUS

While in *War* Josephus makes no reference to relationships between the Pharisees and Maccabean monarchs before Alexandra Salome, in *Antiquities* he introduces a story, unrelated to the narrative in which it occurs, about a break between John Hyrcanus and the Pharisees. This same story, told about Jannaeus, also occurs in the Babylonian Talmud. Josephus's story is as follows:

> As for Hyrcanus, the envy of the Jews was aroused against him by his own successes and those of his sons; particularly hostile to him were the Pharisees, who are one of the Jewish schools, as we have related above. And so great is their influence with the masses that even when they speak against a king or high priest, they immediately gain credence. Hyrcanus too was a disciple of theirs, and was greatly loved by them. And once he invited them to a feast and entertained them hospitably, and when he saw that they were having a very good time, he began by saying that they knew he wished to be righteous and in everything he did tried to please God and them—for the Pharisees profess such beliefs; at the same time he begged them, if they observed

19 Josephus, *Antiquities,* trans. L. Feldman (Cambridge: Harvard University Press, 1965), 18:11–17, pp. 9, 11, 13, 15.

him doing anything wrong or straying from the right path, to lead him
back to it and correct him. But they testified to his being altogether
virtuous, and he was delighted with their praise. However, one of the
guests, named Eleazar, who had an evil nature and took pleasure in
dissension, said, "Since you have asked to be told the truth, if you wish
to be righteous, give up the high-priesthood and be content with
governing the people." And when Hyrcanus asked him for what reason
he should give up the high-priesthood, he replied, "Because we have
heard from our elders that your mother was a captive in the reign
of Antiochus Epiphanes." But the story was false, and Hyrcanus was
furious with the man, while all the Pharisees were very indignant.

Then a certain Jonathan, one of Hyrcanus's close friends, belonging
to the school of Sadducees, who hold opinions opposed to those of the
Pharisees, said that it had been with the general approval of all the
Pharisees that Eleazar had made his slanderous statement; and this,
he added, would be clear to Hyrcanus if he inquired of them what
punishment Eleazar deserved for what he had said. And so Hyrcanus
asked the Pharisees what penalty they thought he deserved—for, he
said, he would be convinced that the slanderous statement had not
been made with their approval if they fixed a penalty commensurate
with the crime—, and they replied that Eleazar deserved stripes and
chains; for they did not think it right to sentence a man to death for
calumny, and anyway the Pharisees are naturally lenient in the matter
of punishments. At this Hyrcanus became very angry and began to
believe that the fellow had slandered him with their approval. And
Jonathan in particular inflamed his anger, and so worked upon him
that he brought him to join the Sadducaean party and desert the
Pharisees, and to abrogate the regulations which they had established
for the people, and punish those who observed them. Out of this, of
course, grew the hatred of the masses for him and his sons, but of
this we shall speak hereafter. For the present I wish merely to explain
that the Pharisees had passed on to the people certain regulations
handed down by former generations and not recorded in the Laws of
Moses, for which reason they are rejected by the Sadducaean group,
who hold that only those regulations should be considered valid which
were written down [in Scripture], and that those which had been
handed down by former generations need not be observed. And concerning these matters the two parties came to have controversies and
serious differences, the Sadducees having the confidence of the wealthy
alone but no following among the populace, while the Pharisees have
the support of the masses. But of these two schools and of the Essenes
a detailed account has been given in the second book of my *Judaica*.

And so Hyrcanus quieted the outbreak, and lived happily thereafter; and when he died after adminstering the government excellently
for thirty-one years, he left five sons.[20]

---

[20] Josephus, *Antiquities*, trans. R. Marcus, 13:288–98, pp. 373, 375, 377.

It is instructive to compare the foregoing account with the Talmud's story about Alexander Jannaeus. The two stories are too close to be wholly unrelated, yet they differ in spirit and in detail. Both Josephus and the Talmudic storyteller attempt to explain how the Pharisees broke from the Maccabean dynasty, and both attribute the break to a dramatic event—a banquet that ended badly. Ancient historians routinely explain historical events by reference to personalities, decisive incidents, and individual decisions made on the basis of whim or temperament.

> It is taught: The story is told that Yannai [Jannaeus] the King went to Kohalit in the wilderness and conquered there sixty towns. When he returned, he rejoiced greatly, and invited all the sages of Israel.
>
> He said to them, "Our forefathers would eat salt fish when they were engaged in the building of the Holy House. Let us also eat salt fish as a memorial to our forefathers."
>
> So they brought up salt fish on golden tables, and they ate.
>
> There was there a certain scoffer, evil-hearted and empty-headed, and Eleazar ben Poirah was his name.
>
> Eleazar b. Poirah said to Yannai the King, "O King Yannai, the hearts of the Pharisees are [set] against you."
>
> "What shall I do?"
>
> "Test them by the plate that is between your eyes."

[The reference is to the high priest's medallion ("plate between your eyes"). Jannaeus is both king and high priest, but the Pharisees claimed that Jannaeus's mother had been taken captive and raped, and therefore could not be the mother of a high priest, who had to be born of a virgin. Hence the king was not fit to be high priest. If the Pharisees were "tested" as to the matter, they would have to make a public admission of their disloyalty to the king-priest. Since the government of Jewish Palestine was based in the Temple of Jerusalem, the head of government ("king") also had to be head of the Temple ("high priest"). If Alexander Jannaeus could not be the latter, he could not head the state. So the "test" amounted to an examination of the loyalty of the Pharisees to the throne.]

> He tested them by the plate that was between his eyes.
>
> There was there a certain sage, and Judah b. Gedidiah was his name. Judah b. Gedidiah said to Yannai the King, "O King Yannai, Let suffice for you the crown of sovereignty [kingship]. Leave the crown of the [high] priesthood for the seed of Aaron."
>
> For people said that his [Yannai's] mother had been taken captive in Modin. The charge was investigated and not found [sustained]. The sages of Israel departed in anger.
>
> Eleazar b. Poirah then said to Yannai the king, "O King Yannai, That is the law [not here specified, as the punishment inflicted on

Judah] even for the ordinary folk in Israel. But you are King and high priest—should that be your law too?"

"What should I do?"

"If you take my advice, you will trample them down."

"But what will become of the Torah?"

"Lo, it is rolled up and lying in the corner. Whoever wants to learn, let him come and learn."

The evil blossomed through Eleazar b. Poirah. All the sages of Israel [= the Pharisees] were killed.

The world was desolate until Simeon b. Shetah came and restored the Torah to its place.[21]

This story is told from the rabbinical viewpoint. The "sages of Israel" are rabbis, Pharisees. The little colloquy about what will become of "the Torah" can only come come out of a rabbinical setting. Similarly, the "desolation" of the world is the absence of rabbinical instruction.

Solomon Zeitlin holds that the Talmudic story is older than the version of Josephus; it could have been written "only at a time when the kings were not high priests, which was from the time of Herod onwards."[22]

At any rate, there is an important lacuna in the Talmudic version: *that is the law* takes for granted the details available only in Josephus's account. But the relationship between the two versions is not clear. Either Josephus copied from a Hebrew source, or the Talmudic narrator copied from Josephus, or both have relied on a third authority. The story interrupts and contradicts Josephus's narrative, for Hyrcanus lived on happily after the disgrace. One should have expected some more appropriate heavenly recompense.

Again we observe in *Antiquities* stress upon the Pharisees' enjoying mass support, while only the rich listen to the Sadducees. The difference between the two parties, common in Hellenistic politics, is the disparity between the wealthy few and the virtuous many. Whoever hopes to govern Palestine had best rely upon the leaders of the latter.

THE PHARISEES

AND ALEXANDRA SALOME

The version in *Antiquities* of the Pharisees-in-power story is strikingly revised in favor of the Pharisees:

And when the queen saw that he was on the point of death and no longer held to any hope of recovery, she wept and beat her breast,

---

21 b. Qid. 66a.

22 Solomon Zeitlin, *The Rise and Fall of the Judaean State* (Philadelphia: Jewish Publication Society, 1962), Vol. 1, pp. 168–170.

lamenting the bereavement that was about to befall her and her children, and said to him, "To whom are you thus leaving me and your children, who are in need of help from others, especially when you know how hostile the nation feels toward you!"

Thereupon he advised her to follow his suggestions for keeping the throne secure for herself and her children and to conceal his death from the soldiers until she had captured the fortress. And then, he said, on her return to Jerusalem as from a splendid victory, she should yield a certain amount of power to the Pharisees, for if they praised her in return for this sign of regard, they would dispose the nation favorably toward her.

These men, he assured her, had so much influence with their fellow-Jews that they could injure those whom they hated and help those to whom they were friendly; when they spoke harshly of any person, even when they did so out of envy; and he himself, he added, had come into conflict with the nation because these men had been badly treated by him.

"And so," he said, "when you come to Jerusalem, send for their partisans, and showing them my dead body, permit them, with every sign of sincerity, to treat me as they please, whether they wish to dishonor my corpse by leaving it unburied because of the many injuries they have suffered at my hands, or in their anger wish to offer my dead body any other form of indignity. Promise them also that you will not take any action, while you are on the throne, without their consent. If you speak to them in this manner, I shall receive from them a more splendid burial than I should from you; for once they have the power to do so, they will not choose to treat my corpse badly, and at the same time you will reign securely." With this exhortation to his wife he died, after reigning twenty-seven years, at the age of forty-nine.

Thereupon Alexandra, after capturing the fortress, conferred with the Pharisees as her husband had suggested, and by placing in their hands all that concerned his corpse and the royal power, stilled their anger against Alexander, and made them her well-wishers and friends. And they in turn went to the people and made public speeches in which they recounted the deeds of Alexander, and said that in him they had lost a just king, and by their eulogies they so greatly moved the people to mourn and lament that they gave him a more splendid burial than had been given any of the kings before him. Now although Alexander had left two sons, Hyrcanus and Aristobulus, he had bequeathed the royal power to Alexandra. Of these sons the one, Hyrcanus, was incompetent to govern and in addition much preferred a quiet life, while the younger, Aristobulus, was man of action and high spirit. As for the queen herself, she was loved by the masses because she was thought to disapprove of the crimes committed by her husband.

Alexandra then appointed Hyrcanus as high priest because of his greater age but more especially because of his lack of energy; and she permitted the Pharisees to do as they liked in all matters, and also commanded the people to obey them; and whatever regulations, introduced by the Pharisees in accordance with the tradition of their fathers, had been abolished by her father-in-law Hyrcanus, these she again restored. And so, while she had the title of sovereign, the Pharisees had the power.

For example, they recalled exiles, and freed prisoners, and, in a word, in no way differed from absolute rulers. Nevertheless the queen took thought for the welfare of the kingdom and recruited a large force of mercenaries and also made her own force twice as large, with the result that she struck terror into the local rulers round her and received hostages from them. And throughout the entire country there was quiet except for the Pharisees; for they worked upon the feelings of the queen and tried to persuade her to kill those who had urged Alexander to put the eight hundred to death. Later they themselves cut down one of them, named Diogenes, and his death was followed by that of one after the other, until the leading citizens came to the palace, Aristobulus among them—for he was obviously resentful of what was taking place, and let it be plainly seen that if only he should get the opportunity, he would not leave his mother any power at all—, and they reminded her of all that they had achieved in the face of danger, whereby they had shown their unwavering loyalty to their master and had therefore been judged worthy by him of the greatest honors. And they begged her not to crush their hopes completely, for, they said, after escaping the dangers of war, they were now being slaughtered at home like cattle by their foes, and there was no one to avenge them. They also said that if their adversaries were to be contented with those already slain, they would bear with equanimity what had taken place, out of genuine devotion to their masters; but if, on the other hand, these men were to continue in the same course, let them, they begged, at least be given their freedom; for they would never bring themselves to seek any means of safety but what should come from her, and would welcome death in her palace so long as they might not have disloyalty on their conscience. It would be disgraceful both for them and for her who ruled as queen, they added, if, being abandoned by her, they should be given shelter by the enemies of her husband; for Aretas the Arab and the other princes would consider it of the utmost value to enlist such men as mercenaries, whose very name, they might say, had caused these princes to shudder before they had heard it [spoken aloud]. But if this could not be, and she had determined to favor the Pharisees above all others, let her, as the next best thing, station each of them in one of the garrisons, for, if some evil genius were thus wroth with the house of Alexander, they at least would show themselves [loyal] even though living in humble circumstances.

Speaking in this vein at great length, they called upon the shades of Alexander to take pity on those who had been killed and those who were in danger, whereupon all the bystanders burst into tears. And Aristobulus in particular made plain his sentiments by denouncing his mother bitterly. But still they themselves were to blame for their misfortunes, in allowing a woman to reign who madly desired it in her unreasonable love of power, and when her sons were in the prime of life. And so the queen, not knowing what to do consistent with her dignity, entrusted to them the guarding of the fortresses with the exception of Hyrcanis, Alexandreion and Machaerus, where her most valuable possessions were.[23]

In *War* Alexandra listened to the Pharisees "with too great deference," and they took advantage of her. They ran the government, but she paid. They wreaked terrible vengeance on their enemies, so many had to flee. Now we have Alexander Jannaeus, archenemy of the Pharisees, telling the queen to put the Pharisees in power! Since everyone follows them, she can govern the country effectively if she can win their support. Josephus waxes lugubrious on this very point. No longer do the Pharisees take advantage of the woman's ingenuousness. Now they are essential for her exercise of power. Even Alexander Jannaeus himself would have had a better time of it had he won their support. He advises her to let them dishonor his corpse if necessary, and above all to do anything they tell her. In place of a credulous queen, we have a supine one; in place of conniving Pharisees, we have powerful leaders of the whole nation. The Pharisees are won over, and they win over the masses, even to the extent of eulogizing Jannaeus. What do the Pharisees do with their power? They teach the people to live in accordance with "the tradition of their fathers." John Hyrcanus's and Alexander Jannaeus's work is undone, exiles are called back, prisoners are set free. To be sure, the queen organized a professional army. Josephus adds that the Pharisees sought to avenge themselves upon their enemies, killing one of them and then more, and so the account of Aristobulus's protection of the Pharisees' enemies is included. Somehow, the Pharisees fall away from the account. The mass slaughter of *War,* in which the Pharisees killed anyone they wanted, is shaded into a mild persecution of the Pharisees' opposition.

IN HEROD'S COURT

The Pharisees now have a different, and more important, place in the account of Herod's reign. They have foresight, and seek to oppose Herod. No one takes for granted that the Pharisees can be bribed. Their foresight, not their love of money, warned them that Herod's family was destined for

---

[23] Josephus, *Antiquities,* trans. R. Marcus, 13:399–418, pp. 429, 431, 433, 435, 437.

a bad end (which everyone knew by 95 A.D.). The Pharisees are accused of corrupting people at court, not of being corrupted. Some of them are put to death on that account. The passage is cited on pp. 7–8.

The Pharisees as Politicians

How shall we make use of the materials supplied by Josephus? First we must ask what details may we account for by reference to Josephus's own interests? What does Josephus tell us because he wants to make a particular case? What is credible in Josephus's picture?

To what party did Josephus adhere? Our comparison of the *War* with the *Antiquities* answers the question. Morton Smith points out:

> In the *War,* written shortly after the destruction of Jerusalem, Josephus still favors the group of which his family had been representative—the wealthy, pro-Roman section of the Priesthood. He represents them . . . as that group of the community which did all it could to keep the peace with Rome. In this effort be once mentions that they had the assistance of the chief Pharisees, but otherwise hardly figure on the scene. In this account of the reign of Salome-Alexandra he copies an abusive paragraph of Nicholas of Damascus, describing the Pharisees as hypocrites whom the queen's superstition enabled to achieve and abuse political power.
>
> In his account of the Jewish sects he gives most space to the Essenes. (Undoubtedly he was catering to the interests of Roman readers, with whom ascetic philosophers in out-of-the-way countries enjoyed a long popularity.) As for the others, he merely tags brief notices of the Pharisees and Sadducees onto the end of his survey. He says nothing of the Pharisees' having any influence with the people, and the only time he represents them as attempting to exert any influence (when they ally with the leading priests and other citizens of Jerusalem to prevent the outbreak of the war), they fail.
>
> In the *Antiquities,* however, written twenty years later, the picture is quite different. Here, whenever Josephus discusses the Jewish sects, the Pharisees take first place, and every time he mentions them he emphasizes their popularity, which is so great, he says, that they can maintain opposition against any government. His treatment of the Salome-Alexandra incident is particularly illuminating: he makes Alexander Jannaeus, Salome's husband and the lifelong enemy of the Pharisees, deliver himself of a deathbed speech in which he blames all the troubles of his reign on the fact that he had opposed them and urges the queen to restore them to power because of their overwhelming influence with the people. She follows his advice and the Pharisees cooperate to such extent that they actually persuade the people that Alexander was a good king and make them mourn his passing!

What motivated Josephus's rewriting of *War* so as to place the Pharisees into a position of nearly absolute power in later Maccabean times? Smith answers this question:

> It is almost impossible not to see in such a rewriting of history a bid to the Roman government. That government must have been faced with the problem [after 70 A.D.]: Which group of Jews shall we support?...To this question Josephus is volunteering an answer: The Pharisees, he says again and again, have by far the greatest influence with the people. Any government which secures their support is accepted; any government which alienates them has trouble. The Sadducees, it is true, have more following among the aristocracy...but they have no popular following at all, and even in the old days, when they were in power, they were forced by public opinion to follow the Pharisees' orders. As for the other major parties, the Essenes are a philosophical curiosity, and the Zealots differ from the Pharisees only by being fanatically anti-Roman. So any Roman government which wants peace in Palestine had better support and secure the support of the Pharisees.
>
> Josephus's discovery of these important political facts (which he ignored when writing the *Jewish War*) may have been due partly to a change in his personal relationship with the Pharisees. Twenty years had now intervened since his trouble with Simeon ben Gamaliel, and Simeon was long dead. But the mere cessation of personal hostilities would hardly account for such pointed passages as Josephus added to the *Antiquities*. The more probable explanation is that in the meanwhile the Pharisees had become the leading candidates for Roman support in Palestine and were already negotiating for it....[24]

Having accounted for Josephus's picture of the Pharisees, are we able to make use of any elements of that picture in an account of their history? We must discount all of his references to the influence and power of the Pharisees, for, as Smith points out, these constitute part of his highly tendentious case in behalf of the rabbis of Yavneh, the Pharisees' heirs, and not objective data about the pre-70 party.

The picture of the *War* therefore contains two important facts. First, the Pharisees had been a political party, deeply involved in the politics of the Hasmonean dynasty. They were opponents of Alexander Jannaeus, but we do not know why, and supported Alexandra Salome, who put them into power, but we do not know for what purpose.

---

[24] Morton Smith, "Palestinian Judaism in the First Century," in *Israel: Its Role in Civilization,* ed. Moshe Davis (New York: Harper & Row, Publishers, 1956), pp. 75–76. Note also Gustav Hölscher, *Die Quellen des Josephus für die Zeit vom Exil bis zum jüdischen Kriege* (Leipzig, 1904), pp. 81–84. Hölscher notes Talmudic parallels to Josephus's stories and concludes that Josephus was a Pharisee and drew upon the "oral tradition" of the Pharisaic party, thus accounting for those parallels.

In the first century A.D., individual Pharisees remained active in political life. Simeon ben Gamaliel and other Pharisees certainly took a leading role in the conduct of the war. But, strikingly, Josephus makes no reference to the group's functioning *as a party* within the revolutionary councils. We may conclude that Simeon and others were members of the group, but not the group's representatives, any more than Judah the Pharisee represented the Pharisaic group in founding the Fourth Philosophy. The Pharisees then probably did not constitute an organized political force. Evidently the end of the Pharisaic political party came with Aristobulus, who slaughtered many of them, and was sealed by Herod, who killed even more. From that point forward, so far as Josephus is concerned, the Pharisees as a group no longer played a role in the politics and government of Jewish Palestine.

Second, the Pharisees also constituted a philosophical school. Smith's observation (p. 8) that Jews thought of groups in their society which were distinguished by peculiar theories and practices as different schools of the national philosophy helps us understand the foundations of the Pharisaic polity. As a political party, the Pharisees presumably stood for a particular perspective within the national philosophy. They probably claimed they ought to rule because they possessed true and wise doctrines. The specific doctrines alluded to by Josephus, however, seem quite unrelated to the political aspirations of the group. It is not clear why people who believed in fate and in the immortality of the soul should rule or would rule differently from those who did not, nor is it clear how such beliefs might shape the policies of the state. But evidently what characterized the group—these *particular* beliefs—and what rendered their political aspirations something more than a power-grab were inextricably related, at least in the eyes of their contemporaries.

Josephus thus presents us with a party of philosophical politicians. They claim to have ancient traditions, but these are not described as having been orally transmitted, or attributed to Moses at Sinai or claimed as part of the Torah. They were excellent lawyers, marked off from other groups by a few philosophical differences. As a party they functioned effectively for roughly the first 50 years of the first century B.C. While individuals thereafter are described as Pharisees, the group seems to end its political life as a sect with the advent of Herod.

When we reflect on Josephus's Pharisees, we should expect them to continue as a political group after the fall of the Maccabees, with emphasis on certain doctrinal questions on which all Pharisees agree. We should not suppose that what is important about being a Pharisee is ritual behavior: keeping dietary laws, observing holy days and the Sabbath, and similar wholly unpolitical and unphilosophical matters. Yet, as we shall now see, the Gospels' Pharisees, although including important politicians, primarily concerned themselves not with philosophy but with matters of religious ritual.

4

The Gospels' Pharisees: "Brood of Vipers"

Survey of the Gospels' Traditions about the Pharisees_____

New Testament scholarship routinely addresses its problems to rabbinical literature, making use of sayings and stories in that literature concerning the life of Jesus and the history of the early Church. We now reverse the question: What can be learned from the New Testament in the study of Pharisaism?

When we next meet the Pharisees, in the Gospels, they are characterized not as philosopher-politicians, but as a table-fellowship sect within Judaism, that is, a group of people who keep the same dietary laws and therefore may eat together. Pharisaic table-fellowship required keeping everywhere the laws of ritual purity that normally applied only in the Jerusalem Temple, so Pharisees ate their private meals in the same condition of ritual purity as did the priests of the holy cult. The Pharisees laid further stress upon proper tithing of foods. The Gospels say much else about the Pharisees, but these are the main points that survive when we discount the hostile polemic.

The Gospels' stories about the Pharisees are set in the first 40 years of the first century A.D., but they derive from the second half of the century. While they speak of the Pharisees in the time of Jesus, they were composed, it is generally agreed, between *ca.* 50 and *ca.* 90 A.D. The narrators assume a violently antagonistic view of the Pharisees, while at the same time giving them a central place in the governance of the Jewish community. After 70 A.D. the Pharisees' rabbinical heirs at Yavneh did exercise considerable influence, in consequence of their accession to power with Roman support. Hence the Gospels' picture of the Pharisees as the leading opponents of Jesus reflects the situation of the nascent Church, which found in the Pharisees a major competitive force preventing conversion of Jews to faith in Jesus as messiah by supplying a different interpretation of both Scriptures and contemporary events.

The Pharisees thus are condemned for opposing Jesus, and guilty of not having been Christians. One learns much in the synoptic traditions, John, and Acts about the attitudes of the early Christian community toward the Pharisees and the relationships of the Pharisees toward the Christians. Viewed as an autonomous sect, and not in relationship to the early Church, the Pharisees are of no great interest to New Testament writers. Nonetheless, the New Testament picture of the Pharisees is not entirely without historical value.

Our interest in the New Testament is neither to prove that the Pharisees were not hypocrites or a brood of vipers, nor to dismiss the Gospels' evidence on account of obvious bias, but simply to review the data and to find which elements may illuminate the historical Pharisees. For that purpose, we shall first distinguish among the several sorts of traditions and locate those of special interest. I discern five kinds of materials: first, those in which the Pharisees are represented as enemies of Jesus, forming part of the narrative background; second, and closely related, stories in which the Pharisees criticize Jesus; third, condemnations of Pharisaic hypocrisy in general terms; fourth, representations of Pharisees and Christians in agreement, either in general or on particular matters of doctrine; and finally, traditions in which the Pharisees are condemned for specific practices or beliefs. This last corpus is of greatest interest.

THE PHARISEES AS THE
ENEMIES OF JESUS,
PART OF THE NARRATIVE BACKGROUND

In the first group of stories, the Pharisees are assigned a hostile role, but are not central actors. They are merely part of the narrative background. It is taken for granted that the Pharisees are enemies of Jesus, as they try to provoke him, or trap him, or raise sensitive issues for his comment. In all these stories, Jesus easily overcomes the Pharisaic challenge. For example, the question of loyalty to the Roman government and payment of taxes which faced the early Church is answered by an enigmatic saying at which all marvel. Likewise, the Pharisees "test" Jesus by asking about the biblical law of divorce. They do not press the issue; having appeared as the hostile questioners, they fade into the background, and Jesus supplies his sermon. Then the disciples raise the same issue and Jesus gives a more direct, but similar answer, saying that divorce is wrong. The texts are as follows:

Mt. 21:45. When the chief priests and the Pharisees heard his parables, they perceived that he was speaking about them [but could not arrest him].

Lk. 11:53–4. As he went away from there, the scribes and the Pharisees began to press him hard, and to provoke him to speak of many things, lying in wait for him, to catch at something he might say.

Other pertinent passages are as follows: Mt. 27:67; Lk. 17:20, 19:39; Jn. 1:24, 4:1, 7:32, 7:45, 8:3, 8:12–13, 11:46–7, 11:57, 12:19, 12:42–3, 18:3; Mt. 12:38–40; Mt. 16:1–4; Mk. 8:11–12; Lk. 11:16, 29–30; Lk. 7:36–9, 26:6–13; Mk. 14:3–9; Jn. 21:1–8.

Mk. 12:13–17 (note also Mt. 22:15–22; Lk. 20:19–26). And they sent to him some of the Pharisees and some of the Herodians, to entrap him in his talk. And they came and said to him, "Teacher, we know that you are true, and care for no man; for you do not regard the position of men, but truly teach the way of God. Is it lawful to pay taxes to Caesar, or not? Should we pay them, or should we not?"

But knowing their hypocrisy, he said to them, "Why put me to the test? Bring me a coin, and let me look at it."

And they brought one. And he said to them, "Whose likeness and inscription is this?" They said to him, "Caesar's."

Jesus said to them, "Render to Caesar the things that are Caesar's, and to God the things that are God's" And they were amazed at him.

Mk. 10:2–10 (note also Mt. 19:3–12; Lk. 16:18). And Pharisees came up and in order to test him asked, "Is it lawful for a man to divorce his wife?"

He answered them, "What did Moses command you?"

They said, "Moses allowed a man to write a certificate of divorce, and to put her away."

But Jesus said to them, "For your hardness of heart he wrote you this commandment. But from the beginning of creation, 'God made them male and female.' 'For this reason a man shall leave his father and mother and be joined to his wife, and the two shall become one.' So they are no longer two but one. What therefore God has joined together, let no man put asunder."

And in the house the disciples asked him again about this matter. And he said to them, "Whoever divorces his wife and marries another, commits adultery against her; and if she who divorces her husband marries another, she commits adultery."

PHARISEES CRITICIZE JESUS

The Pharisees come to the fore in the second group of stories, in which they openly challenge things Jesus says or does. Appropriately, the issues are more directly concerned with Pharisaic life and practice. The questions in the earlier materials faced all Jews; in the following, they concern Sabbath observance, on which Pharisaism had its particular doctrines in addition to those held in common by all Jews. The matter involves Jesus's healing on the Sabbath. Some say he is a sinner for not keeping the Sabbath; others say the miracles themselves authenticate his actions, and so he cannot be regarded as a sinner.

> *Jn. 9:13–17.* Now they brought to the Pharisees the man who had formerly been blind. Now it was a Sabbath day when Jesus made the clay and opened his eyes.
> The Pharisees again asked him how he had received his sight, and he said to them, "He put clay on my eyes and I washed and I see."
> Some of the Pharisees said, "This man is not from God, for he does not keep the Sabbath."
> But others said, "How can a man who is a sinner do such signs. . . ."

Other relevant passages are as follows: Mt. 9:11, 14, 9:34; Lk. 5: 17–26; Jn. 9:40.

PHARISEES CONDEMNED
IN GENERAL TERMS

A separate category of materials contains sayings in which the Pharisees are condemned, but make no reply. They are represented as the enemies and most formidable opposition of John and Jesus. John calls them "brood of vipers." "The leaven of the Pharisees" appears as a negative image, but no one seems to know just what this means, so Luke defines it as "hypocrisy." They are likewise described as lovers of money, self-righteous, proud of their religious virtue, and certain of their merit. Jesus is then quoted as saying that he who exalts himself will be humbled, and he who humbles himself will be exalted. The same saying is attributed to Hillel: "My self-abasement is my exaltation, and my exaltation is my self-abasement." However, in Hillel's case the expression is not set into a polemical context.

> *Mt. 3:7.* But when he [John the Baptist] saw many of the Pharisees and Sadducees coming for baptism, he said to them, "You brood of vipers! Who warned you to flee from the wrath to come?"

> *Mt. 5:20.* [Jesus:] "Unless your righteousness exceeds that of the scribes and Pharisees, you will never enter the kingdom of heaven."

Mt. 6:16. [Jesus:] "Beware of the leaven of the Pharisees. . . ."

Mk. 8:15. "Take heed, beware of the leaven of the Pharisees and the leaven of Herod."

Lk. 7:30. But the Pharisees and the lawyers rejected the purpose of God for themselves, not having been baptized by him [John].

Lk. 12:1. "Beware of the leaven of the Pharisees, which is hypocrisy. . . ."

Lk. 16:10–14 (note also Mt. 19:16–30; Lk. 18:9–14). "He who is faithful in a very little is faithful also in much; and he who is dishonest in a very little is dishonest also in much. If then you have not been faithful in the unrighteous mammon, who will entrust to you the true riches? And if you have not been faithful in that which is another's, who will give you that which is your own? No servant can serve two masters; for either he will hate the one and love the other, or he will be devoted to the one and despise the other. You cannot serve God and mammon."

The Pharisees, who were lovers of money, heard all this, and they scoffed at him. But he said to them, "You are those who justify yourselves before men, but God knows your hearts; for what is exalted among men is an abomination in the sight of God."

Lk. (Acts) 18:9–14 (note also Mt. 6:5; Mk. 11:25). He also told this parable to some who trusted in themselves that they were righteous and despised others: "Two men went up into the temple to pray, one a Pharisee and the other a tax collector. The Pharisee stood and prayed thus with himself, 'God, I thank thee that I am not like other men, extortioners, unjust, adulterers, or even like this tax collector. I fast twice a week, I give tithes of all that I get.' But the tax collector, standing far off, would not even lift up his eyes to heaven, but beat his breast saying, 'God, be merciful to me a sinner!' I tell you, this man went down to his house justified rather than the other, for every one who exalts himself will be humbled, but he who humbles himself will be exalted."

PHARISEES AND CHRISTIANS
IN AGREEMENT

Luke-Acts preserves a different picture of the Pharisees. They appear as allies of the Christians and friends of Jesus. In fact, they warn Jesus of Herod's enmity. In Acts the alliance of Pharisees and Christians is quite explicit. Gamaliel is made to say that there may be something in the Christians' beliefs. Paul appeals to the Pharisees for support. He is represented as a Pharisee, and claims that he is persecuted because of that, for he believes in resurrection of the dead, just as they do. Then the Pharisees, like Gamaliel earlier, find grounds for supporting the Christians. Jesus likewise espouses belief in the resurrection of the dead. Nicodemus, his friend, was a Pharisee. In all, the tradition of Luke-Acts, with echoes elsewhere, presents a striking contrast to stories told about Pharisees as enemies of Jesus and sayings assigned to Jesus and John in which the Pharisees are made to exemplify evil traits.

> *Lk. 13:31.* At that very hour some Pharisees came and said to him, "Get away from here, for Herod wants to kill you. . . ."

> *Acts 5:34–9.* But a Pharisee in the council named Gamaliel, a teacher of the law held in honor by all the people, stood up and ordered the men to be put outside for a while. . .[saying], "For if this plan. . .is of men, it will fail; but if it is of God, you will not be able to overthrow them. You might even be found opposing God!"

> *Acts 23:6–9.* But when Paul perceived that one part were Sadducees and the other Pharisees, he cried out in the council, "Brethren, I am a Pharisee, a son of the Pharisees; with respect to the hope and the resurrection of the dead I am on trial." And when he had said this, a dissension arose between the Pharisees and the Sadducees; and the assembly was divided. For the Sadducees say that there is no resurrection nor angel nor spirit; but the Pharisees acknowledge them all. Then a great clamor arose; and some of the scribes of the Pharisees' party stood up and contended, "We find nothing wrong in this man. . . ."

> *Acts 26:5* [Paul:] "They have known for a long time—that according to the strictest party of our religion I have lived as a Pharisee. And now I stand here on trial for hope in the promise made by God to our fathers. . . . Why is it thought incredible by any of you that God raises the dead?"

Other relevant passages are as follows: Jn. 3:1 (Nicodemus was a Pharisee); Acts 15:5; Mt. 22:34–40; Mk. 12:28–34; Lk. 10:25–28. To these should be added the following, in which Jesus is represented as espousing belief in resurrection of the dead, against the contrary view of the Sadducees: Mt. 22:23–33; Mk. 12:18–27; Lk. 20:27–40; Acts 4:1–2.

What is striking in all the foregoing is that we are given little material evidence on the character and beliefs of the Pharisaic sect, excluding belief in resurrection. The Pharisees serve as a narrative convention. Whenever the narrator needs someone to ask a question that allows a stunning response on the part of Jesus, he calls forth the Pharisees. When a villain is needed to exemplify obviously unsavory spiritual traits, the Pharisees serve quite well. The favorable stories in which the Pharisees and Christians stand together do little to change the picture. The only characteristic trait that emerges is belief in the resurrection of the dead. That is all the Christians and the Pharisees have in common. In the following stories, by contrast, the Pharisees' own practices and convictions come into view.

PHARISEES CONDEMNED
FOR SPECIFIC PRACTICES OR BELIEFS

The final group of stories differs from the foregoing in its attention to details of the Pharisees' actual beliefs and practices, primarily as they pertain to conduct at meals. What the Pharisees do, and what Jesus does not do, when enjoying table-fellowship comprises the subject of important stories. In quantity and character these materials, which can be divided into six groups, exhibit important differences from the rest.

In the first instance, Jesus and his disciples eat with sinners and tax collectors, people who do not keep the law. It is unlikely that these people observe the laws of ritual purity at meals or tithe their food, though that is not the point of the stories. Pharisaic law explicitly excludes tax collectors from the Pharisaic table-fellowship.

In the second group, included with the first group in the examples, the question of fasting is raised. The Pharisees fast, but the Christians do not. Jesus is made to explain that fact.

The third group concerns preparation of food. Observance of the Sabbath in that connection is introduced: Is it permissible to harvest food on the Sabbath? The story is developed around the saying, "The son of man is lord of the Sabbath," and the Pharisees are not central to the account.

Sabbath observance is also involved in the fourth passage, which is once again about healing.

The fifth, and most interesting, group explicitly concerns ritual purity in eating. The Christian disciples do not wash their hands, thus do not enter a higher stage of ritual purity. The details of the ritual purity laws are unknown to the narrator. He explains—for evidently Mark assumed that the reader would not understand—that in general the Pharisees wash before meals, and wash cups, pots, and bronze vessels. This is all regarded as part of the "tradition of the elders," which the Gospels and Josephus assign to the Pharisees. But one would not have to know a great deal about Pharisaic purity rules to know that the Pharisees maintained such practices. The narrator obviously has little more to report than that simple fact. As we consider some of the details of tithing and purity rules represented by the rabbinic traditions about the Pharisees, we shall be struck by their complexity of detail, the subtlety and sophistication of their articulation to cover every aspect of everyday life. The Gospels' picture will then seem rather remote and unfocused. But the purpose of the narrator is to contrast purity rules with ethical laws, for one is claimed to be in conflict with the other. Then the larger question of ritual defilement through the eating of food is raised. This is not merely a matter of prohibited foods, such as not eating pork or certain kinds of fish. The issue is ritual defilement, and again ritual purity is set into tension with moral rules: evil thoughts, pride, and so on.

The sixth group now relates to the moral character of the Pharisees. While they keep the ritual purity laws, they neglect other important precepts of the Torah, and are therefore incapable of bringing men to salvation. In this group of stories, the most important detail is the polemic against ritual tithing. The Pharisees tithe their food, but neglect "the weightier matters of the law, justice and mercy and faith." But then Jesus is made to say that there is no conflict between the one and the other—"These you ought to have done, without neglecting the others"—so the tension between ethics and ritual is relaxed. As with ritual purity, the implication is to clean the inside, "that the outside also may be clean."

When the generalized polemic is excluded, three important issues thus remain: Sabbath observance, ritual purity, and tithing.

Mk. 2:15–23 (note also Mt. 9:10–17; Lk. 5:29–39). And as he sat at table in his house, many tax collectors and sinners were sitting with Jesus and his disciples; for there were many who followed him. And the scribes of the Pharisees, when they saw that he was eating with sinners and tax collectors, said to his disciples, "Why does he eat with tax collectors and sinners?"

And when Jesus heard it, he said to them, "Those who are well have no need of a physician, but those who are sick; I came not to call the righteous, but sinners."

Now John's disciples and the Pharisees were fasting; and people came and said to him, "Why do John's disciples and the disciples of the Pharisees fast, but your disciples do not fast?"

And Jesus said to them, "Can the wedding guests fast while the bridegroom is with them? As long as they have the bridegroom with them, they cannot fast. The days will come, when the bridegroom is taken away from them, and then they will fast in that day. No one sews a piece of unshrunk cloth on an old garment; if he does, the patch tears away from it, the new from the old, and a worse tear is made. And no one puts new wine into old wineskins; if he does, the wine will burst the skins, and the wine is lost, and so are the skins; but new wine is for fresh skins."

Mt. 12:1–14 (note also Mk. 2:15–28, 3:1–6; Lk. 6:1–11, 14:1–6). At that time Jesus went through the grainfields on the Sabbath; his disciples were hungry, and they began to pluck ears of grain and to eat. But when the Pharisees saw it, they said to him, "Look, your disciples are doing what is not lawful to do on the Sabbath."

He said to them, "Have you not read what David did, when he was hungry, and those who were with him: how he entered the house of God and ate the bread of the Presence, which it was not lawful for him to eat nor for those who were with him, but only for the priests? Or have you not read in the law how on the Sabbath the priests in the temple profane the Sabbath, and are guiltless? I tell you, something greater than the temple is here. And if you had known what this means, 'I desire mercy, and not sacrifice' [Hos. 6:6], you would not have condemned the guiltless. For the Son of man is Lord of the Sabbath."

Mt. 12:1–14 And he went on from there and entered their synagogue. And behold, there was a man with a withered hand. And they asked him, "Is it lawful to heal on the sabbath?"

He said to them, "What man of you, if he has one sheep and it falls into a pit on the sabbath, will not lay hold of it and lift it out? Of how much more value is a man than a sheep! So it is lawful to do good on the sabbath."

Then he said to the man, "Stretch out your hand." And the man stretched it out, and it was restored, whole like the other.

But the Pharisees went out and took counsel against him, how to destroy him.

Mk. 7:1–13 (note also Mt. 15:1–20; Lk. 11:37–41). Now when the Pharisees gathered together to him, with some of the scribes, who had come from Jerusalem, they saw that some of his disciples ate with hands defiled, that is, unwashed. (For the Pharisees, and all the Jews, do not eat unless they wash their hands, observing the tradition of the elders; and when they come from the market place, they do not eat unless they purify themselves; and there are many other traditions which they observe, the washing of cups and pots and vessels of bronze.)

And the Pharisees and the scribes asked him, "Why do your disciples not live according to the tradition of the elders, but eat with hands defiled?" And he said to them, "Well did Isaiah prophesy of you hypocrites, as it is written,

'This people honors me with their lips,
but their heart is far from me;
in vain do they worship me,
teaching as doctrines the precepts of men.'
You leave the commandment of God, and hold fast the tradition of men."

And he said to them, "You have a fine way of rejecting the commandment of God, in order to keep your tradition! For Moses said, 'Honor your father and your mother'; and, 'He who speaks evil of father or mother, let him surely die'; but you say, 'If a man tells his father or his mother, What you would have gained from me is *Corban* (that is, given to God) then you no longer permit him to do anything for his father or mother, thus making void the word of God through your tradition which you hand on. And many such things you do."

And he called the people to him again, and said to them, "Hear me, all of you, and understand: there is nothing outside a man which by going into him can defile him; but the things which come out of a man are what defile him."

And when he had entered the house, and left the people, his disciples asked him about the parable.

And he said to them, "Then are you also without understanding? Do you not see that whatever goes into a man from outside cannot defile him, since it enters, not his heart but his stomach, and so passes on?" (Thus he declared all food clean.)

And he said, "What comes out of a man is what defiles a man. For from within, out of the heart of man, come evil thoughts, fornication, theft, murder, adultery, coveting, wickedness, deceit, licentiousness, envy, slander, pride, foolishness. All these evil things come from within, and they defile a man."

Mt. 23:1–36 (note also Mk. 12:38–40; Lk. 20:45–7). Then said Jesus to the crowds and to his disciples, "The scribes and the Pharisees sit on Moses' seat; so practice and observe whatever they tell you, but not what they do; for they preach, but do not practice. They bind heavy burdens, hard to bear, and lay them on men's shoulders; but they themselves will not move them with their finger. They do all their deeds to be seen by men; for they make their phylacteries broad and their fringes long, and they love the place of honor at feasts and the best seats in the synagogues, and salutations in the market places, and being called rabbi by men.

"But you are not to be called rabbi, for you have one teacher, and you are all brethren. And call no man your father on earth, for you have one Father, who is in heaven. Neither be called masters, for you have one master, the Christ. He who is greatest among you shall be your servant; whoever exalts himself will be humbled, and whoever humbles himself will be exalted.

"But woe to you, scribes and Pharisees, hypocrites! because you shut the kingdom of heaven against men; for you neither enter yourselves, nor allow those who would enter to go in.

"Woe to you, scribes and Pharisees, hypocrites! for you traverse sea and land to make a single proselyte, and when he becomes a proselyte, you make him twice as much a child of hell as yourselves.

"Woe to you, blind guides, who say, 'If any one swears by the temple, it is nothing; but if any one swears by the gold of the Temple, he is bound by his oath.' You blind fools! For which is greater, the gold or the temple that has made the gold sacred? And you say, 'If any one swears by the altar, it is nothing; but if any one swears by the gift that is on the altar, he is bound by his oath.' You blind men! For which is greater, the gift or the altar that makes the gift sacred? So he who swears by the altar, swears by it and by everything on it; and he who swears by the temple, swears by the throne of God and by him who sits upon it.

"Woe to you, scribes and Pharisees, hypocrites! for you tithe mint and dill and cummin, and have neglected the weightier matters of the law, justice and mercy and faith; these you ought to have done, without neglecting the others. You blind guides, straining out a gnat and swallowing a camel!

"Woe to you, scribes and Pharisees, hypocrites! for you cleanse the outside of the cup and of the plate, but inside they are full of extortion and rapacity. You blind Pharisee! first cleanse the inside of the cup and of the plate, that the outside also may be clean.

"Woe to you, scribes and Pharisees, hypocrites! for you are like white-washed tombs, which outwardly appear beautiful, but within they are full of dead men's bones and all uncleanness. So you also outwardly appear righteous to men, but within you are full of hypocrisy and iniquity.

"Woe to you, scribes, and Pharisees, hypocrites! for you build the tombs of the prophets and adorn the monuments of the righteous, saying, 'If we had lived in the days of our fathers, we would not have taken part with them in shedding the blood of the prophets.' Thus you witness against yourselves, that you are sons of those who murdered the prophets. Fill up, then, the measure of your fathers. You serpents, you brood of vipers, how are you to escape being sentenced to hell? Therefore I send you prophets and wise men and scribes, some of whom you will kill and crucify, and some you will scourge in your synagogues and persecute from town to town, that upon you may come all the righteous blood shed on earth, from the blood of innocent Abel to the blood of Zechariah the son of Barachiah, whom you murdered between the sanctuary and the altar. Truly, I say to you, all this will come upon this generation."

This last point is most striking, for it links the anti-Pharisaic polemic to the destruction of the Temple. The Pharisees persecute the prophets, wise men, and scribes; they drive the messengers of God out of the synagogue. Surely the competition between the Pharisees and the Christian missionaries for the loyalty of the mass of Jews lies at the foundation of these sayings. The destruction of the Temple here finds explanation and takes a central place in the Christian indictment of Pharisaism. The Pharisaic leadership has led to the catastrophe, so repudiating that leadership and following the Christian way will lead beyond it. Such an assertion takes on heavy meaning in the aftermath of the destruction, for, as noted, it was then that the Pharisaic party assumed leadership of more considerable parts of the Jewish community than earlier.

In summary, the materials before us are not all of the same sort. Stories in which the Pharisees occur as part of the narrative background take for granted that the Pharisees were Jesus's enemies. These stories are contradicted by the materials, primarily in Luke-Acts, which represent the early Church as including Pharisees and standing with them on an important issue of sectarian difference, resurrection of the dead. The picture of Acts does nothing to prepare us for so hostile a role as is attributed to the Pharisees in the Gospels. There the Pharisees, sometimes along with the chief priests, are presented as conspiring to persecute Jesus, or to trip him up with difficult questions, or to make him show himself hostile to Rome.

Another sort of story has Jesus debate with the Pharisees on grounds for divorce and on Jesus's failure to give a sign from heaven.

The Pharisaic critique of Jesus focuses on three issues. First, why do Jesus's disciples eat with tax collectors? Second, why do Jesus's disciples not fast? Third, why does Jesus violate the Sabbath by healing on the holy day? The third theme recurs in the specific critique of the Pharisees. The general condemnation is composed of mere invective: The Pharisees are a "brood of vipers," one should beware of the "leaven" of the Pharisees "which is hypocrisy." Pharisees love money. Pharisees regard themselves as better than other men by reason of their religious observances.

For our purposes, the important data derive not from the polemical narrative materials, but from the condemnation of the Pharisees for specific religious practices. The most interesting information comes from Mk. 7:1–23, on ritual purity in eating and on the dietary laws, and Mt. 23:1–36, on the Pharisees' emphasis on ritual purity of dishes and their exact tithing. These passages take for granted specific Pharisaic rites, and direct criticism against them. They tell us not only that the early Christian community found itself in conflict with the Pharisaic party, but that Pharisees known to the Gospel story-tellers carried out important rites which are quite irrelevant to the doctrinal issues, important to the Christians, in the Pharisaic-Christian relationship.

The Pharisees and Ritual Purity

Mk. 2:15–27 and 3:1–6 are controversy dialogues. A single action, like plucking corn or healing on the Sabbath, is carefully described. Then the opponent seizes on the action. Bultmann observes, "Just as these latter situations are...imaginary, i.e. not reports of historical occasions but constructions giving lively expression to some idea in a concrete event—even so does the same judgment apply to those situations in which the reported action is in itself more likely, that is to say to the plucking of corn and the miracles of healing."[1]

Bultmann holds that the life situation producing such stories is the apologetic and polemic necessity of the Palestinian Church. The purpose of the stories is to defend the conduct of the disciples, meaning the Church: they pluck corn on the Sabbath, they do not fast, they eat with unwashed hands. But did Jesus do all these things? Bultmann contends that if any part of the controversy dialogues does go back to Jesus, it is the decisive saying, e.g., The Son of man is Lord of the Sabbath, or Did not he who made the

---

1 Rudolf Bultmann, *The History of the Synoptic Tradition,* trans. John Marsh (New York: Harper & Row, Publishers, 1968), p. 39.

outside make the inside also? Further, Bultmann observes, "There is an active tendency seeking always to present the opponents of Jesus as Scribes and Pharisees,"[2] despite the presence of Pharisees inside the Church.

In Mt. 23:1–36, the accusation is that the Pharisees seek outward purity. Their purity rules are full of anomalies. They purify the outside of the cup, but not the inside; they tithe little things but neglect weighty matters of law. Bultmann states, "But the oldest material is clearly in the brief conflict sayings which express in a parable-like form the attitude of Jesus to Jewish piety, e.g. Mk. 7:15, 3:4, Mt. 23:16–19, 23f., 25f. In my view this is the first time that we have the right to talk of sayings of Jesus, both as to form and content."[3]

The point of the materials is that the Pharisees do things in the wrong way—hypocritically. But their teachings are accepted.[4] Davies comments that "the characteristics condemned in the Pharisees [in Mt. 23] are almost precisely those decried in the Sermon on the Mount," Mt. 7:15–21, 23:2–3; Mt. 7:1ff., 23:4.[5] The "woes" on the Pharisees "serve as a counterbalance to the Beatitudes. The yoke of Jesus, which is easy...is contrasted with that of the Pharisees."[6]

Davies further notes that the Pharisaic-Christian encounter depicted in the Gospels reflects the situation after 70, when the Pharisaic movement controlled the "seat of Moses," at Yavneh, at the very same time that the Gospels were reaching final form. Davies concludes, "...the possibility is a real one that the form of the SM [Sermon on the Mount] was fashioned under their impact [that of the rabbis of Yavneh]. It is our suggestion that one fruitful way of dealing with the SM is to regard it as the Christian answer to Jamnia [Yavneh]. Using terms very loosely, the SM is a kind of Christian...counterpart to the formulation taking place there.... It was the desire and necessity to present a formulation of the way of the New Israel at a time when the rabbis were engaged in a parallel task for the Old Israel that provided the outside stimulus for the Evangelist to shape the SM."[7]

What then is to be learned from the Gospels' picture of the Pharisees?

---

2 Ibid., p. 52.

3 Ibid., p. 147.

4 W.D. Davies, *The Setting of the Sermon on the Mount* (Cambridge: Cambridge University Press, 1964), p. 106.

5 Ibid., p. 291.

6 Ibid., p. 292.

7 Ibid., p. 315. Note also Benjamin W. Bacon, *Studies in Matthew* (New York: Holt, Rinehart and Winston, Inc., 1930), pp. 246 ff.; Krister Stendahl, *The School of St. Matthew* (Uppsala: C.W.K. Gleerup, 1954) pp. 23–26. The most thorough account of the Pharisees in the New Testament is Wolfgang Beilner, *Christus und die Pharisäer* (Vienna: Herder & Co., 1959). On Mt. 15:1–20, Mk. 7:1–23, see pp. 74–88. The literary analysis throughout seems to me impeccable.

First, they laid great stress on eating with the right people, specifically those who obeyed the purity laws.

Second, they held a "tradition of the elders" about this matter, which, required that one wash hands before eating and perform other ritual ablutions. It also required that dishes be purified—not merely washed—in connection with meals.

The Pharisees further laid stress on eating the right kinds of food. Some foods may render unclean (defile), and these are not to be eaten. They tithed with great care, and so prepared foods for eating. Tithing was a dietary law, rendering food ritually acceptable, just as washing hands made the man unclean, and washing dishes made the utensils ritually acceptable.

So, apart from the partisan issues, the central traits of Pharisaism concerned observance of dietary laws. Men became Pharisees because they observed those laws. Nicodemus or Gamaliel were Pharisees by virtue of their right doctrines and ritual observances, not their politics. Pharisees furthermore ate only with other Pharisees, to be sure that the laws were appropriately observed. Among the extremely complex issues posed by the materials rapidly reviewed here, these are the matters of importance for our inquiry. The Gospels' Pharisees—aside from the invective—are a table-fellowship sect. As we shall now see, the Gospels' picture conforms to the rabbinical traditions about the Pharisees, which center upon the laws of tithing and ritual purity, defining what and with whom one may eat, that is, table-fellowship.

5

The Rabbinical Traditions
About the Pharisees

An Overview _____

While the synoptic Gospels' picture of the Pharisees was complete by
ca. 80 A.D., the rabbinical traditions occur in much later documents. The
earliest, the Mishnah, reached final form in *ca*. 200 A.D.[1] Those documents
—Mishnah, Tosefta, the two Talmuds—contain numerous sayings and
stories which cannot be dated with any certainty, for they are not attributed
to specific masters. Even if they were, we would have no way of verifying the
accuracy of those attributions. Some of the sayings and stories allude to
conditions in Temple times; others contain no indication of the particular
time and place to which reference is made. The corpus of anonymous rabbinical traditions compiled in the third and later centuries may contain
significant materials deriving from pre-70 times. But we shall concentrate on
those sayings and stories which indubitably allude to Pharisees before 70 A.D.

Only two Pharisees known in the rabbinical literature, Gamaliel (Acts
5:34) and Simeon b. Gamaliel (Josephus, *Life*, 191), are explicitly mentioned outside of the corpus of rabbinical literature. By contrast, other first
century men described as Pharisees, such as Nicodemus, Paul, and Josephus,
are never referred to in rabbinic literature. We are therefore unable to

1 See p. 158.

correlate directly the traditions found in rabbinical literature with those in the Gospels and Josephus.

The rabbinical traditions under study concern 15 men and the Houses, or circles of disciples, of Shammai and Hillel. They consist of approximately 371 separate items—stories, sayings, or allusions—versions of which occur in approximately 655 different pericopae, or completed units of tradition. Of these, 280, in 462 pericopae (comprising about 75 per cent of the total), pertain to Hillel and people associated with Hillel, such as Shammai and the Houses of Hillel and Shammai. A roughly even division of the materials would give 23 traditions in 40 pericopae to each name or category, so the disparity is enormous. Exact figures cannot be given, for much depends upon how one counts the components of composite pericopae or reckons with other imponderables. The figures in the table suffice to indicate that the disproportionately greater part of the rabbinical traditions about the Pharisees pertains to Hillel and people involved with him.

Master	Number of Traditions	Number of Pericopae
Simeon the Just—*ca.* 300 B.C.	10	30
Antigonus of Sokho—*ca.* 200 B.C.	2	2
Yosi b. Yoezer—*ca.* 150 B.C.	4	10
Yosi b. Yohanan—*ca.* 150 B.C.	6	13
Joshua b. Perahiah—*ca.* 100 B.C.	3	6
Nittai the Arbelite—*ca.* 100 B.C.	2	2
Judah b. Tabbai—*ca.* 80 B.C.	7	26
Simeon b. Shetah—*ca.* 80 B.C.	13	38
Shemaiah-Abtalion—*ca.* 40 B.C.	11	18
Shammai—*ca.* 20 B.C.	15	25
Menahem—*ca.* 20 B.C.	2 ⎫ 61	3 ⎫ 156
Hillel—*ca.* 20 B.C.	33 ⎭	89 ⎭
Shammai + Hillel—*ca.* 20 B.C.	11	39
Gamaliel—*ca.* 20 A.D.–40 A.D.	26	41
Simeon b. Gamaliel—*ca.* 40 A.D.–70 A.D.	7	13
Houses of Shammai and Hillel—*ca.* 10 B.C.–70 A.D.	219	300
	371	655

Pharisaic Law

By Pharisaic law I mean those legal sayings in Talmudic literature attributed either to Pharisaic masters before 70 A.D. or to the Houses of Shammai and Hillel. A legal saying is a statement of what one must or must not do in ordinary, everyday life. It may pertain to adjudication of civil disputes, conduct of the Temple cult, the manner of issuing a writ of divorce, the way to say one's prayers, tithing of food, the preservation of ritual purity, or the purification of something which has been defiled or made unclean. Thus, laws pertained to a wide range of commonplace matters, many of which currently would not be regarded as subject to legislation at all. Most of the nearly 700 pericopae pertaining to pre-70 Pharisees concern legal matters, and the largest number of these relate to, first, agricultural tithes, offerings, and other taboos, and, second, rules of ritual purity—that is, sectarian interests.

Laws that made a sect sectarian were either those which were interpreted and obeyed by the group in a way different from other groups or from common society at large, or those which were observed only by the group. In the latter category are the purity laws, which predominate in the Pharisaic corpus.

These purity laws were the center of sectarian controversy. The Pharisees were Jews who believed one must keep the purity laws outside of the Temple. Other Jews, following the plain sense of Leviticus, supposed that purity laws were to be kept only in the Temple, where the priests had to enter a state of ritual purity in order to carry out such requirements as animal sacrifice. They likewise had to eat their Temple food in a state of ritual purity, while lay people did not. To be sure, everyone who went to the Temple had to be ritually pure. But outside of the Temple the laws of ritual purity were not observed, for it was not required that noncultic activities be conducted in a state of Levitical cleanness.

But the Pharisees held that even outside of the Temple, in one's own home, the laws of ritual purity were to be followed in the only circumstance in which they might apply, namely, at the table. Therefore, one must eat secular food (ordinary, everyday meals) in a state of ritual purity *as if one were a Temple priest*. The Pharisees thus arrogated to themselves—and to all Jews equally—the status of the Temple priests, and performed actions restricted to priests on account of that status. The table of every Jew in his home was seen as being like the table of the Lord in the Jerusalem Temple. The commandment, "You shall be a kingdom of priests and a holy people," was taken literally: Everyone is a priest, everyone stands in the same relationship to God, and everyone must keep the priestly laws. At this time, only the Pharisees held such a viewpoint, and eating unconsecrated food as if one were a Temple priest at the Lord's table thus was one of the two significations that a Jew was a Pharisee, a sectarian.

The other sign was meticulous tithing. The laws of tithing and related agricultural taboos may have been kept primarily by Pharisees. Our evidence here is less certain. Pharisees clearly regarded keeping the agricultural rules as a chief religious duty. But whether, to what degree, and how other Jews did so is not clear. Both the agricultural laws and purity rules in the end affected table-fellowship; that is, as noted they were "dietary laws."

Since tithes and offerings either went to the Levites and priests or had to be consumed in Jerusalem; and since the purity rules applied only in the Temple, the Pharisees manifestly claimed that laymen were better informed about priestly and Temple laws than the Temple priesthood. In this connection, Morton Smith observes:

> Differences as to the interpretation of the purity laws and especially as to the consequent question of table-fellowship were among the principal causes of the separation of Christianity from the rest of Judaism and the early fragmentation of Christianity itself. The same thing holds for the Qumran community, and, within Pharisaic tradition, the [Pharisaic] *havurah* [fellowship]. They are essentially groups whose members observe the same interpretation of the purity rules and therefore can have table fellowship with each other. It is no accident that the essential act of communion in all these groups is participation in common meals.[2]

Since food which had not been properly grown or tithed could not be eaten, and since the staple of the diet was agricultural products—grain, olives— and not meat, the centrality of the agricultural rules is in no small degree on account of precisely the same consideration: What may one eat, and under what circumstances?

Smith states, "The obligation to eat only tithed food was made the basis of elaborate regulations limiting table-fellowship in a way comparable even to the effect of the purity laws."[3] The normative religion of the country, Smith notes, "is that compromise of which the three principal elements are the Pentateuch, the Temple, and...the ordinary Jews who were not members of any sect." The Pharisaic laws virtually ignore the second, treat the third as an outsider, and are strangely silent concerning the first. They supply no rules about synagogue life, reading the Torah, and preaching in synagogues. It would be difficult to maintain that the sect exercised influence in the life of synagogues not controlled by its own members.

The Pharisaic laws we have are therefore the laws we *should* have: the rules of a sect concerning its own sectarian affairs, matters of importance primarily to members of the group. Let us now rapidly review the legal traditions attributed to the masters before 70 A.D.

The first names on the list quoted about (p. 82), Simeon the Just and Antigonus of Sokho, leave no laws. Yosi b. Yoezer, a priest, laid down rules concerning cleanness of fluids in the Temple slaughterhouse and the ritual status of a kind of locust, and corpse uncleanness (cited below, p. 119). To Yosi b. Yoezer and Yosi b. Yohanan and the rest of the chronological pairs

2 Morton Smith, "The Dead Sea Sect in Relation to Ancient Judaism," *New Testament Studies,* Vol. 7, 1961, pp. 347–60.
3 Ibid., p. 353.

are attributed opinions on the laying on of hands in a sacrifice during festivals that coincide with the Sabbath (pp. ·104–11). They also decreed cleanness upon the land of the peoples and upon glassware. That is, foreign countries were ritually unclean; glassware was susceptible of uncleanness. Joshua b. Perahiah ruled on the ritual uncleanness of Alexandrian wheat. Judah b. Tabbai and Simeon b. Shetah declared metalware capable of becoming unclean. To Simeon is also attributed a decree regarding the marriage contract. Shemaiah and Abtalion ruled on a Temple rite, and issued laws about giving Heave-offering and on preparing animals for use in the festival. They further gave an opinion on the acceptability of a ritual pool.

This is the sum of the laws attributed to Pharisees before Hillel: purity rules, Temple rites, agricultural taboos. Only the marriage contract stands outside of the sectarian framework, and precisely what is attributed to Simeon is unclear. So the early laws, whether authentic or not, conform to the pattern one discerns in evidence pertinent to later times.

Shammai's rulings follow the Gospels' legal agenda. They pertain to Sabbath observance, phylacteries, Heave-offering, Second-Tithe uncleanness, ploughing in the Seventh Year, uncleanness from a bone in a "tent" (covered area), the requirement that children observe the festival of *Sukkot* (Tabernacles) and the Day of Atonement, and the liability of a person's agent for misdeeds done at his bidding. Only the last item is outside of the pattern.

Hillel's laws and legal exegesis pertain to Passover observance: eating the required Passover foods together, sacrificing the *pesah,* the Paschal offering, on the Sabbath; to uncleanness: touching an insect in a ritual pool, declaring an itch to be clean; to Seventh Year and Jubilee Law; to interest; to liability for tithes; and to expounding the language of the marriage contract. Only interest and the marriage contract stand outside of the established pattern.

Shammai and Hillel together rule on the retroactive uncleanness of a menstruant, which is important in assessing the ritual cleanness of dishes she may have touched; the liability of a loaf of bread for a priestly offering; the acceptability of a ritual pool for cleansing what has been made unclean; uncleanness of hands; and uncleanness in vintaging grapes for the vat—all as expected.

Gamaliel I made rulings quite different from the foregoing, such as one on the right of a woman to remarry on the testimony of one witness to the fact that her first husband has died. He was asked concerning giving *peah* (the corner of the field left for the poor, an agricultural taboo), and made an ordinance about the Sabbath observance of the Temple's calendar-witnesses. He issued ordinances on annulling divorces, using nicknames in writs of divorce, and collecting the money stipulated in a marriage contract. Gamaliel's laws thus pertain not to sectarian matters, but to the affairs of ordinary folk, which is what one would expect from an important civil authority, a member of the Temple Sanhedrin.

From Simeon b. Gamaliel, his son, we have no legal sayings, only reports of how he lowered the price of doves used in the Temple cult, gave *peah,* and managed to live in the same alley with a nonbeliever, with respect to the Sabbath limit. The latter two items are of sectarian interest. The first puts Simeon into the Temple as a major official, in conformity with Josephus's picture. If he made and effected such a ruling, it was not as a Pharisee. The legal traditions of the named masters thus tend to conform to the pattern suggested above: sectarian rules primarily pertaining to matters of sectarian interest.

Laws attributed to the Houses of Shammai and Hillel are much more abundant, but do not change the picture. The Houses' rulings pertaining either immediately or ultimately to table-fellowship involve preparation of food, ritual purity relating directly to food or indirectly to the need to keep food ritually clean, and agricultural rules concerning the proper growing, tithing, and preparation of agricultural produce for table use. The agricultural laws relate to producing or preparing food for consumption, assuring either that tithes and offerings have been set aside as the law requires, or that conditions for the nurture of crops have conformed to biblical taboos. Of the 341 individual Houses' legal pericopae, no fewer than 229, approximately 67 per cent of the whole, directly or indirectly concern table-fellowship. The rest are scattered through all other areas of legal concern, forming a striking disproportion.

The Houses' laws of ritual cleanness apply in the main to the ritual cleanness of food, and of people, dishes, and implements involved in its preparation. Pharisaic laws regarding Sabbath and festivals, moreover, involve in large measure the preparation and preservation of food.

We find no such concentration of interest by the Houses in any other aspect of everyday life. Ritual considerations in respect to sexual relations do figure, but these are a minor part of the matter, and the menstrual uncleanness that prevents sexual relations also makes a women unclean for the preparation of food.

We should have expected to find more Houses' laws about family matters. Levirate marriage (Deut. 25:5–10), the disposition of the wife's property, annulling the vows of a wife, the remarriage of a widow, exercising the minor's right of refusal of an arranged marriage, and similar topics are represented only in one or two rulings. These laws affect strikingly fundamental matters. It is hardly possible that for many centuries Jews had not known laws about marital life. In some cases, especially Gamaliel's rulings in respect to divorce documents, we may suppose the Pharisees have taken over and made their own the rulings of the civil authorities, including

Gamaliel himself. Levirate marriage, on the other hand, apparently involved considerations internal to the sect itself. Perhaps some of the family law rulings were primarily for members of the group; others may represent ratification by the group of laws pertaining to everyone and issued by other officials.

Oaths and vows, which figure in the Christian indictment of Pharisaism, play a smaller role in the Houses' traditions than their place in that indictment would have led us to anticipate. Vows were made and carried out. Party members would have been governed by sectarian rules, while Jews not in the Pharisaic group would have turned to Temple priests for instruction in keeping or annulling the rows.

Ritual and liturgical rules not involving table-fellowship are episodic: reciting the *Shema* (below, p. 111), a liturgy for the New Year that coincides with the Sabbath, or the remote need to rule on the circumcision of a child born circumcized (below, p. 139).

Two civil laws—all the Pharisaic rulings on that matter—relate to assessment of damages. They do not leave the impression that Pharisees bore heavy responsibilities in the public administration of civil justice.

If the Pharisees were primarily a group for Torah study, as the Dead Sea Scrolls' writers describe themselves, then we should have expected more rules about the school, perhaps also about scribal matters. In fact, we have only one, about sneezing in the schoolhouse. Surely other, more fundamental problems ought to have presented themselves. Neither do we find much interest in defining the master-disciple relationship, including the duties of the masters and the responsibilities and rights of the disciple, the way in which the disciple should learn his lessons, and similar matters of importance in later times.

This brings us to a puzzling fact: Nowhere in the rabbinic traditions of the Pharisees do we find a reference to gatherings for ritual meals, or table-fellowship, of the Pharisaic party, apart from an allusion to the meeting of several *havurot* [fellowship groups] in the same hall. This surely supplies a slender basis on which to prove that the Pharisaic party actually conducted communion meals, especially since no Pharisaic ritual meal is ever mentioned.

By contrast, the Qumranian laws, which make much of purity, also refer to communion meals and the right or denial of the right of access to them.

The whole editorial and redactional framework of the rabbinical traditions is silent about ritual meals and table-fellowship. The narrative materials say nothing on the matter. So the laws concentrate attention on rules and regulations covering all aspects of a ritual meal, the myth or rites of which are never described or even alluded to. The Pharisaic group evidently did not conduct table-fellowship meals *as rituals*. The table-fellowship laws pertained not merely to group life, but to daily life quite apart from a sectarian setting and ritual occasion. The rules applied to the home, not merely to the synagogue or Temple. While the early Christians gathered for ritual meals which became the climax of their group life, the Pharisees apparently did not.

The very character of the Pharisees' sectarianism therefore differs from the quality of the sectarianism of the Christians. While the communion meal embodied and actualized sectarian life for the Christians, the expression of the Pharisees' sense of self-awareness as a group apparently was not a similarly intense ritual meal. Eating was not a ritualized occasion, even though the Pharisees had liturgies to be said at the meal. No communion ceremony, no rites centered on meals, no specification of meals on holy occasions characterize Pharisaic table-fellowship.

The one communion-meal about which we do find legislation characterized all sects, along with the rest of the Jews: the Passover *Seder*. The Pharisees may have had *Seder* rules separate from, and in addition to, those observed by everyone else, but that is not the same thing as a sectarian communion meal.

Pharisaic table-fellowship therefore was a quite ordinary, everyday affair. The various fellowship rules had to be observed in a wholly routine daily circumstance, without accompanying rites other than a benediction for the food. The Christians' myths and rituals rendered table-fellowship into a much heightened spiritual experience: *Do these things in memory of me.* The Pharisees told no stories abo ⁺ purity laws, except (in later times) to account for their historical deveҡ.ɔment (e.g., who had decreed which purity rule?). When they came to table, so far as we know, they told no stories about how Moses had done what they now do, and they did not "do these things in memory of Moses our rabbi."

In the Dead Sea commune, table-fellowship existed upon much the same basis as among the Pharisees: appropriate undertakings to keep ritual purity and consume properly grown and tithed foods. Priests, not laymen, said the blessings. Indeed, Qumran's table-fellowship depended upon the presence of a priest: "Let there not lack among them a man who is a priest, and let them set before him, each according to his rank" (IQS vi, 2–8) ; "And then when they set the table to eat or prepare the wine to drink, the priest shall first stretch out his hand to pronounce a blessing on the first-fruits of bread and wine" (IQSa ii, 11–22). Only those who knew the secret doctrine of the sect were fully accepted in table-fellowship. Sinners were excluded, whether the sins pertained to the rituals of the table or otherwise. The "Messiah of Israel," blessed the bread after the priests, then the others blessed according to their rank. The blessing of the meal is an important rite, but the Qumranian table meal references do not seem to include a ceremony equivalent to the Eucharist. In this respect they appear to be somewhat similar to the Pharisaic meal.[4] As we know it, the Qumranian meal was liturgically not much different from the ordinary Pharisaic gathering, the rites pertaining solely to, and deriving from, the eating of food.

The Dead Sea sect's meal would have had some similarity to the Eucharist if it had included some sort of narrative about the Temple cult, or stories about how the sect replicates the holy Temple and eats at the table of God, how the founder of the community transferred the Temple's holiness out of unclean Jerusalem, how the present officiants stand in the place of the High Priest of Jerusalem, and how the occasion calls to mind some holy event of the past. But we have no allusions to the inclusion of such mythic elements in the enactment of the community meal. Josephus's Essenes have a priest pray before the meal and afterward: "At the beginning and the end they do honor to God as the provider of life." The primary difference between this and the Pharisaic table rite is the prominence of priests in the life of the group. The table-fellowship of Qumranians and Pharisees thus exhibits less of a ritual embodiment of sacred myth than does that of the early Christians.

On the other hand, both Christians and Pharisees lived among ordinary folk, while the Qumranians did not. In this respect the commonplace character of Pharisaic table-fellowship is all the more striking. The sect ordinarily did not gather *as a group* at all, but in the home. All meals required ritual purity, but Pharisaic table-fellowship took place in the same circumstances as did all nonritual table-fellowship. Members of the sect were engaged in workaday pursuits like everyone else.

This fact made the actual purity rules and food restrictions all the more important, for keeping the law alone set the Pharisees apart from the people among whom they lived. Not in the wilderness on festivals or on Sabbaths alone, but on weekdays and in the towns, without telling myths, or reading holy books (Torah talk at table is attested to only later), or reenacting first things, Pharisaic table-fellowship depended solely on observance of the law. The observance, apart from the meal itself, was not marked off by benedictions or other rites extrinsic to the eating of food.

The setting for law observance was the field and the kitchen, the bed and the street. The occasion for observance occurred every time a person picked up a common nail, which might be unclean, or purchased a *seah* of wheat, which had to be tithed—by himself, without priests to bless his deeds or sages to instruct him. So keeping the Pharisaic rule required neither an occasional exceptional rite at, but external to, the meal, as in the Christian sect, nor taking up residence in a monastic commune, as in the Qumranian

[4] But note Matthew Black, *The Scrolls and Christian Origins* (New York: Charles Scribner's Sons, 1961), pp. 102 ff. See also J. van der Ploeg, "The Meals of the Essenes," *Journal of Semitic Studies*, 2 (1957), 163–75.

sect in Judaism. It imposed perpetual ritualization of daily life, and constant, inner awareness of the communal order of being.

Since Pharisaic legalism is taken for granted in every account of ancient Judaism, it is important to see of just what that legalism consisted, and to assess its impact upon everyday life. The legalism concerned dietary laws. Its impact extended far beyond the table, however, for purity required one always to remain aware of the rules of table-fellowship. A person always knew he was part of the sect, and expressed his loyalty to it in each commonplace situation. Since the Pharisees claimed that the laws they kept were not "sectarian," but derived from the Torah of Moses at Sinai, they would have said they kept the rules and regulations of the Creator of the World, and their laws constituted perpetual observance of his will. Obviously, God cared for more than what went into the mouth and down into the belly and out again. But part of the Torah which originally pertained to the priests in the Temple, and now was meant to sanctify all Israel and transform each man into a priest and the whole nation into a holy people, had to do with eating: the sanctification of the body and of the body of believers.

The Missing Traditions

The rabbinical traditions of the Pharisees may be characterized as self-centered. They are the internal records of a sect concerning its own life, sectarian laws, and partisan conflicts. Curiously, stories of what happened outside of the party are omitted. Almost nothing in Josephus's picture of the Pharisees seems closely related to the rabbis' portrait of them except for a few stories in common and the rather general allegation that the Pharisees had "traditions from the fathers," a point made also by the Synoptic story-tellers. The rabbis' Pharisaic conflict stories, moreover, do not tell of Pharisees opposing Essenes and Christians, but chiefly of Hillelites opposing Shammaites. Pharisaic laws deal *not* with the governance of the country, but with the party's rules for table-fellowship. The political issues are not whether one should pay taxes to Rome or how one should know the Messiah, but whether in the Temple the rule of Shammai or that of Hillel should be followed in a minor festal sacrifice (as if the Pharisees ran the Temple!).

If we were confined to only the rabbinical traditions about the Pharisees, we could not have reconstructed a single significant public event of the period before 70—not the rise, success, and fall of the Maccabees, or the Roman conquest of Palestine, or the rule of Herod, or the reign of the procurators, or the growth of opposition to Rome, or the proliferation of social violence and unrest in the last decades before 66 A.D., or the outbreak of the war with Rome. Nor should we gain a picture of the Pharisees' philosophy of history or theology of politics.

We should not even know how Palestine was governed, for the Pharisees' traditions according to the rabbis do not refer to how the Pharisees governed the country. Unlike Josephus, the rabbis never claim that the Pharisees ran pre-70 Palestine, at least not in stories told either about named masters or about the Houses. Neither do they tell us how the Romans ran it. Furthermore, sectarian issues are barely mentioned, and other sects (apart from the Sadducees) not at all. The growth of Christianity makes its first impact on rabbinical traditions well after 70 A.D.

The rabbis' Pharisees are mostly figures of the late Herodian and Roman periods, a nonpolitical group whose chief religious concerns, as noted, were for preservation of ritual purity in connection with eating secular (not Temple) food, and for observance of dietary laws, especially those pertaining to the proper nurture and harvest of crops. Their secondary religious concern was with proper governance of the party itself.

By contrast, as we saw, Josephus's Pharisaic materials pertain mostly to the years from the rise of the Maccabees to their fall. They were a political party which tried to get control of the government of Jewish Palestine, not a little sect separated from society by observance of laws of common table-fellowship. Josephus's Pharisees are important in the reigns of John Hyrcanus and Alexander Jannaeus, but drop from the picture after Alexandra Salome.

On the other hand the Gospels' Pharisees, appropriately, are much like those of the rabbis and belong to the Roman period. Their legal agenda is virtually identical: tithing, purity laws, Sabbath observance, vows, and so on.

The rabbinical and New Testament traditions begin where Josephus's narrative leaves off, and the difference between them leads us to suspect that the change in the character of Pharisaism from political party to table-fellowship sect comes with Herod and his contemporary, Hillel. If Hillel was responsible for directing the party out of its activist, political concerns and into more irenic and quietistic paths, then we can understand why his figure dominates the subsequent rabbinic tradition. Since Hillel evidently was a contemporary of Herod, we may commend his wisdom, for had the Pharisees persisted as a political force, they would have come into conflict with Herod, who would certainly have wiped them out. Hillel's policy may have been shaped by remembrance of the consequences to the party of its conflict with Alexander Jannaeus, when many Pharisees were killed and later avenged themselves on their enemies in like manner.

We have very sparse materials about masters before Hillel. This suggests that few Pharisees survived Jannaeus's massacres, and that those few did not perpetuate the policies or decisions of their predecessors. Hillel and his followers chose to remember one master, Simeon b. Shetah, who was on good terms with Alexandra Salome, but not his followers, who were almost certainly on bad terms with Aristobulus and his descendents, leaders of the national resistance to Rome and to Antipater's family (note Josephus's story of Aristobulus's protection of the Pharisees' victims, p. 51). As Herod's characteristics became clear, the Pharisees must have found themselves out of sympathy with both the government and the opposition. At this moment Hillel arose to change what had been a political party into a table-fellowship sect, not unlike other publicly harmless and politically neutral groups.

All this is more than mere conjecture, but less than established fact. We do know that the vast majority of rabbinic traditions about the Pharisees relate to the circle of Hillel, and certainly the best attested and most reliable part of the corpus, the opinions of the Houses of Shammai and Hillel, reaches us from that circle's later adherents. The pre-Hillel Pharisees are not known to us primarily from the rabbinic traditions, and when we begin to have a substantial rabbinic record, it concerns a group very different from Josephus's pre-Hillelite, pre-Herodian party.

Attestations

How are we to tell which stories and sayings come first, and which ones were made up later, in the formation of rabbinical traditions about the Pharisees? In what way may we make use of these materials for reconstruction of a picture of the historical Pharisees? Having gained a perspective on what we do not have, let us now make use of what we do know.

Since the rabbinical traditions about the Pharisees derive from a period of time extending from 70 A.D., if not before, to *ca.* 600 A.D., we will do best to concentrate our attention on the first century of the traditions, from 70 to *ca.* 170. This may conveniently be divided into two strata, derived first from Yavneh (*ca.* 70–125 A.D.), and second from Usha (*ca.* 140–170 A.D.). We shall very briefly look at the stratum produced by the circle of Judah the the Patriarch (*ca.* 170–210 A.D.).

On what basis do we justify assigning a tradition to a specific time and school? I rely upon a simple and primitive means of *attestation,* that is, the effort to find a *terminus ante quem*—a point before which a tradition had to have been available—for the substance, form, and wording of a pericope. We shall generally seek evidence outside of the structure of the pericope itself, and, if possible, external even to the collection in which it appears. That evidence should indicate the time at which a saying or story was known. Attestation refers to determination of the time and circle in which a pericope reached the condition in which we have received it. What is thereby attested is the form and wording of the pericope, not the contents or the traditions that may lie behind it.

There are three ways in which it may be shown that a pericope has reached its present form and phrasing.

First, the pericope may be cited by an authority entirely external to the rabbinic tradition. That sort of positive verification is presently unavailable to us. The Houses of Shammai and Hillel are never referred to in the other extant contemporary documents, e.g., New Testament, Qumranian writings, Apocrypha-Pseudepigrapha, and Josephus. Some masters occur in Josephus's' narrative, particularly Simeon b. Gamaliel. But such external references merely show that these men were known as individuals outside of rabbinical circles.

Second, the final date of compiling a collection in which a story first occurs commonly supplies the final date for the present form of all the materials in that collection; subsequent changes will be limited to textual corruption (minor) and interpolations (probably rare). Hence Mishnah-Tosefta, which for convenience we assign to *ca.* 200 and 250 A.D., gives the *terminus ante quem* for the bulk of the rabbinic traditions about the Pharisees.

Third, and most important, are internal evidences in the rabbinical traditions. These are, mainly, attribution to named masters after 70 A.D. of comments or sayings about pericopae assigned to pre-70 Pharisees. If a later master refers to the substance and language of the pericope itself, but evidently stands outside of both, we may suppose that the pericope was known to him, and therefore comes before or in his time in pretty much its present form and wording.

If a Yavnean master actually participates in deciding the issue of a dispute between Houses, the pericope in its present form probably did not arise much before his time. An earlier form may have been available to him, but his appearance in the structure of the dispute supplies a firm *terminus post quem*: the dispute in its *present* state cannot come before that master. This also suggests that the dispute may derive from the circle of his disciples. I have assigned both pericopae in which named masters actually participate, and those on which named masters comment, but from which they stand apart, to the same master's stratum, unless evidence for a more precise estimate was available. For instance, both Aqiba's appearance in the structure of a pericope, and his comment on an apparently completed pericope, or on one which he himself evidently completed, are interpreted in the same way for purposes of attestation: The pericope belongs to the Aqiban part of the Yavnean stratum. That is an imprecision to be specified at the outset.

My reasoning for this sort of internal attestation is based on a number of unproved assumptions.

First, I assume that later masters commonly tried to assign sayings to the man who said them, not to some earlier and more prestigious authority. If something is attributed to Gamaliel II, I assume either that Gamaliel II actually said it, or that the tradents of his circle with his approval assigned it to him—for our purposes it comes down to the same thing. That assumption demonstrably is not always reliable. We have instances in which the

Mishnah attributes to a man words which the Tosefta says were made up by a later authority. But the limited number of such instances of pseudo-attribution suggests that in the main attributions of traditions are reliable. Hence it is merely an assumption that if Gamaliel II said to comment on a Houses-pericope, the tradition was indeed known to him.

If the later rabbi's comment takes into account the actual language of the pericope, it is a further assumption that the pericope in its present form was available to him. Without further evidence I do not suppose that a later tradent made the language of the earlier Houses conform to the comment of the later master. We do have evidence of the fabrication *of* Houses-disputes out of opinions of later masters *about* the opinions of the Houses. Moreover, such fabrications involve direct attributions to the Houses of specific statements. In such a case the probability is that the later master not only supplied the *terminus ante quem,* but was the actual creator of the pericope.

It seems to me impossible that the whole literature is pseudepigraphic in an extreme sense: that it is the product *only* of the final circle of redactors or editors. I take for granted that Yavnean materials were shaped at Yavneh, then handed on to Usha; Ushan materials were shaped at Usha, then handed on to the circle of Judah the Patriarch, editor of the Mishnah. So I take very seriously attribution of a saying to a named authority in a particular school and time. While no one can show that the named authority actually said such a thing, it seems to me beyond reasonable doubt that circles of his disciples believed he did, and moreover assumed that what he said was true. Hence by "Aqiba" or "Joshua" we may mean the Aqiban circle or the Joshuan circle. That may make biography difficult, but it permits other kinds of reasonably accurate historical inquiry. Those circles presumably did redact and hand on what now is in their master's name, and what they handed on reflects what they believed about law and history. Their beliefs may or may not accurately reflect historical reality, but it is likely to reflect their own situation.

An example of the consequences of this reasoning is as follows: Rava and Abbaye, fourth century Babylonian masters, discuss the identity of the Hasmonean king who troubled the Pharisees, e.g., b. Qid. 66a (above, p. 59). We may therefore suppose the pericope lay before them in something like its present condition. Of course, a later editor may have revised the pericope to conform to the opinions of those masters.

A second example, already alluded to, appears in a reference by a post-70 master to the present formulation of a legal issue in a Houses-dispute. This tells us, first, that the issue was debated in his circle; second, that it was believed the Houses had faced the same problem and ruled on it; third, that Yavneans, Ushans, or the circle of Judah the Patriarch had materials before them in pretty much their present form and did not thereafter revise them;

and finally, that they decided the law and gave the decision to the Hillelites. I certainly cannot claim that this sort of attestation is definitive, but it seems to me the best we can now hope for.

Some argue that the essential contents of a pericope, not merely the form and wording, are verified if we find reason to believe they accurately reflect the conditions of the time of which the tradition speaks. Thus Josephus's stories of the later Hasmoneans' relations to the Pharisees may be alleged to verify the accuracy of the rabbinic stories of tension between Yannai the King and Simeon b. Shetah (above, p. 59). It is undeniable that Josephus and the rabbinical tradents possessed traditions about tension between Yannai (Jannaeus) and Pharisees. But those traditions are not before us. All we have are two quite separate sets of stories, and we cannot claim that the detailed Talmudic version is attested because of similarities to Josephus, for the similarities (excluding b. Qid. 66a) are only in generalities. The details, that is, the actual course of events which the Talmudic pericopae report, remain unsupported.

Certain sorts of internal evidences prove less than they may seem at first glance. If a story takes for granted that the Temple is still standing, it would be foolish to conclude that it was actually written before 70, for that ignores the ability of a later narrator to avoid obvious anachronism. If people believed Hillel flourished in Temple times, they obviously did not make up stories about how Hillel had walked through the Temple ruins. Verisimilitude cannot be confused with authenticity. Internal evidence, particularly that deriving from what the narrator has set out to tell us, cannot be regarded as decisive or probative.

Conclusion

We have now considered four loosely related matters.

First, we reviewed the character of the rabbinical traditions about the Pharisees: Where do they occur? How many such traditions are in our hands? To what men and events do they relate? We saw that the rabbinical traditions focus upon a few masters, spread over approximately two centuries. They deal primarily with the legal traditions of those masters, and particularly with laws about table-fellowship.

We then asked, What is the meaning of those Pharisaic dietary laws which predominate in the rabbinical traditions about the Pharisees? How did they affect everyday life? What do they tell us about the character of the Pharisaic sect, by contrast with the Christian and the Dead Sea sects?

We afterwards turned to the very opposite consideration: What traditions ought we to have expected which in fact we do not have? That question produced the answer: We know practically nothing, from the rabbinical traditions about the Pharisees, concerning the public life of Jewish Palestine.

We thus gained an insight into the nature of the sectarian traditions. A sect preserved information primarily about its own affairs and considered of importance only its private concerns. Just as the Christians' traditions about the Pharisees concentrated attention not upon the Pharisees themselves but upon the relationships of Jesus and the Christian community to the Pharisees, so the rabbis' stories and sayings reveal an equivalent self-centeredness.

Our fourth problem, quite unrelated to the first three, was one of method: How do we find our way among the complicated rabbinical traditions to discern the order in which they appeared? Is it possible to isolate one stratum of materials from other strata? The answer—the method of attestation just proposed—prepares the way for our next two chapters. There we deal with rabbinical traditions about the Pharisees attested to during the periods 70 to 125 A.D. and 140 to 170 A.D., respectively. We shall ask, What are the predominant traits and concerns of the tradents of each of these periods? How do their traditions about Pharisaic Judaism before 70 A.D. relate to their own interests, and what elements of their traditions may testify concerning the character of pre-70 Pharisaism? These same questions, you will recall, were asked concerning the traditions of Josephus and those found in the New Testament.

6

Traditions of Yavneh
(70–125 A.D.)

Yavneh

The historical importance of the academy at Yavneh cannot be over-estimated. The rabbis of Yavneh laid the foundations for the classical form of Judaism which predominated from the first century to the twentieth and is likely to characterize the Judaic religious tradition so long as Judaism endures. Their achievements include preservation of the pre-70 Pharisaic tradition and development of the legal corpus which guided Judaism thence-forward, and which was eventually redacted as the Mishnah of Judah the Patriarch. The Yavneans furthermore laid down the main outlines of the Judaic Prayerbook, the *Siddur,* used from then to now. The shape of Judaic piety is thus of their making. They are also credited with the final canonization of the Hebrew Scriptures. Important elements of the doctrine, theology, and ethics of rabbinic Judaism first appear in sayings and stories assigned to the masters of Yavneh. So without exaggeration we may regard the period of Yavneh as the seedtime of classical Judaism.

The stunning achievements of the rabbis of Yavneh came in response to the catastrophe of their own day, the destruction of the Temple. They transformed the disaster into the occasion for regeneration. When the rabbis at Yavneh affirmed their faith that the Torah remained the will of their unvanquished God, they made certain that for 20 and more centuries

Judaism would endure as a living religion, and the Jews as a vital people. The founder of the Yavneh academy, Yohanan ben Zakkai, in setting out to restore the broken heart of the people, began a revolution of the spirit which has yet to run its course.

With the fall of Jerusalem in 70 A.D., destruction of the Temple, and the end of the autonomous Jewish government based there, many Jews and gentiles supposed that the life of the old Israel had come to an end. The political and religious crisis seemed overwhelming. How to worship God without sacrifice? How to maintain the community life of the Jewish people without a sovereign government?

For the Christian Jews, the author of the Epistle to the Hebrews gave one answer: The perfect priest, Christ, is also the final, perfect sacrifice, and the old cult is no longer needed. As to the polity of old Israel, the Christians held it had lasted until the coming of the Messiah and ended with the crucifixion of Jesus and the Jews' rejection of Christ. The ruler's staff (Gen. 49:10) had finally departed from Judah.

For other Jews these answers explained nothing. The surviving Pharisees of Jerusalem, assembled at Yavneh by Yohanan ben Zakkai, offered another viewpoint: The old order endures. The Lord still is served, sin is expiated, and reconciliation is achieved through the new sacrifice, which is deeds of lovingkindness:

> For we have another atonement, which is like sacrifice, and what is it? Deeds of lovingkindness, as it is said, *For I desire mercy and not sacrifice* (Hos. 6:6).

So stated Yohanan ben Zakkai, standing amid the ruins of the Temple. As to the polity of Israel, it persists in the academy founded by Yohanan at Yavneh, which preserves an unbroken relationship with the old Sanhedrin in Jerusalem.[1] The Torah of Moses endures at Yavneh.

The academy, formed by Yohanan and his leading disciples, Eliezer ben Hyrcanus and Joshua ben Hananiah, was situated in a coastal town, Yavneh, to which the Romans had sent Jewish loyalists during the war. It had a mixed population of Jews and pagans and seemed a safe place in which to concentrate displaced elements of the rebellious population. When Yohanan and his disciples escaped from Jerusalem before the end of the siege, they found refuge there and shaped a political and religious program for the new age in which the old institutions and beliefs were no more. They were joined by remnants of other groups in pre-70 Pharisaism, including survivors of the Houses of Shammai and Hillel, and the descendants and circle around Simeon b. Gamaliel.

[1] See Jacob Neusner, *Life of Yohanan ben Zakkai* (Leiden: E. J. Brill, 1970) and *Development of a Legend: Studies on the Traditions Concerning Yohanan ben Zakkai* (Leiden: E.J. Brill, 1970).

Their religious program consisted of, first, study of Torah—the ancient Scriptures and the unwritten doctrines and rules ("traditions of the fathers") called by later rabbinic Judaism "the oral Torah"; second, practice of the commandments of the Torah; and third, performance of good deeds. Yohanan did not manage to establish a political system for surviving Jewry. His successor as head of the Yavnean group, Gamaliel II, son of Simeon ben Gamaliel I, the Pharisaic leader in pre 170 times, and grandson of Gamaliel I mentioned in Acts 5:34, eventually won Roman approval for an autonomous, loyalist Jewish regime. That government was under rabbinical control and headed by Gamaliel himself and his descendants at Yavneh. The regime was to supervise the internal affairs of Palestinian Jewry.

The Yavnean academy lasted from 70 to *ca.* 125. In the unrest provoked thereafter by Bar Kokhba, a messianic revolutionary who led a new war against Rome from 132 to 135 A.D., the old regime collapsed. The greatest Yavnean rabbi of the day, Aqiba, recognized Bar Kokhba as the Messiah, and so the irenic and collaborationist regime established by Yohanan ben Zakkai and Gamaliel II fell because of Aqiba's pressure from within and the weight of a new messianic movement to oppose Roman rule in Palestine.

Yavneh thus represents the crucial period in the history of ancient Judaism. For us, the work of Yavneh, carried on by rabbis who claimed to possess the oral traditions of pre-70 Pharisaism, is especially important, for it is at Yavneh that we *first* find attestations for rabbinical traditions about the pre-70 Pharisees.

In the whole corpus of materials attributed to, or told about, pre-70 masters, we find not a single cross-reference. No pre-70 Pharisee ever alludes to a teaching, story, or saying of another pre-70 Pharisee, except within the same pericope. Yohanan ben Zakkai, allegedly the disciple of Hillel, rarely refers to anything he learned from Hillel. None of the named masters, such as Yosi ben Yoezer, Simeon ben Shetah, or Gamaliel, ever alludes to a decree issued by the other named masters, nor do the Houses of Shammai and Hillel make reference to traditions of the masters who precede Shammai and Hillel. Even Gamaliel I and Simeon ben Gamaliel I, who come at the end of 150 years of Pharisaic teaching, seem to know nothing about the specific rules laid down in the names of antecedent masters, or about the disputes of the Houses of Shammai and Hillel. The contrast with the Yavnean stratum is extraordinary, for Yavnean masters copiously allude to pre-70 materials. The work of Yavneh thus included the effort to preserve and organize the legacy of Jerusalemite Pharisaism.

This seems a natural response to the old city and its institutions being in ruins. The survivors sought to preserve what could be saved, to make permanent in fixed laws what had seemed as stable as the stones of the old city—the Pharisaic way of life. Just as the destruction of Jerusalem and the end of the old order provoked the composition of Josephus's writing and of

1037

elements of the Gospel traditions, so it led to the earliest formation of the rabbinical record of Pharisaism.

The Houses of Shammai and Hillel

The record begins with materials about the inner life of Pharisaism, the disputes of the Houses of Shammai and Hillel. After the Pharisaic masters, Shammai and Hillel, who had flourished at the end of the first century B.C., circles of their disciples persisted within the Pharisaic sect.

The earliest Yavneans, around Yohanan ben Zakkai, do not seem to have been part of the Shammaite and Hillelite circles. While later traditions call Yohanan a disciple of Hillel, in no saying attributed to him does Yohanan state, "Thus have I received from my master, Hillel." Similarly, Gamaliel II never alludes to his supposed ancestor, Hillel, although, as noted, later patriarchs of his line, particularly after the Bar Kokhba War, claim to have been descended from Hillel and hence from the messianic seed of David, to which Hillel is assigned descent in the female line. So it was taken for granted that Gamaliel, Simeon, and Gamaliel likewise were Hillel's children.

The traditions attested at Yavneh, on the other hand, give a detailed picture of the disputes of the Houses of Shammai and Hillel. This suggests that disciples of those Houses, surviving the War, joined Yohanan in the work of Yavneh and began to record and preserve the traditions they had learned before 70.

These traditions must have been handed on before that time according to the interests and practices of the respective Houses. The laws of the Qumran community are coherently organized by theme and contain no rulings contrary to those accepted by the community. So, I should imagine, the laws of the House of Shammai and of the House of Hillel were laid out along whatever thematic or other principles of organization seemed appropriate in the respective Houses. They would *not* have been preserved in antithetical relationship with the contrary opinions of the opposing House. Thus we should expect the Shammaite traditions on the Sabbath to be a list of Sabbath laws, given without contrary opinions of the Hillelite House:

> As to the Sabbath,
> > One does not do so-and-so.
> As to tithing,
> > One tithes such-and-such.

The Houses' laws deriving from, and well attested at, Yavneh, however, give the two Houses' respective opinions in opposition to one another:

As to the Sabbath,
  The House of Shammai say, "One does not do so-and-so,
  And the House of Hillel say, "One does so-and-so."

The pericopae of these two Houses, as observed, constitute the largest corpus of materials attributed to pre-70 masters. Nearly all elements in that corpus exhibit common form and structure and uniform style. The traditions of the two Houses are invariably combined in the form of a dispute between them on points of law. The dispute form involves a superscription which states the legal problem, followed by brief rulings attributed to the House of Shammai and the House of Hillel, in that order.

A secondary form is the debate, in which the Hillelites normally come first; the Shammaites have the last word and win the argument. Here the sayings generally are developed and not compressed into a few words or balanced against one another.

The Houses' opinions are usually phrased in direct discourse or intensive verbs. For example:

> House of Shammai
>   say unclean
>   declare unclean
>   declare liable; say, liable
>   declare unfit
>   declare ready to receive uncleanness
> House of Hillel
>   say, clean
>   declare clean
>   declare free of liability;
>   say, free of liability
>   declare fit
>   declare *not* ready to receive uncleanness

In later times masters observed the literary phenomena represented by the fixed order and rigid forms of the Houses' disputes:

> R. Abba in the name of Samuel [a third century Babylonian rabbi] said, "For three years there was a dispute between the House of Shammai and the House of Hillel.
>
> "One said, 'The law is in agreement with us,' and the other said, 'The law is in agreement with us.'
>
> "Then an echo came forth and said, 'Both are the words of the living God, but the law follows the words of the House of Hillel.'"
>
> Since both are the words of the living God, what entitled the House of Hillel to have the law established in agreement with their words?

Because they were kindly and modest. They studied their own rulings and those of the House of Shammai. They were even so humble as to mention the words of the House of Shammai before their own.[2]

On what account did the House of Hillel prove worthy that the law should be established according to their words?
R. Judah b. R. Pazzi said, "Because they placed the words of the House of Shammai ahead of their words.
"And not only so, but they also saw [the point of] the words of the House of Shammai and retracted their own opinions."[3]

Clearly, it was regarded as preferable to come first. It also was held that an echo from heaven had pronounced the decision:

An echo went forth and said, "These and these are the words of the living God, but the law is according to the words of the House of Hillel."
Where did the echo go forth?
R. Bibi in the name of R. Yohanan [a third century Palestinian rabbi] said, "In Yavneh did the echo go forth."[4]

To be sure, Hillelites believed in heavenly echoes, and Shammaites did not. While in this form the Houses are at parity, the Shammaites in fact predominate. They give the first ruling, and, in a debate, the final, decisive argument.

The problem of dating pericopae is complicated by the fact that the Houses' dispute form was pseudepigraphically employed over a period of roughly a century, from *ca.* 70 to *ca.* 170, and somewhat less commonly thereafter. We do not know whether the form was used before 70 as well. But it seems unlikely, for none of the pericopae can be verified or attested by reference on the part of named masters before 70, who, as noted, never comment directly on materials attributed to the Houses or even on legal issues addressed by the Houses. Further, the individual Houses, apart from their opposition, presumably preserved their rules without allusion to contrary opinions.

All we can hope to find is a plausible date for the creation and first usage of the Houses' dispute form itself. It obviously cannot come before the time of Shammai and Hillel—*ca.* 10 A.D. But it also cannot date after the time of Aqiba and Tarfon—*ca.* 90 A.D.—for both refer to and therefore attest the existence of Houses' disputes. Eliezer b. Hyrcanus and Joshua b. Hananiah also comment on Houses pericopae, which pushes the *terminus* of the form back by about 15 years, to *ca.* 75 A.D. These two masters sometimes are

2 b. Eruv. 13b.
3 y. Suk. 2:8.
4 y. Yev. 6:6.

identified with, or regarded as equivalent to, the Houses of Shammai and Hillel. Perhaps the form itself appeared even before their time, right at the outset of the Yavnean period.

The Hillelites predominated at Yavneh, certainly by 90 A.D., and possibly after 70, for Yohanan b. Zakkai was alleged to have been Hillel's disciple. By contrast, no important Yavnean was assigned to Shammai as a disciple. (Eliezer is called a sympathizer.) Since the Hillelites told stories both to account for Shammaite predominance in pre-70 Pharisaism, and also to explain the later predominance of the Hillelites ("heavenly echo came to Yavneh"), it stands to reason that the Shammaites predominated before 70, the Hillelites shortly afterward. This is further suggested by one-sided, if limited, evidence that Simeon b. Gamaliel I followed Shammaite rules and therefore sympathized with the House of Shammai, as did his son, Gamaliel II.

My guess is that the Houses' forms were first worked out at Yavneh, when the parties were nearly equal in influence but the Shammaites still enjoyed a measure of power, so they could persist in taking precedence. It was at that time and place that the parties had to come together to determine normative law, and that authorities of sufficient stature to impose the necessary compromises actually assembled.

The reconstruction undertaken at Yavneh required the conciliation of both parties in order to achieve unification of Pharisaism for the purpose of assuming and exercising the new power and responsibility gained in the aftermath of the destruction. Yohanan b. Zakkai and Gamaliel II afterwards may have sought to conciliate the Shammaites in the redaction of existing legal materials. The generation of Gamaliel II, Eliezer, Joshua, Tarfon, and Aqiba, as noted, is the first to refer to Houses disputes in their present form. Yavneh's accomplishments thus evidently include not only formation of elements of the *Siddur* and perhaps canonization of parts of Scripture, but also the redaction, in the Houses' form, of parts of the Oral Torah of Pharisaism. This Oral Torah would at first have consisted primarily of Houses' pericopae, arranged in patterns to permit easy memorization. But it is the *form,* not the substance, of Houses' pericopae which reached the final stage of development.

Some Yavnean Traditions

Approximately 65 rabbinical traditions about the pre-70 Pharisees are attested at Yavneh. These concern primarily legal questions, and not matters of history, doctrine, or faith. The kinds of law for which Pharisaic derivation is claimed pertain to the Temple cult, tithing, Sabbath and festival observance, liturgy, uncleanness rules, and family law—the legal agenda reviewed above (pp. 82–90). We find almost no civil law, which means that the early Yavneans either did not have, or did not choose to preserve and attribute to the pre-70 Pharisees, traditions about the adjudication of property disputes. There is no criminal law at all. The laws we do have are those we should have expected on the basis of New Testament allusions to the Pharisees, and the proportions are exactly right: most pertain, first, to tithing and uncleanness rules, second, to Sabbath and festival observance. Let us now examine examples of some of the kinds of law attributed by Yavnean rabbis to pre-70 Pharisaism, particularly to the Houses of Shammai and Hillel.

TEMPLE LAW:
THE LAYING ON OF HANDS

The following pericope, about laying hands on a Temple offering before slaughter on the festival day, is fundamental to the rabbinical traditions about the Pharisees. We begin with a "chain of tradition" (above, p. 9), in which the heads of the Pharisaic sect are listed and given opinions on this question. Then we shall see a Mishnaic form (*ca.* 200 A.D.) of a dispute in which the same issue is worked out in a different manner, together with later developments of the same issue. Then we shall examine the Tosefta's version (*ca.* 250 A.D.) of the matter, including a classic debate between the Houses of Shammai and Hillel.

The early attestation of Yavneh comes at the very end: Abba Saul, a Yavnean master, has an account of the opinion of the House of Hillel different from that given in the Mishnah. This tells us that the foregoing tradition had taken shape in his time, evidently in competition with others. Finally, I have included a pertinent story about Hillel and Shammai's disciples in the Temple.

> A. 1. Yosi b. Yoezer says [on a festival day] not to lay [hands on the offering before it is slaughtered]. Yosi b. Yohanan says to lay [hands].
>
> 2. Joshua b. Perahiah says not to lay [hands]. Nittai the Arbelite says to lay [hands].
>
> 3. Judah b. Tabbai says not to lay [hands]. Simeon b. Shetah says to lay [hands].
>
> 4. Shemaiah says to lay [hands]. Abtalion says not to lay [hands].
>
> 5A. Hillel and Menahem did not differ, but Menahem went forth, and Shammai entered in.
>
> 5B. Shammai says not to lay [hands]. Hillel says to lay [hands].
>
> B. The former were *Nasis* [Patriarchs], and the latter, fathers of the court [chief magistrates].[5]

---

5 M. Hag. 2:2.

This chain of tradition lists the Pharisaic masters, giving each an opinion about laying hands:

1. Yosi + Yosi
2. Joshua + Nittai
3. Judah + Simeon
4. Shemaiah + Abtalion
5A. Hillel + Menahem
5B. Shammai + Hillel

The list of names and opinions contains no allusion to the offices the several authorities held. The subscription (B) then tells us that the first named were patriarchs, while the second named were heads of the court, that is, second to the patriarch. The issue of which authority takes precedence does not figure in the body of the pericope, since it is irrelevant to its contents. Furthermore, the pattern is inconsistent. The first name should always say not to lay on hands, so Shemaiah has the wrong opinion for his position in the list.

To understand this list, we must know several facts.

First, after 70 A.D., particularly after 140, the rabbinical government of Palestine was headed by the *Nasi,* or patriarch, first, at Yavneh, by Gamaliel II, next, at Usha, by Simeon b. Gamaliel II, his son. The most important, at the end of the second century A.D., was Judah the Patriarch, who stands behind the Mishnah.

In Simeon's time (*ca.* 140), the claim was made that the patriarchal family is descended from Hillel. The head of the government therefore had a strong interest in reshaping earlier materials to give as important a place as possible to Hillel. He certainly had to be represented as the patriarch of own day. We shall now see how this was accomplished.

The tradition before us was reworked, for the little group at the end (Hillel-Menahem, then Shammai-Hillel) is difficult. Hillel-Menahem break the pattern; this is probably a later insertion, for Hillel should say *not to lay on hands,* since he was supposed to have been *Nasi.* We shall see a story on this very point, in which Hillel is represented as following Shammai's practice.

Clearly, in the pericope before us Hillel is presumed to be *Nasi,* despite his having the wrong opinion. But if we drop the interpolation of Hillel-Menahem, we find that the form calls for merely *Shammai/Hillel: not to lay/lay,* and that is surely the authentic reading according to the foregoing pattern. Therefore the original list had Shammai as *Nasi.* I cannot guess why Shemaiah's opinion has been reversed.

In Tos. Hag., which is according to the teaching of Meir, a major authority at Usha, *ca.* 150 A.D., provides a far better solution to the problem

of making Hillel *Nasi* in traditions which originally had him as father of the
court. Meir works with the original list, containing five pairs of names, and
preserves the opinions as originally attributed to the authorities—not to lay,
then to lay. But at the end he simply claims that the first three *not to lay*
names were patriarchs, and the last two *to lay* names were also patriarchs—
a neat solution. It requires much less doctoring of the original list than inclusion of the little Hillel-Menahem-Shammai-Hillel set.

> They differed only on the laying of hands.
> "They are five pairs. The three of the first pairs who said not to
> lay on hands, and the two of the last pairs who said to lay on hands
> were *Nasis*. The second ones [mentioned] were heads of the court," so
> R. Meir.
> R. Judah [bar Ilai] said, "Simeon b. Shetah [was] *Nasi*. Judah b.
> Tabbai [was] head of the court."[6]

Meir thus has five pairs:

1. *Nasi* (not to lay) + head of court (to lay)
2. *Nasi* (not to lay) + head of court (to lay)
3. *Nasi* (not to lay) + head of court (to lay)
4. *Nasi* (to lay) + head of court (not to lay)
5. *Nasi* (to lay) + head of court (not to lay)

Meir's list is the same as M. Hag. 2:2 as far as Shemaiah and Abtalion. He
presumably did not include Hillel-Menahem, for that would have made
Hillel-Shammai a *sixth* pair. But for the last pair he had a "to lay"-*Nasi* in
first place. Was it Shammai or Hillel? Probably Hillel, since the "not to
lay"/"to lay" antithesis is primary to the tradition, and there seems no
strong reason for changing the attributions. So we have two forms of the
list, one which can be reconstructed from M. Hag. 2:2, the other from
Meir's report.

Meir's tradition can be explained as a secondary development from the
other, motivated by the desire of the Hillelites to represent Hillel as head
of the government, *Nasi*. What the M. Hag. tradition accomplished by
inserting the Hillel-Menahem pair before Shammai and Hillel was done in
Meir's tradition by simply reversing the customary order and putting Hillel
before Shammai.

Judah b. Ilai, another important Ushan authority, differs only with
reference to Judah b. Tabbai and Simeon b. Shetah. The latter, he says,
was *Nasi*.

The list of M. Hag., excluding Menahem and the subscription, could

---

6 Tos. Hag. 2:8.

not have been shaped later than the time of Meir and Judah, since both refer to it. Judah the Patriarch in his Mishnah follows Meir, and therefore has as *Nasis* Yosi b. Yoezer, Joshua, *Judah*, Shemaiah, and Hillel. Since he thought he descended from Hillel, it was natural to explain matters as he did in the subscription. But the subscription in M. Hag. 2:2 cannot come before Meir and Judah, who do not cite it verbatim. It appears to be Judah the Patriarch's summary of Meir's comment.

The following tradition now represents the Houses as debating the same issue. The House of Shammai say that one brings the peace offerings on the festival day but does not lay hands on them—just what Shammai had said. The reason is that the person who lays hands on the animal places his weight upon it, and one may not make use of animals—even to such an extent—on the festival day, the law of which is like the Sabbath in that it required one's animals to enjoy rest. One therefore lays on hands on the preceding day. At issue are the festal offerings. The whole offerings are not brought at all on the festival-day, because they are not consumed by the man who brings them. Since the pilgrim derives no benefit from them on the festival day, they are left over and offered afterward. There is no need to set aside the sanctity of the festival on their account.

The House of Hillel is consistent with Hillel: All the offerings are brought, the man who brings them lays on hands, and all are then sacrificed.

> A. The House of Shammai say, "They may bring Peace-offerings [on a festival day] and do not lay the hands thereon; but [they do] not [bring] Whole-offerings."
> And the House of Hillel say, "They may bring [both] Peace-offerings and Whole-offerings and lay their hands thereon."[7]

The Tosefta now supplies a substantial supplement to the relatively brief Mishnaic version of the Houses' dispute. The several arguments are explained in sequence:

> A. What is the laying on of hands concerning which they differed?
> B. The House of Shammai say, "They do not lay on hands on the festival, and as to peace offerings, the one who celebrates through them lays hands on them on the day *before* the festival."
> The House of Hillel say, "They bring Peace-offerings and Whole-offerings and lay hands on them [as in the Mishnah]."

Thus, as noted, the issue is, Do you lay on hands on the festival day? The opinion of the House of Shammai is that you do not, therefore you do so the day before the festival. The opinion of the House of Hillel is that you do lay on hands, therefore no provision is made for the day before the festival.

7 M. Hag. 2:3.

The superscription (A) refers to M. Hag. 2:3 and distinguishes among the several disputes therein combined. The laying on of hands to which reference is made pertains to festival offerings. As to the pilgrim's offering, he lays on hands on the preceding day. The House of Hillel say one brings Peace offerings and sacrifices and lays on hands, just as in the Mishnah. So the revisions pertain primarily to the Shammaite saying:

M. Hag.:	A.	They bring Peace-offerings and do not lay on hands.
	B.	They do not bring Whole-offerings.
Tos. Hag.:	A.	They do not lay on hands on the festival [on *any* offerings].
	B.	As to the festival offering, they lay on hands on the *preceding* day.

The clarification therefore serves M. Hag. clause A: When *do* they lay on hands? Tos. underlines the ruling and explains how to carry out the sacrifice. The Hillelite position is unchanged. So the principle under discussion is whether or not one lays hands on the sacrifice on the festival day, debated by the pairs (M. Hag. 2:2) as well as by the Houses. But no one debated *whether* to bring offerings on the festival.

A debate now follows the introductory statement of the dispute:

> C. The House of Hillel said, "Now, if at a time that you are not permitted to work for an ordinary person, you *are* permitted to work for the Highest One [the Sabbath]—when you *are* permitted to work for an ordinary person, are you not permitted to work for the Highest One?" [Therefore the whole-offering should be made.]
>
> The House of Shammai said to them, "Vow- and free-will-offerings will prove [the matter], for you *are* permitted to do them for an ordinary person, and you are not permitted to do them for the Highest One."

In Part C, the Hillelites argue that one may not work on the Sabbath, even in connection with preparation of food, yet one *may* offer the perpetual and supplementary sacrifices. On the festival, when one *is* permitted to work for an ordinary person, one should be permitted to lay on hands; consideration of Sabbath rest does not enter.

The Shammaites reply that even when one *is* permitted to work for the ordinary person, that is, on the festival, one *still* does not offer vow- and free-will sacrifices, a law with which the Hillelites agree.

Now the Hillelites take up this last point, and distinguish between vow- and free-will offerings and the pilgrim's sacrifice, which is at issue:

> D. The House of Hillel said to them, "No, if you say so concerning vow- and free-will-offerings, whose time is *not* set, will you say so

concerning the pilgrim's sacrifice, whose time *is* set?" [Thus only now may the sacrifice be offered.]

The House of Shammai said to them, "So too with the pilgrim's sacrifice—sometimes its time is *not* set, for he who did not celebrate it on the first day of the festival may offer [it] the whole festival and [even] the last day of the festival [according to your view]."

E. Abba Saul gives a different version in the name of the House of Hillel: "If when your stove is closed [you cannot cook on the Sabbath], the stove of your Lord is open [sacrifices *are* offered], when your stove is open [you can cook on festivals], will not the stove of your Lord [also] be open?"[8]

In Part D, the Hillelites distinguish between vow- and free-will offerings and the pilgrim's sacrifice. The time for those offerings *is* set. The Shammaites deny that this is invariably the case. There the debate ends, with the Shammaites having the last word and winning the argument.

The revision of Abba Saul, a Yavnean authority, is of great importance, for the debate must thereby be dated back to Yavneh and cannot be regarded as a second century expansion of first century legal sayings. This shows not only that the dispute form existed, but also that the debate form had already taken shape. Therefore, the debate comes quite early in the formation of traditions.

Abba Saul holds that the House of Hillel say vow- and free-will offerings *are* sacrificed on the festival day, for "when your stove is open" all the more so will the stove of the Master be open for vow- and free-will offerings.

Immediately following is a story of Hillel, who laid on hands on the sacrifice in the courtyard and then assured Shammaites that it was a female and needed merely for peace offerings, and so pretended he was a Shammaite. The Hillel story comes after, and illustrates, the legal dispute of the Houses. Thus a law or exegesis is turned into a narrative, "historical" account illustrating the same law or exegesis.

A. The story is told concerning Hillel the Elder, who laid hands on the whole-offering in the courtyard [of the Temple, thus transgressing the Shammaite rule], and the disciples of Shammai collected against him.

B. He said to them, "Come and see that it is [merely] a female, and I must make it [as] a peace-offering [not as a whole-offering, which the Shammaites prohibit]."

He put them off with words, and they went their way.

Thus Hillel seemed to break the Shammaite rule. But when confronted by the disciples of Shammai, he explained that his action did not violate the

8 Tos. Hag. 2:10.

law. The offering was not a whole-offering, but merely a peace-offering, and to this they had no objection. They therefore supposed Hillel followed Shammaite law. Consequently, people supposed Hillel had reversed himself and that the rule should be according to the House of Shammai.

> C. Forthwith the hand of the House of Shammai was strengthened, and they [the court] sought to establish the law according to them [the Shammaites].
>
> D. And there was Baba b. Buta, who was of the disciples of the House of Shammai, but who knew that the law [was] according to the words of the House of Hillel in every place. He went and brought the whole "flock of Qedar" [best sheep] and set them up in the courtyard, and he said, "Whoever needs to bring whole-offerings and peace-offerings, let him come and take and lay on hands."
>
> They came and took the beast and offered up whole-offerings and laid hands on them.
>
> E. On that very day the law was established according to the words of the House of Hillel, and no one protested at the matter.[9]

The pericope is a supplement to M. Hag. 2:2–3: Shammai says, "He may not lay on hands [on the whole-offering]," and Hillel says, "He may." Instead of supplying arguments to support his viewpoint, Hillel here simply dissimulates, for Shammai's House agree that a pilgrim's peace offerings *do* require laying on of hands.

The first story ends with part B. Then comes a connecting clause, tying the foregoing incident to the effort to effect the law as the Shammai House taught it. Baba b. Buta, a disciple of Shammai, but a good Hillelite (!), thereupon foiled the effort. Part E supplies a happy ending, stressing that no one protested.

The pericope as a whole is a fantasy, shaped within the theory that the Temple was in the hands of the Pharisees. Shammai's disciples therefore could criticize Hillel's procedures in making the appropriate sacrifice and vice versa.

This is a Hillelite dramatization of the legal dispute on sacrifices between the two Houses, in two acts. The first, parts A-B, tells how Hillel conformed to Shammaite law, laying on hands as the Shammaites said was proper, but otherwise not. Part C draws the consequence of that fact: It is an interlude underlining that Hillel's conformance to Shammaite law led to the decision being made to follow Shammai. Part D is the second act, in which Baba b. Buta rescues the situation by forcing the issue. Large numbers of people thereupon followed the Hillelite view of law. Part E, balancing part C, provides the denouement. In its present form the story cannot derive from Shammaite circles, which probably would not have recorded that Hillel "put them off with words, and they went on their way."

9 Tos. Hag. 2:11.

Since the Temple was not in Pharisaic hands, stories that told otherwise were likely to have been shaped later on, when the facts of the case either no longer mattered or had been forgotten. But the formulation of stories on the basis of fantasies is not unheard of, and we cannot regard the facts of the matter as decisive in suggesting dates for stories such as this one.

What is more important is that it is taken for granted the Hillelites are now in power. Baba b. Buta "knew" what was only a fact much later on, when the House of Shammai had lost all control over the formation of new traditions (even though old ones continued to be preserved). Since this is self-evidently a Hillelite story, I imagine it must come later than the period in which the House of Shammai proved an effective force within Pharisaism. Still, the possibility remains that this is how Hillelites always told their stories, and the foregoing considerations are not decisive one way or the other.

LITURGY:

RECITING THE SHEMA

One of the most important problems facing the masters at Yavneh was how to conduct Jewish liturgy, so much of which had formerly centered upon the Temple cult. Yohanan ben Zakkai issued a number of decrees to preserve for synagogue life the rites and rituals formerly conducted only in the Jerusalem Temple. One of the most striking liturgical discussions concerns how to recite the *Shema* ("Hear O Israel, the Lord our God, the Lord is one"), which faithful Jews said (and say) morning and night. The Houses are supposed to have debated the proper way of doing so—specifically, the proper posture in which the prayer is to be said.

The pericope follows in logical sequence upon discussions of *when* one must read the *Shema* night and morning, in which Eliezer, Gamaliel, and Joshua appear. The next set of pericopae deals with other matters. So the primary issue pertaining to the *Shema* in early Yavnean discourse concerned *when,* then *how* the *Shema* was to be read. Obviously, all parties assumed one does indeed read the *Shema* morning and night. But the issues of when and how one does so ought also to have been settled long before, if it were a routine private devotional practice, and if all details of religious life were supposed to be determined precisely by law. To teach, "It is your duty to recite the *Shema* morning and night—just how and when you do it is to be settled by your own piety and common sense," was probably the practice of the ordinary folk.

Separation of the Pharisees from the practices of common piety had to be a long and gradual process, since new, precise laws in all details of religious life could not be invented at once. So this common but unspecified pious practice lies in the general background against which the Houses' disputes may be seen as genuine points of precise definition and differentiation. Among them, the manner in which one recites the *Shema* does not look like an issue faced for the first time in early Yavneh. Issues facing the Houses and the early Yavneans are closely related. The evident absence of experience in the matter raises the possibility that the Houses and early Yavneans were working out what was to them a liturgical practice that was fundamentally new, not in basics but in precise definitions. In taking over the governance of cultic life, just as they apparently took over and preserved the pilgrim festivals—Tabernacles, Passover, Pentecost— which were formerly centered in the Temple, the later Houses and early Yavneans had to work out rules for what had been primarily in the hands of priests. This accounts for some of their innovations, but more are accounted for by the determination to extend the rule of precise laws to all those areas of life formerly left to the judgment of the pious individual.

The issue is attested by several Yavneans, in quite unrelated pericopae, as follows:

A. The House of Shammai say, "In the evening every man should recline and recite [the *Shema*], but in the morning he should stand up, for it is written, *And when thou liest down and when thou risest up* (Deut. 6:7)."

The House of Hillel say, "Every man recites it in his own way, for it is written, *And when thou walkest by the way.*

"If so, why is it said, *And when thou liest down and when thou risest up?* But [the reference is to] the time that men [usually] lie down and the time that men [usually] rise up."

B. R. Tarfon said, "I was coming on the way, and I reclined to recite [the *Shema*] in accordance with the words of the House of Shammai, and I put myself in jeopardy by reason of robbers."

They said to him, "You were worthy to be liable for your own [punishment] because you transgressed the words of the House of Hillel."[10]

The Scriptural proof texts look like interpolated glosses. None is required for the House of Shammai, which, as often, rely on the obvious meaning of the Scripture. But the House of Hillel differ from that meaning and therefore require the explanation of how their position squares with the plain sense of the Scriptural commandment.

The story (part B) of R. Tarfon, a Yavnean and teacher of Aqiba, supplies a firm *terminus ante quem* for the foregoing materials, possibly in their present form, for the same verbs occur in both the legal saying and the story. This suggests Tarfon, or the person responsible for the story about him, wished to underline knowledge of, or make reference to, the actual words of the House of Shammai.

10 M. Ber. 1:3.

The point of the story is that anyone who follows the view of the House of Shammai deserves to be punished and die, a sure sign that the issue was vivid, and that many did agree with the House of Shammai. We do not know who "they" are, but it hardly matters. Tarfon says precisely what "they" do through his story about supernatural punishment for following Shammai; "they" underline the lesson by generalizing on the consequences of transgressing the words of the House of Hillel.

Another pertinent account is as follows:

> R. Ishmael and R. Eleazar b. Azariah were dwelling in one place, and R. Ishmael was reclining, and R. Eleazar b. Azariah standing up. The time of reciting the *Shema* came. R. Ishmael stood up and R. Eleazar b. Azariah lay down.
> R. Ishmael said to him, "What is this, Eleazar?"...
> He [Ishmael] said to him, "You lay down to carry out the words of the House of Hillel, and I stood up to carry out the words of the House of Shammai."
> "Another matter, so that the disciples should not see and permanently establish the law according to your words."[11]

For our purposes, what is important is the further indication of a firm *terminus ante quem* for the pericope on the subject. Both masters were important Yavnean authorities in the early second century. For the Mishnah, Judah the Patriarch preferred the more explicit Tarfon subscription: If you follow the opinion of the House of Shammai, you deserve supernatural punishment. The supplement, in the Tosefta, takes this for granted, but is less explicit.

FAMILY LIFE:

GROUNDS FOR DIVORCE

We have already seen that the Pharisees are represented by Mark 2:2–10 as debating with Jesus about the appropriate grounds for divorce (p. 69). Here we have the equivalent pericopae from Yavneh, first a dispute, then an amplification through a debate. Aqiba supplies the *terminus ante quem*, since his saying takes the foregoing for granted and then provides a still more lenient rule in the tradition of the House of Hillel.

> [*When a man takes a wife and marries her, if then she finds no favor in his eyes because he has found some matter of indecency in her, and he writes her a bill of divorce and puts it in her hand...* (Deut. 24:1).]
> From here—

11 Tos. Ber. 1:4.

A. The House of Shammai say, "A man should not divorce his wife unless he has found in her some indecency, as it is said, *Because he has found some matter of indecency in her.*"

And the House of Hillel say, "Even if she spoiled his soup, as it is said, *Because he has found some matter of indecency in her.*"

B. The House of Hillel said to the House of Shammai, "If *matter* is said, why is *indecency* said,? And if *indecency* is said, why is *matter* said? For if *matter* were said and *indecency* were not said, I might say, 'She who goes forth on account of a *matter* [of any kind] will be permitted to marry, and she who goes forth on account of *indecency* [in particular] will not be permitted to remarry.'

"And do not be surprised, for if she was prohibited from that which had been permitted to her [her husband], should she not be prohibited from that which had already been prohibited to her [any other man]? Scriptures says *indecency, and she goes forth from his house, and she goes and marries another man.*

"And if *indecency* were said and *matter* were not said, I might say, 'On account of *indecency* she will go forth, on account of [any other] *matter,* she will not go forth.' Scripture says, *Matter, and she goes forth from his house.*"

C. R. Aqiba says, "Even if he found another prettier than she. . . ."[12]

The passage recurs in the following:

The House of Shammai say, "A man should not divorce his wife unless he has found in her some indecency, as it is said, *Because he has found some matter of indecency in her.*"

The House of Hillel say, "Even if she spoiled his soup, as it says, *Because he has found some matter of indecency in her.*"

R. Aqiba says, "Even if he found another prettier than she, as it says, *If she find no favor in his eyes* (Deut. 24:1)."[13]

Sifré Deut. 269, part B, contains only the Hillelite view. We may take it for granted that the Shammaites' argument has been dropped, or no one has bothered to invent one. But its main outlines are evident in the primary pericope (part A) itself: the text specifies only adultery as a proper ground for divorce, just as Jesus notices. The Hillelites' reinterpretation of the Scripture has to be spelled out to counter the obvious sense of the Scripture itself.

But the failure of the tradents to supply the Shammaites with an appropriate reply seems to me probative evidence that while part A is within the joint Houses' tradition, part B derives from Hillelite circles only, and probably from the Aqiban tradents. Judah the Patriarch, editor of the

---

12 Sifré Deut. 269.
13 M. Git. 9:10.

Mishnah, has excluded part B from the Mishnah because he normally leaves out exegeses. But he has kept the Houses' pericope intact, also a common phenomenon. As noted, Aqiba provides a *terminus ante quem* for part A; he stands well within the Hillelite tradition, extending the ruling to a more extreme case than is given to the Hillelites.

The language of the House of Hillel, "Even if. . . ," indicates dependence of the Hillelite lemma on the Shammaite one, for by itself the Hillelite saying would not be comprehensible. The Shammaites' opinion is spelled out in full: "A man should not divorce. . .unless. . .as it is said." The Hillelites respond to the *whole* of the foregoing: "Even if. . . ." This represents a different form from the common *Statement of law—House of Shammai—House of Hillel.* In such statements, dropping the opinion of the first of the Houses would not on the face of it render that of the second incomprehensible, since both Houses relate to a single antecedent statement of the legal issue or theme. Here, by contrast, the House of Hillel give a kind of gloss to the House of Shammai. This leads to the supposition that the Shammaite opinion was already framed in precisely the form and language selected by Shammaites—hence the inclusion of a strong exegetical foundation—and never thereafter changed. But the Hillelites did not merely gloss the foregoing. They also supplied a complete response which does not permit the Shammaites a reply. The pericope as a whole shows us what Hillelites were prepared to do, and not do, with completed Shammaite traditions. They obviously have not falsified or doctored the Shammaite pericope, but preserved it whole. They have commented on the substance, and added a fictitious colloquy.

In Mark 10:2–10, on divorce (p. 69), Jesus is tested by the Pharisees. The narrative introduction is appropriately brief. The argument rests on the assumption, common to both parties, that Scriptural rules do apply: One may write a certificate of divorce and put the wife out. Jesus is then constrained to explain the agreed-upon principle, which he does through further Scriptural exegesis. Formally, the dispute differs in no significant respect from a standard Houses' debate such as the one before us.

The type of pericope—a legal dispute—and the form—a debate—seem identical in both traditions. Bultmann observes that the counterquestion is in no sense a counterargument, and the Scriptural reference does not really answer the opponents, but is subject to their criticism.[14] But this is similar to the debate before us. The second party to the debate accepts the premises of the first, then builds a case upon the shared premises. Naturally therefore, the Scriptures will be cited in common, then interpreted differently.

---

14 Rudolf Bultmann, *The History of the Synoptic Tradition,* trans. John Marsh (New York: Harper & Row, Publishers, 1968), p. 27.

AGRICULTURAL LAW:

UNCLEAN HEAVE OFFERING

While the Gospels say the Pharisees laid great stress on exact tithing, they give no hint of the complexity and sophistication of Pharisaic agricultural laws. The authors of the Gospels cannot have had profound knowledge of those laws; if they had, they would have formulated, from their viewpoint, a much more severe indictment. The following complex example deals with the sort of far-fetched and remote situation of interest to the Yavnean tradents.

Heave offering has been separated from the crop and set aside for presentation to the priest. A small part of it, made unclean by contact with a source of ritual uncleanness, has fallen into a much larger quantity of clean Heave offering. Is the whole mass rendered unclean? Or is the small quantity of unclean Heave offering neutralized by reason of its minuteness, and to be disregarded? The practical result is that unclean Heave offering cannot be consumed by the priest to whom it belongs, but must be left to rot. Clean Heave offering is available to him for use. But the Pharisees did not make rules for the priesthood, and the issue is a matter of legal theory, rather than of significant practical advantage. The passage is as follows:

A. [If] one *seah* [small measure] of unclean Heave-offering fell into a hundred *seahs* of clean Heave-offering—

The House of Shammai forbid. [That is, the unclean matter is sufficient to render the whole prohibited for priestly use.]

And the House of Hillel permit [it]. [That is, the small quantity is diluted, and the priest may enjoy the produce.]

B. The House of Hillel said to the House of Shammai, Since clean [Heave-offering] is forbidden to non-priests, and also unclean [Heave-offering] is forbidden to priests, if the clean can be neutralized, cannot the unclean be neutralized also?"

The House of Shammai said to them, "No! If common [unconsecrated] produce, to which leniency applies and which *is* permitted to non-priests, neutralizes what is clean, should Heave-offering, to which stringency *does* apply and which is forbidden to non-priests, neutralize what is unclean!"

C. *After they had agreed*—

R. Eliezer says, "It should be taken up and burned."

And the Sages say, "It is lost through its scantiness [and therefore the diluted mixture is permitted to priests]."[15]

The issue is clear: Is the unclean Heave offering neutralized in the clean? According to the Shammaites it must be left to rot; the priests cannot

---

[15] M. Ter. 5:4.

use it ("prohibit"). The argument of the Hillelites (part B) is that clean Heave offering is prohibited to nonpriests, and unclean is prohibited to priests. Since clean Heave offering *is* capable of being neutralized when it falls into 100 times its quantity of unconsecrated food, so the unclean Heave offering should be neutralized in clean Heave offering. The Shammaites reply that common produce can indeed serve to neutralize what is clean, but clean Heave offering, to which more stringent rules apply, cannot serve to neutralize unclean. It is a false analogy.

Part C begins with an agreement but does not specify who agreed with whom. Normally, part B would have ended the argument—the Shammaites would have the last word and win. Later masters assume that the House of Shammai agreed with the House of Hillel. But "After they agreed" is nothing more than a joining formula, to tie R. Eliezer b. Hyrcanus's opinion —in the present tense!—to the antecedent elements. Part C actually is a separate pericope, awkwardly tied to the superscription of the whole:

> [If] one *seah* of unclean Heave-offering fell into hundred *seahs* of clean Heave-offering—
> R. Eliezer says, "It should be taken up and burned."
> The sages say, "It is lost [neutralized] through its scantiness."

The word-choices differ from the foregoing, but the positions are the same:

> Eliezer = House of Shammai
> Sages = House of Hillel

That is, the man must take up a *seah* and give it to the priest, as in the case of clean Heave offering that is neutralized, but the *seah* is not to be eaten, but rather to be burned like unclean Heave offering. Hence Eliezer forbids the unclean Heave offering to the priest, just as do the House of Shammai. The sages' position, that it is lost (neutralized) through its scantiness, is identical with the Hillelite position. There is no necessity to to supply further Heave offering; the whole is regarded as Heave offering, and the priests consume it in a state of cleanness. The substance of part C, excluding the curious redactional formula, "after they had agreed," therefore is a separate and complete pericope which duplicates or is duplicated by part B. The differences are in word choice, but the law is the same.

Both versions stand in direct relationship to the opening problem, given in the superscription, concerning *seah* of unclean Heave offering that has fallen into 100 *seahs* of clean Heave offering. Which version comes first? The word choices of the Houses' opinions, "prohibit/permit," are curiously inappropriate to the argument. One has to know that "prohibit" will mean that the unclean Heave offering is *not* neutralized in the clean Heave offering, and is therefore "prohibited" for priestly use. By contrast, Eliezer's language is entirely appropriate: "It should be taken up and burned." This exact specification of the fate of the unclean Heave offering answers the problem set in the topic sentence.

Similarly, the Hillelite use of "permit" is generalized and irrelevant to the immediate context, while the sages' language, "It is lost through its scantiness," satisfactorily completes the topic sentence. Two separate versions have been combined awkwardly, the Houses' dispute and argument and the Eliezer-sages formally conventional ruling. Since the latter (part C) renders more precise and clear what the former leaves generalized and unclear, it seems to me likely that the latter improves upon, and comes later than, the former. But this is merely a suggestion. Yavneh surely supplies the *terminus ante quem*.

AGRICULTURAL LAW:
FLEECE

Another sort of law concerns the definition of biblically ordained requirements of gifts of agricultural produce to the priests and Levites. Here the law concerns giving a fleece offering. The pericope before us defines a rather fundamental question, far less complex and sophisticated than the one about the unclean Heave offering.

> [...*And the first of the fleece of your sheep you shall give him* (Deut. 18:4).]
> And how many sheep must he have so that he will be liable for the first of the fleece?
> The House of Shammai say, "Two ewes, as it is said, *In that day a man shall keep alive a young cow and two sheep* (Is. 7:21)."
> And the House of Hillel say, "Five, as it is said, *And five sheep already dressed* (I Sam. 25:18)."
> R. Aqiba says, "*First fleece*—two. *Of your flock*—four. *You will give to him*—lo, five."[16]

The exegeses are glosses; in the Houses' pericopae it is rare to find an exegesis integral to the Houses' opinions. The original pericope would have looked something like this:

> How many sheep—first of fleece:
> House of Shammai: *Two*
> House of Hillel: *Five.*

Aqiba's opinion provides a striking example of the Aqiban exegetical convention of parsing a verse and supplying numerical values to its elements.

[16] Sifré Deut. 166.

Elsewhere, when the Aqibans do provide a later exegesis in support of the existing Hillelite ruling, they attribute their exegesis to the Hillelites. Here, by contrast, a distinction between the opinion of Hillel's House and the exegetical foundation for that opinion, supplied by Aqibans, is carefully preserved. The reason is that both Houses have already been given appropriate Scriptures. Had the pericope been presented without such exegesis, we might have found Aqiba's words placed in the mouth of the House of Hillel.

UNCLEANNESS LAW:
THE TEMPLE

As we have seen, the Pharisees presumed to legislate about the purity rules pertaining to the Temple, although the Temple was in the hands of the priesthood, not of the Pharisees. The following collection of rules about Temple cleanness is attributed to Yosi b. Yoezer (*ca.* 150 B.C.), the first in the chain of the Pharisaic leaders of M. Hag. 2:2. It is satisfactorily attested by an allusion of Eliezer b. Hyrcanus, and therefore ought to have been in its present form by early Yavnean times. But the pericope, even in its present form, comes from a much earlier period; it represents the sort of tradition handed on in earliest Pharisaic times—simple, on a single theme, without contrary opinions.

> A. R. Yosi b. Yoezer of Seredah testified concerning (1) the *Ayil*-locust is clean, and (2) *that the* liquids in the Temple shambles are clean, and (3) that he who touches a corpse becomes unclean.
> B. And they called him "Yosah the permitter."[17]

We do not have definitive evidence of the fixed forms in which teachings were transmitted before 70 A.D., but these materials are apt to provide a model. The teaching probably began simply, "Yosi b. Yoezer...testified," with three things composing the list. We do not know who called him "the permitter" (or lenient), or who held an opposite view, that the locust *was* capable of ritual uncleanness, and that the liquids *were* susceptible. We may imagine someone, possibly the Temple priests, whose sayings were not preserved in Pharisaic tradition, taught that the liquids (blood, water) could receive uncleanness.

The tradition probably is an accurate record of what early generations of Pharisees attributed to Yosi b. Yoezer. Perhaps he himself, as a priest, had issued such rulings. If he did so, it was not in the Temple, but in the Pharisaic party, hence the teaching contains one of the Pharisaic disputes with the Temple authorities.

---

17 M. Ed. 8:4.

If Temple officials held the opposite, we may assign to them both the hypothetical contrary ruling *and* the epithet. Presumably the Pharisaic tradents did not regard the epithet as particularly hostile, and since it would have been known outside of their circles, they had no reason to suppress it. So Temple authorities applied a stricter rule than did the Pharisees: The locust *could* receive uncleanness, and purity rules *did* pertain to the liquids of the Temple slaughterhouse—a considerable inconvenience. The Temple in all respects must be kept inviolable, and the sanctity rules applied as strictly as possible. This indeed later characterized the priestly Sadducees' view of the purity laws. They saw the laws as strict, but affecting only the Temple. The Pharisees interpreted those laws leniently, but regarded them as applicable everywhere, even in connection with common meals. The Essenes were equally strict, but kept the laws only in their commune, where it was relatively easy to do so.

In the original form, prior to that before us, the sayings probably were given as a unit, for they consist of closely related uncleanness rules on locust, liquid, and corpse. All pertain to the chief legal issue about which Pharisaic tradition attributed teachings to the early masters. The unifying principle was not the legal theme by itself, but also the combination of three Temple cleanness rulings attributed to Yosi b. Yoezer. The logia may have originally circulated separately and been put together only later. If so, the earlier form of Pharisaic traditions was presumably extremely brief, constituting one-sentence, simple logia containing rules of Temple (uncleanness) law, mainly concerning matters of detail (locust, liquid). The Temple for centuries had carried on its affairs according to Scriptural purity rules as interpreted by the priests' traditions. If the Pharisees took matters of detail seriously, it must have been because Temple authorities and Pharisaic opinion separated primarily on these matters. Of course we do not know why the Pharisees believed that the *Ayil*-locust was pure. Temple authorities would also have regarded the liquid of the slaughterhouse as capable of receiving uncleanness. Why did the Pharisees maintain otherwise? More important, why and how did it become a partisan issue? We do not know.

Now we see the attestation:

> Rabbi Eliezer says, "Uncleanness in no way pertains to liquids. You may know that this is so, for behold, Yosi ben Seredah [sic] gave testimony concerning the waters of the slaughter-house that they are clean."
> Rabbi Aqiba says. . . .[18]

Eliezer cites the materials redacted in M. Ed. 8:4. Aqiba and Eliezer thus supply the earliest possible *terminus ante quem*.

[18] Sifra Shemini 8:5.

UNCLEANNESS LAW:

FOOD

Since the Pharisees obeyed the laws of cultic purity outside of the cult, even in their own homes, it was important to define when various sorts of food might become fit to receive ritual uncleanness. One such dispute comes from Yavneh:

> When do fish become susceptible to uncleanness?
> The House of Shammai say, "After they are caught."
> The House of Hillel say, "After they are dead."
> R. Aqiba says, "If they could live [if they were put back into the water, they are not susceptible to uncleanness.]."[19]

This is another sort of standard dispute: When does an item become susceptible to uncleanness (or, elsewhere, enter the state of cleanness)? The Shammaite position is that since fish do not require slaughtering, they are capable of receiving uncleanness as soon as they are caught, even while alive. Aqiba is essentially in line with the Hillelite view, as usual.

The Yavnean Stratum

We cannot claim to know all that the Yavneans said and thought, for materials first attested in later strata, or occurring for the first time in Mishnah-Tosefta or even afterward, *may* have roots in traditions known at Yavneh or before that time. Furthermore, rabbinical traditions not attributed or referring to specific pre-70 Pharisees and the Houses have not been considered at all. However, what is the configuration of the tradition *indubitably* known and regarded as authoritative and normative at Yavneh? We cannot extrapolate from the known to the unknown, or allege that the materials not explicitly related to pre-70 Pharisaism, or not attributed to any named authority, play no part in Yavnean (and Ushan) reflections on pre-70 Pharisaism.

Of a historical nature are the references to Yosi b. Yoezer's uncleanness rulings, and a very few other traditions. On such a basis, we simply could not reconstruct a coherent account of pre-70 Pharisaism. We find no effort at periodization, no attention to the lists of authorities of the party (except Abba Saul's involvement in M. Hag. 2:2), no overview of what had gone before 70. The pericopae of a historical character are random and episodic.

The primary concern of Yavneans was with the Houses and their laws. The Houses obviously persisted in Yavneh as discernible groups, and their

[19] M. Uqs. 3:8.

disagreements on law clearly contributed to setting the agenda for Yavnean discussion. The work of Yavneh consisted, first, in establishing viable forms for the organization and transmission of the Houses' materials. These forms obliterated whatever antecedent materials were available, for, as noted, we may assume the respective Houses shaped autonomous materials, not merely in antithetical relationship to the opposition, and handed them down in coherent units. The Yavneans, second, made considerable progress in redacting antecedent materials in the forms they had created. The Yavnean stratum is virtually exhausted by those materials.

The earliest attested materials are apt to represent the historical Pharisees' legal agenda, in theme and probably also in substance. The laws of tithing and ritual purity, as we should have expected on the basis of the testimony of the Gospels, are well attested. They are highly developed, sophisticated, and detailed, and pertain to subtle and difficult questions, not to the definition of such basic matters as in the way one recites the *Shema*. They evidently depend upon ancient traditions within Pharisaism. This is not surprising, since the early masters of Yavneh, particularly Yohanan b. Zakkai, had been important teachers in pre-70 Jerusalemite Pharisaism.

While many new legal and theological problems required attention at Yavneh, old Pharisaic traditions certainly were carried forward and accurately set down for posterity.

7

Traditions of Usha
(140–170 A.D.)

Usha

The messianic war led by Bar Kokhba in 132–135 and endorsed by Aqiba proved to be a complete disaster. While the Jews fought with exceptional courage, they had no chance against the superior legions of Rome, then at the height of its power. The Jews' courage therefore prolonged the hopeless struggle and produced utter devastation of the Judean part of Palestine. Henceforward, the main centers of Jewish settlement would be in Galilee. Other parts of the country were denuded of Jewish population and resettled by gentiles. Since the war had been essentially religious and messianic in motivation, in its aftermath the Romans instituted a period of severe repression and for a brief time made the practice of Judaism a capital crime. By 140 the former benign policy had been restored; the Romans rebuilt the autonomous, collaborationist Jewish regime to govern the inner life of the Palestinian Jews in accord with the teaching of the Torah as interpreted by the rabbis. The Romans reestablished the loyalist patriarchate, placing in power Simeon b. Gamaliel II, the son of Gamaliel II, who had served so well at Yavneh. At Usha the patriarch Simeon reassembled the rabbinical masters, most of them the surviving disciples of Aqiba. The Aqibans, who had at Yavneh championed the viewpoint of the House of Hillel, were now in complete control.

Some Ushan Traditions_____

From a legal viewpoint, those rabbinical traditions about the Pharisees first attested at Usha do not significantly alter the picture yielded by those from Yavneh. The area and kinds of law on which the Houses legislated do not appreciably expand. What becomes commonplace is the revision of earlier materials of the Houses. Some later Yavnean pericopae contain a few items in which a master alleges the Houses did not really differ about the matter in question, but rather were in complete agreement, very often on the Hillelite side. The real difference concerned a much finer point of law. In the Ushan stratum this mode of interpretation of Houses' pericopae becomes commonplace, and, as we shall see, in the circle of Judah the Patriarch (170–210 A.D.) it predominates to the near exclusion of all other sorts of commentary.

This means that, in their study of the Houses' materials, the Ushans and the men around Judah the Patriarch were prepared both to revise what they had, and to investigate the legal principles underlying the antecedent materials, extending actual disputes to most ambiguous matters. This mode of study signifies that these investigators found the Houses' materials especially interesting as sources for legal theory, without reference to the actualities of the earliest disputes, if they had access to such information to begin with. It further implies that the historical Houses lay sufficiently in the background for legal theory, rather than practical politics, to become the focus of inquiry.

At the same time, the Ushans gave considerable effort to the working out and redaction of historical materials. Indeed, most historical stories about the Pharisees for which we have any attestation at all first occur at Usha. The Ushans, aware of the need to reconstruct out of the remnants of pre-140 rabbinic traditions a viable theological, legal, and political structure, sought to establish historical continuities between themselves and the earlier masters. They accomplished this in part by telling fables about the pre-70 masters, and by attempting to systematize and organize their history, not merely their legal traditions.

The Ushans included in the normative tradition as much as they could about ancients, back as far as Moses. The Mosaic origins of the Oral Torah, and the history of the Oral Torah from Moses to Usha itself, supplied the primary theme of Ushan historians. That signifies awareness of a break in continuity with the past, just as the Yavneans' apparent indifference to historical questions tends to suggest a sense that nothing much had changed. It is still another mark of the abyss separating pre- from post-Bar Kokhban times. The real break in the history of the Pharisaic-rabbinic movement probably comes, not at 70, with the destruction of the Temple, but at 140, with the devastation of southern Palestine and reconstitution of the rabbinic movement and the patriarchal government in Galilee.

THE HOUSES' DISPUTES

The disputes of the Houses were now a matter of a legal study, not of political importance. The House of Shammai's followers had completely passed from the scene. Advocates of their legal theory persisted, but posed no important challenge to the complete predominance of the Hillelites, established at Yavneh by Aqiba, who were in complete control. It was possible to record the following fantastic statement:

> Not withstanding that these [the House of Shammai] forbid what the others [the House of Hillel] permit, and these declare ineligible whom the others declare eligible [for marriage], yet the House of Shammai did not refrain from marrying women from the House of Hillel, nor the House of Hillel from marrying women from the House of Shammai.
> [Despite] all [the disputes about what is] clean and unclean, wherein these declare clean what the others declare unclean, neither refrained from preparing [food in ritual] cleanness with one another.[1]

So we are told the Houses intermarried, even though such marriages would have produced *mamzerim,* illegitimate children. In addition, they would lend one another cooking pots, despite disputes on purity laws. The picture is incredible. If the disputes came to so little that the Houses ignored the practical consequences of violating their own rulings, why should the disputes have been carried on at all? Why should the Houses have troubled to register their contrary views of law, if they did not intend to live by them? The saying is not meant to denigrate the disputes—that much is clear—but rather to deny their practical results in social life. Since the Shammaites take, or are given, the more stringent side in the great number of disputes, the assertion seems on the face of it to be directed toward them. But the specific case to which allusion is made has the Hillelites declaring Shammaite children to be *mamzerim* [illegitimate], and yet supposedly allowing their children to marry such *mamzerim*! In a community so conscious of genealogical purity as Palestinian Jewry, that is simply unbelievable.

One must ask, When would such an assertion have been made, by whom, and for what purpose? It is in the language of historical narrative, so we cannot suppose the intention was to settle the disputes by a legal compromise. Indeed, nothing is compromised at all. It was important to say such a thing at a time that someone was attempting to unify the Houses, within the rest of the Jewish community, for action in a common purpose. The Houses by now could not have been so vigorous, or their disputes so vital, as in the past. The statement looks like an epitaph on a dying age:

1 M. Yev. 1:4.

Whatever the disputes may have been, the parties ignored their practical consequences and really loved one another.

Those Yavneans who held that following Shammaite rulings would be punishable by Heaven would have been surprised by this allegation. Therefore, it needs to be placed at a time in which the Houses' disputes no longer divided the Pharisaic-rabbinical movement, but were still vividly remembered as remnants of an older age. That time was most likely toward the end of Yavneh, on the eve of the Bar Kokhba War, when the historical Houses were a dim memory. Disputes continued to be shaped within the literary-redactional framework of the Houses, but they tended to serve as convenience names to which opposing viewpoints could be assigned, and by which the acceptable law (Hillel) could be ascertained without logical difficulty. It had become important to obliterate old disputes in the face of the current problem concerning the messianic hopes associated with Bar Kokhba. The Aqibans who backed Bar Kokhba may well have asserted that the old Houses really loved one another, and remaining followers of the Shammaites should be free to join as equals in the new cause. Since followers of the Hillelites would have regarded them as illegitimate, it was necessary to assert the contrary.

But the purity laws also had significant practical consequences. Now, for the first time in a century, the Houses were able to eat with one another and trust that the purity laws were kept—or did not matter. The pericope would have entered the tradition and persisted long afterward, alongside contrary views of the practical consequences of the Houses' disputes. Having located an appropriate time, we may therefore suppose the assertion derives from an Aqiban authority. This theory is virtually certain, since Simeon b. Yohai, an Ushan, refers to the saying, so it had reached final form by Ushan times.

DISPUTES ARISE BECAUSE
OF POOR STUDENTS

If the disputes of the Houses amounted to so little, why did they arise at all? Were not the old masters, founders of the Houses, in disagreement? In the following saying, an effort is made to account for the ancient disputes and to prevent the development of new ones:

> When the disciples of Shammai and Hillel multiplied, who had not adequately served [as disciples, and fully learned the masters' Torah], disputes multiplied in Israel, and they become two Torahs....[2]

This clause is intruded into a long logion of R. Yosi [b. Halafta], an important Ushan master, on the origin of disputes in the Oral Tradition.

---

2 Tos. Hag. 2:9.

The logion states that at first there was no dispute in Israel. The high court of 71 was in its chambers, and each town had its court of 23, from which appeals would come to Jerusalem. The legal system was based upon knowledge of traditions; but there were no *conflicting* traditions. If a court had knowledge, it said so; if not, it referred the matter to the higher court. The formula is, "If they heard, they said to them. . . ."

In the end, if necessary, the highest court would take a vote. The majority prevailed, and the law would then be proclaimed in Israel. Then comes "When the disciples. . . ." Afterward, the long account of the judiciary is resumed, including the qualifications for a judgeship and the methods of promotion to the higher courts.

The pericope before us is an independent logion, picked up for the purposes of Yosi's account to explain and date the earliest Houses' disputes. The *terminus ante quem* must be *ca.* 150 A.D. Before that time an unfavorable account of the disputes of the Houses circulated, but we do not know who held it.

THE END OF
THE GRAPECLUSTERS

The Ushan rabbis had a profound (and correct) sense that they had witnessed a turning in the history of Israel. They had survived a bitter war, fought under the leadership of a military messiah. On his coins, Bar Kokhba had made extensive use of the grapecluster, a symbol that occurs only once in Jewish art before his time. It is clear that for Bar Kokhba it was not merely an ornament, but an evocative symbol. The Ushans now took over the same symbol and applied it to themselves:

> When Yosi b. Yoezer of Seredah and Yosi b. Yohanan of Jerusalem died, the grapeclusters ceased, as it is written, *There is not cluster to eat, my soul desireth the first-ripe fig* (Mic. 7:1).[3]

A further reference to the grapecluster is Is. 65:8–9:

> Thus says the Lord, "As the wine is found in the grapecluster, and they say, 'Do not destroy it, for there is a blessing in it,' so will I do for my servants' sake, and not destroy them all. I will bring forth descendants from Jacob, and from Judah the inheritors of my mountains; my chosen shall inherit it, and my servants shall dwell there."

For the rabbinical exegetes, the grapecluster therefore symbolizes the true single and unified Torah, oral and written, revealed to Moses and handed down from him to the Pharisees. That "grapecluster" was lost or hidden

[3] M. Sot. 9:9.

from this time until after Aqiba, from which point controversies marred the formerly united and irreproachable tradition.

We do not know who originally said that the first pairs (M. Hag. 2:2, p. 104) were also the last grapeclusters, and drew from this the inference that the change after Yosi and Yosi was not for the better. We certainly cannot imagine that either Yosi "one day taught his disciples, 'My sons, Yosi and I are the last of the grapeclusters,'" so one must ask, Who so stated and why? Since the Yosi's stood at the head of the M. Hag. list, and since this list cannot come after *ca.* 140 A.D., it looks as if the responsible authority would appear, at the latest, in Ushan times. Now we see a revision:

> It is impossible to set a reproach against any of the grapeclusters that arose for Israel from when Moses died until Yosi b. Yoezer of Seredah and Yosi b. Yohanan of Jerusalem arose. After Yosi b. Yoezer of Seredah and Yosi b. Yohanan of Jerusalem died, and until R. Judah b. Baba arose, it *is* possible to set a reproach against them.[4]

This pericope obviously cannot date from before the middle of the second century A.D., for Judah b. Baba died in the war.

Reproach means division or controversy; the apparent meaning therefore is that until the last of the grapeclusters, the masters were unanimous on all things, but afterward controversy began to multiply in the Torah. The viewpoint is consistent with M. Hag. 2:2. The laying on of hands controversy began with the last of the grapeclusters, and M. Hag. certainly gave rise to this saying.

It is astonishing that a second century tradition, presumably deriving from the circle of the martyred Judah b. Baba, to whom the ordination, in Bar Kokhba's time, of all the surviving students of Aqiba is credited, should have asserted that all the generations of sages from the grapeclusters to Aqiba were *reproachable*! Clearly, important legal issues divided Yavneans and the later Aqibans. No one could have imagined that the ancients were distinguished from the moderns by the absence of controversy among the current or preceding generations. But if some reproach other than mere legal controversy was in mind, it is equally puzzling. We have here what seems to be a rejection of the entire Pharisaic tradition from Yosi and Yosi to, and including, Aqiba.

The saying serves as an interpretation of the meaning of *grapecluster:* What ended? Irreproachability, perfection, absence of division, lack of schism. Immediately following is the assertion that nearly all of Judah b. Baba's deeds were for the sake of heaven, except for a minor one (he violated the law against raising small cattle in Palestine). The inference is

---

4 Tos. B.Q. 8:13.

that from the two Yosi's until Judah b. Baba, not all the deeds of the masters were for the sake of heaven—a strange allegation.

The introduction of the two Yosi's served as a convenient dividing point. Since the grapeclusters are at issue, and since the purpose of the editor of the pericope is to assert that Judah b. Baba had renewed the blessing of the grapeclusters, it was natural to refer to the characterization, known from materials later placed into the Mishnah, of the two men as the end of the old line of tradition and start of the controversies. But if the list of Pharisaic masters at Ushan times *began* with the Yosi's, then it is difficult to understand the reference to them as the end of something old. Rather, they should be said to be the *first* of the grapeclusters, a list of worthies *ending* with Judah b. Baba. In that case, Aqiba and all the other ancients would not be listed among those *not* regarded as grapeclusters, but would be considered models for the coming generation, a sentiment surely appropriate in Judah b. Baba's circle. The grapeclusters then should end with Judah b. Baba—and this Judah the Patriarch obviously could not abide, for he and his generation thereby would have been denigrated. So in preparing the Mishnah he dropped the Toseftan materials entirely, and ended the grapeclusters where they had formerly begun, with the Yosi's.

THE HEAVENLY ECHO

The disciples of Judah b. Baba, who were the masters of Usha, produced a further historical record, this time concerning the end of heavenly communications with Israel (italics indicate Aramaic).

> Simeon the Just heard, *"The decree is annulled which the enemy intended to bring on the Temple,* and Qesgeleges has been killed, and his decrees have been annulled," and he heard these things in the Aramaic language.[5]

The saying comes at the end of a long list of heavenly messages delivered through an echo. In Simeon's instance it is merely stated that "he heard," since earlier in the chapter a number of instances occur in which sages heard heavenly echoes; in a reference to the conclusion of prophecy with Haggai, Zechariah, and Malachi, it is said, "But even so, they would cause them to hear through the echo." An echo heard in Yavneh announced that Hillel was worthy of receiving the holy spirit. In addition, an echo announced at Yavneh that Samuel the Small was worthy of receiving the holy spirit, as follows:

> A. The story is told that the sages entered the house of Guryo in Jericho and heard an echo saying, "There is here a man who is worthy

[5] Tos. Sot. 13:7.

of the holy spirit, but his generation is not sufficiently righteous," and they set their eyes on Hillel the Elder.

B. And when he died, they said concerning him, "Oh the modest man, the pious man, disciple of Ezra."

C. Another time they were sitting in Yavneh and heard an echo saying, "There is here a man who is worthy of the Holy Spirit, but his generation is not sufficiently righteous," and they set their eyes on Samuel the Small.

D. And when he died, they said about him, "Oh the modest [man], the pious [man], disciple of Hillel. . . ."[6]

The Hillel pericope (A) follows the form of the Samuel version (C), and corresponds to it in every detail. Hillel is disciple of Ezra, Samuel of Hillel. We may take for granted that the pericope emanates from heirs of the circle of Samuel the Small, a Yavnean master, and that its intent is to stress that the true disciple of Hillel is not Gamaliel, his descendant, but the pious, modest sage.

The further object is to explain why Hillel and Samuel "his disciple" did not receive the holy spirit: the generation prevented it, but otherwise they both would have received it. We do not know who asserted otherwise, saying that it was a mark of their *own* unworthiness that they did not receive the holy spirit. I cannot imagine it was the patriarchal circle. Probably the Shammaites, confronted by the Hillelite claim that an echo had confirmed their predominance, asserted no one had supernatural confirmation for his laws, not even Hillel. The opposition would have countered that the echo had indeed praised Hillel and explained his failure to prophesy. In the present pericope we have no echo of such a contrary story, and I doubt that such a story was told in a form we can now recover. But the stories of Hillel's rise to patriarch do stress that *all* Israel had access to the holy spirit, so we may suppose that such a story or saying existed, but was subsequently dropped. However, the story may have been told concerning Samuel the Small, and Samuel's defenders may have asserted he was no different from the great Hillel, who also would have received the holy spirit had his generation, like Samuel's, been worthy of it. So the polemic may have served a much later circle of masters, who would have invented the whole pericope.

The Samuel pericope proceeds to relate his dying words in Aramaic: Simeon and Ishmael would be slain with the sword, the companions would be killed, and the rest of the people would be despoiled. The reference now is to the Bar Kokhba War, and hence the whole pericope dates from after that time. The larger framework is a compilation of heavenly message stories, coming in its final form at Usha after the Bar Kokhba War. The introductory materials relate to the alleged cessation of the holy spirit from

6 Tos. Sot. 13:3.

Israel. Even though the holy spirit has ended, the echo continues to connect Israel to Heaven. Then comes Hillel, followed by Samuel the Small, Yohanan the High Priest, and Simeon the Righteous. Intervening is a reference to Judah b. Baba:

> Also concerning Judah b. Baba they sought to say, "Disciple of Samuel," but the hour was confused [the times prevented it].

The whole pericope in final form therefore comes from the Judah b. Baba circle, but antecedent materials were used.

The Hillel materials are in two parts. First (A) comes the story of the sages, then (B) the lament at Hillel's death. The latter has nothing to do with the framework, but was important to the Judah b. Baba tradents, for without a reference to the death scene, their statement about Judah b. Baba would have been irrelevant. Two Hillel stories have thus been joined, one containing the context about heavenly echoes, the other tacked on by the Judah tradents for redactional considerations. We need not doubt that parts A and B circulated separately and were drawn together at Usha, and therefore the *terminus ante quem* of the Hillel stories must be *ca.* 150 A.D.

Having isolated the whole to *ca.* 100–150 A.D., we may ask, Who was eager to suppress the authority of "the holy spirit" at Yavneh? It is the same circle that held it was not the holy spirit but the authority of the sages that would decide the law. This was certainly the House of Shammai, which denied that heavenly echoes gave law.

If we join together the two themes—Hillel would have received the holy spirit if anyone did, and the holy spirit is simply unavailable, and therefore law will be decided by rabbis—the obvious choice for probable origin is the Hillelite group within the patriarchal circle. They were eager to uphold the reputation of Hillel, who by 150 was alleged to be the ancestor of Gamaliel, and anxious to reaffirm the authority of the patriarch even against those who claimed to receive heavenly revelations.

Thus parts A and B of the pericope must (separately) derive from a circle around Samuel the Small. The redactional framework, which occurs later and derives from the period after the Bar Kokhba War, must be provided by the Judah b. Baba circle, which is responsible for joining B to A, D to C. We note that the tendency of some Hillel materials is not only to defend Hillel's reputation, but to deny that anyone could draw upon heavenly revelation in formation of the law. This Shammaite tendency is most reasonably attributed to the patriarchal group. Gamaliel II, not Simeon b. Gamaliel II, was responsible, for the materials were probably in their present form, though separate, before Judah b. Baba's circle joined them together for *its* purpose.

HISTORY OF
THE PATRIARCHS

The list of patriarchs in M. Hag. 2:2 (above, p. 104) attracted the interest of the Ushan historians Meir and Judah. They tried to figure out who had been *Nasi,* or patriarch, in pre-Hillelite times. No one doubted that Hillel had headed the party later on.

> They differed only on the laying of hands.
> "They are five pairs. The three of the first pairs who said not to lay on hands, and the two of the last pairs who said to lay on hands, were *Nasis*. The second ones [mentioned] were heads of the court," the words of R. Meir.
> R. Judah said, "Simeon b. Shetah [was] *Nasi,* Judah b. Tabbai [was] head of the court."
> R. Yosi said, "At first there was no dispute in Israel. . . ."[7]

The motive for attributing to Simeon the position of *Nasi* is unclear to me. I cannot understand what ulterior motive either party to the argument could have had in espousing one position rather than the other. But this makes matters all the more complex, for we have no grounds for conjecture about what either master had in hand as a tradition from olden times.

HISTORY OF THE JERUSALEM TEMPLE
AND ITS CULT

Meir also commented on traditions concerning the conduct of the Jerusalem cult. In the following he gives a "historical" account of who had performed a particularly rare rite:

> A. Who prepared them [the earlier red heifer offerings]?
> "Moses prepared the first, Ezra prepared the second, and five [were prepared] after Ezra," the words of R. Meir.
> But the sages say, "Seven since Ezra."
> B. And who prepared them? Simeon the Just and Yohanan the High Priest prepared two each, and Eliehoenai b. Haqqof and Hanamel the Egyptian and Ishmael b. Phiabi prepared one each.[8]

The *terminus ante quem,* made clear by the reference to Meir, is the middle of the second century. Meir and the sages differ on the question of whether Simeon the Just and Yohanan the High Priest made one or two such offerings. Judah the Patriarch follows the sages, with two attributed

[7] Tos. Hag. 2:8.
[8] M. Par. 3:5.

to each, and one to the three others. Actually, the Tannaim could have had no very firm traditions on the subject.

The pericope is a composite, interrupted by "the words of. . . ." Were it a unitary account, it would have read, "Who had prepared them? Moses the first, Ezra the second, and five/seven after Ezra," plus names. The second (B) And who prepared them?" supplies the continuity broken by the report of the disagreement.

The first "Who prepared them?" follows a reference to the possibility that the high priest could not find remnants of the sacrifices of his predecessors: "If he did not find [remnants of the ashes of] the seven, they might make use of six, five, four, three, two, one." Then comes, "And who prepared them?" It is unlikely that a pericope circulated apart from that question, e.g., in the following language: "Moses made the first, Ezra, the second. . . ." Such a pericope, lacking an explanatory phrase to make clear that the discussion involved the history of the red heifer sacrifice, would have been meaningless. The form before us, therefore, is in the language supplied by the generation responsible for the text, namely, that of Meir or the one immediately following. We do not know how Meir or his opposition knew how many heifers were prepared and who prepared them, since we have no trace of the original tradition. We have merely a reference to the *content* of such a pericope (if any actually existed).

TEMPLE OF ONIAS

Meir and Judah also discussed the founding of the Israelite Temple of Onias, in Egypt, in the days of Simeon the Just. Each authority told his own story without reference to that of the other. Here is the version of Meir:

> A. In the year in which Simeon the Just died, he said to them that he would die.
> They said to him, "How do you know?"
> He replied, "Every Day of Atonement an old man, dressed in white and wrapped in white, met me. He entered with me [into the Holy of Holies] and left with me. But this year an old man, dressed in black and wrapped in black, met me. He entered with me but did not leave with me."
> After the Festival [of Tabernacles] he was ill for seven days and then died.
> And his brethren the priests forbore [to pronounce] the Name in [the priestly] benediction.
> B. In the hour of his departure [from this life], he said to them, "My son Onias shall assume the office [of High Priest] after me."
> His brother Shimei, who was two years and a half older, was jealous

of him and said to him, "Come and I will teach you the order of the Temple service."

He thereupon put on him a gown, girded him with a girdle, placed him near the altar, and said to his brethren, the priests, "See what this man promised his beloved and has now fulfilled: 'On the day in which I assume the office of High Priest, I will put on your gown and gird myself with your girdle.' "

At this his brethren the priests sought to kill him.

He fled from them, but they pursued him. He then went to Alexandria in Egypt, built an altar there, and offered thereon sacrifices in honor of idols.

When the sages heard of this they said, "If this is what happened [through the jealousy] of one who had once assumed the honor [and had been ousted from it]...!"

This is the view of the events according to R. Meir.

C. R. Judah said to him, "That was not what happened, but the fact was that Onias did not accept the office of High Priest because his brother Shimei was two years and a half older than he...."[9]

The context is an anonymous discussion of the status of the Temple of Onias. The responsible authorities are obviously Meir and Judah b. Ilai; indeed, we are explicitly informed that this version of events is Meir's. There follows a completely different version of Onias's history, told by Judah. But all parties seem to agree on the introductory story about Simeon the Just, which comes both separate from, and before, the materials on Onias. Meir and Judah may therefore supply, in addition, the *terminus ante quem* for part A, the middle of the second century A.D.

The Ushan Stratum

In general, the pattern discerned in Yavnean attestations persists. Purity and tithing laws remained the focus of interest, but with one important change. Ushans clearly were involved in the development of a history of pre-70 Pharisaism. Nearly all historical pericopae for which we could find attestations derive from Ushans, particularly Judah b. Baba, Meir, and Judah. Important elements of the rabbinic history of Pharisaism were created in Ushan times.

Otherwise, the earlier proportions are not greatly revised. There is no important increase in Temple, Jerusalem, pilgrimage, and priestly laws. Agricultural tithes and related matters and uncleanness rules continue to constitute the largest part of Ushan attestations. The divisions of law concerning which few rules were attested at Yavneh remain the same at Usha;

[9] b. Men. 10b.

there is no tendency to shape, in the names of the Houses, laws on civil, criminal, and family affairs.

The Houses at Usha therefore do not serve as a mere literary convenience for the formation of laws in easily remembered patterns. The tradents of Yavneh and Usha evidently did not invent pericopae dealing with laws on which they had no traditions from the Houses; they merely reworked Houses' materials, rather than fabricate new laws in the established Houses' pattern. This seems persuasive evidence of the thematic authenticity of rabbinical traditions about the pre-70 Pharisees. It may now be suggested that the pre-70 Houses handed on traditions concerning three areas of law: agricultural tithes, offerings, and taboos; Sabbath and festival law; and cleanness rules. It is also entirely possible that a few family laws were formulated, especially with relationship to Levirate marriage. Whether the *details* of the laws attributed to the Houses actually derive from the pre-70 masters is a more difficult question. But a considerable measure of the *thematic* substance of the pre-70 traditions, particularly those deriving from the Houses, lies before us.

While the Ushans continued to develop Houses' legal disputes, they introduced into the normative tradition important historical themes. The heavenly messages of Simeon the Just and others first occur in Ushan pericopae. The growth of Houses' disputes was attributed to the failure of the disciples. The same theme recurs in the grapecluster materials, certainly an Ushan creation. Since Bar Kokhba had made extensive use of the grapecluster symbol on his coins, and was in fact the first to do so (the symbol occurs only once, on a coin of Archelaus, before his time), it stands to reason that the characterization of Pharisaic masters as grapeclusters, bearers of the abiding blessing, was neither accidental nor irrelevant to the Ushan situation. The claim is that sages, not messiahs, are the source of divine blessing. This theme is then tied into the issue of disputes of the former generations. These are traced to the end of the grapeclusters, with the concomitant warning that new disputes will call into disrepute the work of the Ushans as well, so people had better learn their lessons well and avoid controversy. To this theme is added still another: Hillel, Samuel the Small, and Judah b. Baba would all have received the holy spirit, but the generation was unworthy. At Usha this had obvious implications: those who now claimed to receive the holy spirit were charlatans, since no one, not even the great Hillel, had received it. Furthermore, the unworthiness of the generation prevented it then, and if the current generation did not conform to the Torah, it too could not hope to receive divine communications.

The grapecluster pericope is only one effort to channel the history of ancient times into its relative periods. Another is represented by the Meir-Judah discussion on the Pharisaic chain. Just as the supernatural history was divided into periods, the history of the Pharisaic party itself was also worked out in terms of the names of the presiding authorities in each of its stages. The dispute about the relative places of Judah b. Tabbai and Simeon b. Shetah is closely related to this matter. Meir and Judah seem primarily responsible for provision of a history of Pharisaism, Judah b. Baba for the account of the supernatural history. Preparation of the heifer ceremony is also discussed at Usha. So the four central issues of sacred history—the history of the supernatural, the history of the messianic blessing, the history of the Pharisaic party and of the Oral Torah, and the history of the cult—all were worked out at Usha.

What is the message the Ushan historians give us concerning pre-70 Pharisaism? Let us compose a picture based upon the several stories attested in their names, and see whether we may derive from that composite both the historical account and the message of the Ushan rabbis for their own generation. If we could tell the story as a whole, it would look something like this:

> From the time of Moses onward, the divine blessing inhered in the grapeclusters. These were men who bore the special grace of God. They lasted to the time of the Yosi's. Afterwards, dissensions split the Oral Torah into many parts, and the blessing was lost. But it was restored by Judah b. Baba, who had ordained the surviving students of Aqiba. Those very students now dominate at Usha. So the grapecluster blessing of ancient times has been restored.
>
> If the disciples of Usha's rabbis learn their lessons and satisfactorily teach them, the blessing will persist. And the grapecluster, everyone knows, is the sign of the messiah. So on the unity of the rabbinic group at Usha depends the hope of Israel for the coming of the Messiah—on that unity and *not* on the success of messianic generals.
>
> In the meanwhile, none should suppose that the chain that extends from Usha back to Sinai has been broken. On the contrary, the list of the masters from Sinai onward demonstrates the perfect continuity of the tradition. What began at Sinai endures to this very day.
>
> Heavenly messages came to worthy men in the past—Simeon the Just was even able to tell what was happening at distant places. Hillel told our forefathers that the holy spirit is upon Israel. So those who today want to rely upon the echo and upon the holy spirit may take comfort. However, even Hillel himself did not receive the holy spirit, and the reason was the unworthiness of his contemporaries. Just as the decline of generations and the rise of disputes withdrew the blessing of the grapecluster, and with it the messianic hope, from Israel, so the unworthiness of the generation has deprived Israel of its spiritual gift of receiving revelation.

The stress on sin as the cause for thwarting both the messianic hope and the capacity to receive the marks of divine grace and concern corresponds to the message of the Yohanan b. Zakkai circle after the destruction of the Temple: "Take comfort, for he who punished you for your sins can be relied upon to recognize your penitence and to respond to and reward your regeneration." Here, too, the comfort is that Israel's own sin, and *not* the might of a foreign conqueror, accounts for Israel's present condition.

These primary spiritual concerns for the messiah and for receiving direct divine communications suggest that people claimed to have heavenly messages in Bar Kokhban times. They certainly point toward the messianic claim of Bar Kokhba himself. Aqiba's students could not affirm the master's view that Bar Kokhba had been the messiah, but they did allege that the messianic blessing remained intact, enduring within the rabbinical group itself. This accomplished two important purposes. First, it saved the remnant of the messianic hope from the debacle of Bar Kokhba. Second, it made certain that anyone subject to the influence of the rabbis would reject the notion that someone who was not a rabbi might again enjoy the sponsorship of rabbis in asserting a messianic claim.

The Temple lay in ruins, and prospects rebuilding it were hardly encouraging. Anyone who proposed to build a Temple in some place safer than Jerusalem, as did Onias in Leontopolis, in Egypt, was considered disreputable, and could not hope to enjoy the support of Palestinians or the approval of the rabbis. As a matter of fact, Babylonian Jews did build a Temple at just this time, and evidently considered establishing a sacrificial cult in their own country. They were led by Hananiah, the nephew of the Joshua b. Hananiah, whom we met at Yavneh. So the story of the earlier Temple built in Egypt was strikingly pertinent to the time. The Ushans sent a delegation including important rabbis and priests and informed Hananiah that he had better desist: *From Zion the Torah will go forth, and the word of God from Jerusalem*—and not from Nehar Peqod, in Babylonia, where Hananiah was located.

These, I think, are some of the contemporary motives emerging from the Ushan pericopae on the history of Pharisaism. Of course we cannot claim that Ushan storytellers invented the stories in order to make these very points, because we have no such proof. It is clear, however, that they told such stories to convey a message peculiarly pertinent to their own situation.

What does this mean for the historical credibility of the Pharisaic "histories" of second century A.D. Usha? It seems unlikely that the Ushan rabbis had traditions about pre-70 Pharisaism which were unknown to the Yavnean rabbis. The silence of two generations of masters—from *ca.* 70 to *ca.* 125—on historical questions ought to be suggestive, if not probative, of the unreliability of the Ushans' stories. If we may credibly propose that the stories of Jesus's relationships to the Pharisees reveal the concerns of the early Christian community more accurately than they tell the facts of Jesus's own life and teachings, we must similarly conclude that the Ushans' histories of Pharisaism accurately portray the historical situation of the Ushan rabbis. At best, what the Ushans may have had from the corpus of pre-70 Pharisaic traditions—if they had anything at all—were the names of the pre-70 Masters, as well as the record, handed on from Yavneh, of the disputes of the Houses on a specified legal agenda. For the rest, it is unlikely that the Ushans' Pharisees are anything but the imaginative creation of the Ushan historians.

After Usha: The Circle of Judah the Patriarch (*ca.* 170–210 A.D.)

The next phase in the development of rabbinical traditions about the Pharisees was marked by refinement of the interpretation of the disputes between the Houses of Shammai and Hillel. The general tendency was to claim the Houses had not disputed the issues already defined by the antecedent generations—Yavnean and Ushan rabbis—but rather had debated much more subtle and remote questions. We find little tendency to develop new historical stories or to discuss as live issues the definition of fundamental laws. With the Houses long forgotten except by lawyers, their rivalries and internecine struggles aroused no partisan concern. Hillel had triumphed everywhere.

So the circle of Judah the Patriarch, assembled at Beth Shearim and working on the redaction of the oral traditions into the Mishnah, used the names of the Houses—as had formerly not been the case—for convenience to assign the two most extreme possible opinions on any given legal issue. This made memorizing of decisions easy. Since the law normally followed the House of Hillel, one needed to remember only the definition of the issue, and knowing the possible decisions—liable, free of liability, unclean, clean, and so on—would tell one exactly how to decide a given case. That is why the generation of Judah the Patriarch spent its best efforts on definition of the matters under debate, reformulating the superscriptions that had contained them and reworking the issues in an ever more subtle way.

We shall consider two examples of the tendency of Judah's circle, both produced by his contemporary, Simeon b. Eleazar.

CIRCUMCISION

Evidently the Houses' traditions consisted merely of rulings unaccompanied by a clear definition of what case was at issue. The later masters had to work out the case to which the legal rulings pertained. The best example derives from the circle of Judah the Patriarch. The Houses' opinion consisted of "one does [or, does *not*] have to draw from him a drop of blood as a sign of the covenant." The "covenant" referred to is that of circumcision, and the later masters had to figure out what legal issue led to this decision:

> A. [The rite of circumcision of a] baby born circumcized does not override the Sabbath, for—
>
> The House of Shammai say, "One needs to draw from him [a drop of] blood [as a sign of] the covenant."
>
> And the House of Hillel say, "One does not need [to do so]."
>
> B. R. Simeon b. Eleazar said, "The House of Shammai and the House of Hillel did not dispute concerning one born circumcized. One does need to draw from him a drop of blood of the covenant, because it is a hidden foreskin.
>
> "Concerning what did they dispute? Concerning a proselyte who converted when already circumcized, for—
>
> "The House of Shammai say, 'One needs to draw from him a drop of blood of the covenant.'
>
> "And the House of Hillel say, 'One does not need [to do so].' "[10]

The question is whether various exceptional circumstances of the rite of circumcision override the Sabbath. The basic rule is given anonymously. If the child has a foreskin, the circumcision overrides the Sabbath, but otherwise it does not. The pericope of the Houses is already redacted and attached to the foregoing general rule with *for*. Without the rule, the pericope is complete and follows the normal form, except that it lacks a statement of the problem, so we do not know the antecedent of the House of Shammai's *him*, that is, the legal issue addressed by the Houses. Simeon supplies an alternative theory on that question.

The actual ruling does not explicitly pertain to the Sabbath at all, but to whether or not one draws a drop of blood. Only if we already know that the law follows the House of Hillel, and that the consequence of the Hillelite ruling about *not* drawing blood is that one *also* need not set aside Sabbath regulations on account of such a rite, do we comprehend the redactor's use of the Houses' sayings. Part A is therefore somewhat more complex than it appears on the surface. Its introductory statement could not have been shaped in its present form during the period when the law did not automatically follow the Hillelite House, that is, before 70 (when it probably followed the Shammaites) and presumably for some time thereafter. The presupposition of the redactor suggests a relatively late redaction for part A.

But the original language of the Houses has probably not been changed by the redactor of A or by Simeon. If either had made any changes, he would have had the Houses rule on the issue claimed to be under discussion—Sabbath or convert—rather than on drawing blood, which is

[10] Sifra Tazria 1:5.

peripheral to either issue. So Simeon has preserved the original formulation in his prologue, rejecting the text that must have been before him and substituting a new superscription. In what form would the sayings of the Houses have existed until his time? It had to have been as follows:

> *As to circumcizing one born circumcized:*
> The House of Shammai say, Need to draw blood.
> The House of Hillel say, No need to draw blood.

Then the redactor of A would have augmented the introductory clause:

> As to circumcizing one who was born circumcized, *it does not override the Sabbath.*

In other words, all that was added is *it does not override....* Nothing else need have been altered; adding the clause provided all necessary redactional material. I am impressed with the faithful reproduction of the materials coming down from the Houses; Simeon, in his way, has been just as faithful.

DIVORCE

A further problem was to define the circumstances to which fully articulated disputes between the Houses actually pertained. Although the pericope was by now complete, the lawyers' ingenuity produced new problems for discussion. The Houses had originally discussed the case of a man who divorced his wife and then spent a night with her in the same inn: Does she require a new writ of divorce, or is the original one still valid? The problem is that the couple may have engaged in sexual intercourse, which would establish a new marital connection between them. Then again, they may not have done so. Simeon ben Eleazar here refines the problem by redefining the situation to which the Houses' rulings apply. The Houses did *not* dispute what everyone formerly had supposed. Their argument concerned a situation in which it is quite certain that the couple actually had intercourse. But then one has to ask, Who is to bring evidence in the case? So the Babylonian Talmudic discussion later stipulated that there were witnesses to the act (!):

> If a man divorced his wife and she then lodged with him in an inn—
> The House of Shammai say, "She does not need from him a second bill of divorce."
> And the House of Hillel say, "She needs from him a second bill of divorce."[11]

---

[11] M. Git. 8:9.

M. Git. 8:9 is formally standard; the sayings of the Houses pertain to, and complete, the superscription, and are matched, the difference being the use of the negative in the Shammaite opinion. Simeon redefines matters:

> R. Simeon b. Eleazar said, "The House of Shammai and the House of Hillel did not differ concerning him who divorces his wife, and [then] she spends the night with him in an inn, that she does *not* require from him a second bill of divorce.
> "Concerning what did they disagree?
> "Concerning a situation in which he actually had intercourse [with her]."[12]

According to Simeon b. Eleazar, the dispute does not concern a married couple, for all agree no further bill of divorce is necessary if there is no intercourse. The issue now is, What is necessitated by actual intercourse? The opinions of the Houses are not given. We may assume that the House of Shammai would say no new bill of divorce is needed, and the House of Hillel would require a new one.

In this instance the Shammaite position is made more extreme. Obviously the Hillelites will require a new bill of divorce, just as before. But the Shammaites now treat the act of intercourse as having no legal consequence. The old writ remains valid, even though the couple has engaged in marital relations; the act of intercourse, having no legal implications, is treated as mere prostitution.

The Babylonian Talmud (b. Git. 81a) says that witnesses testify the couple actually had intercourse, or the witnesses saw them alone, thus solving the problem of who is to testify against the validity of the writ of divorce.

The work of the circle of Judah the Patriarch involved more than simply reworking earlier materials. Judah and his circle are responsible for the Mishnah and Tosefta, and therefore for all the traditions concerning the Houses contained in those documents—nearly 80 per cent of the whole corpus of rabbinical traditions about the Pharisees. What was strikingly emphasized in this third stage in the development of the traditions was the effort to rework the superscriptions, the clauses defining the case at hand. In this process, the historical Houses were less of a consideration than the theoretical study of the law.

---

[12] Tos. Git. 8:8.

8

The Pharisees
in History

The historical Pharisees of the period before 70 A.D. have eluded us. Our inquiry time and again brings us to problems of the history of ancient Judaism *after* the destruction of Jerusalem.

Josephus's narrative requires interpretation in the light of his own life in Roman politics after 70.

The Gospels' traditions about the Pharisees show little interest in the Pharisees, except as a convenient basis for polemic or narrative. Information about the Pharisees which the Gospel narrators had to have known for their own purposes consisted of two significant facts: Pharisaic stress on tithing, and Pharisaic commitment to keeping the purity laws outside of the Temple. But the Gospels' superficial knowledge of the details of what the Pharisees actually did hardly suggests much interest in the Pharisaic sect in its own terms.

The rabbinical traditions about the Pharisees prove most complex of all. The legal materials, attested shortly after 70 A.D., have all been reworked in the forms used at Yavneh. The rabbinical history of Pharisaism turns out to be strikingly relevant to the spiritual crisis in the aftermath of the Bar Kokhba War.

So the history of post-70 movements and individuals in Rome, Christianity, and rabbinical Judaism is formative for all three sources of information about pre-70 Pharisaism. That does not mean we know nothing about the Pharisees before the destruction of the Temple, but what we do know in detail is much less than what the sources claim to tell us. It also means that the sources that speak about pre-70 Pharisaic Judaism supply far more accurate information than has been recognized about their own circles.

After 70 A.D., as we have seen, Pharisaism continued in Yavneh, where surviving masters reassembled under the leadership of Yohanan ben Zakkai, and, after his death (*ca.* 80 A.D.), of Gamaliel II. Yohanan had opposed the war against Rome, and Gamaliel would oppose the new rebellion led by Bar Kokhba. Both leaders, therefore, continued the earlier policies of Pharisaism, which had concentrated upon the inner affairs of the Jewish people. The Pharisees had been prepared to allow Rome to manage the relationships between the Jews and other peoples and to include Palestine in the imperial system which maintained world peace.

Yohanan ben Zakkai's view is contained in the following story, which tells how he escaped from besieged Jerusalem:

> Now, when Vespasian came to destroy Jerusalem he said to the inhabitants, "Fools, why do you seek to destroy this city and why do you seek to burn the Temple? For what do I ask of you but that you send me one bow or one arrow, and I shall go off from you?"
>
> They said to him, "Even as we went forth against the first two who were here before thee and slew them, so shall we go forth against thee and slay thee."
>
> When Rabban Yohanan ben Zakkai heard this, he sent for the men of Jerusalem and said to them, "My children, why do you destroy this city and why do you seek to burn the Temple? For what is it that he asks of you? Verily he asks naught of you save one bow or one arrow, and he will go off from you."
>
> They said to him: "Even as we went forth against the two before him and slew them, so shall we go forth against him and slay him."
>
> Vespasian had men stationed inside the walls of Jerusalem. Every word which they overheard they would write down, attach [the message] to an arrow, and shoot it over the wall, saying that Rabban Yohanan ben Zakkai was one of the Emperor's friends.
>
> Now, after Rabban Yohanan ben Zakkai had spoken to them one day, two and three days, and they still would not attend to him, he sent for his disciples, for Rabbi Eliezer and Rabbi Joshua.
>
> "My sons," he said to them, "arise and take me out of here. Make a coffin for me that I might lie in it."
>
> Rabbi Eliezer took hold of the head end of it, Rabbi Joshua took hold of the foot; and they began carrying him as the sun set, until they reached the gates of Jerusalem.
>
> "Who is this?" the gatekeepers demanded.
>
> "It's a dead man," they replied. "Do you not know that the dead may not be held overnight in Jerusalem?"

"If it's a dead man," the gatekeepers said to them, "take him out."

So they took him out and continued carrying him until they reached Vespasian. They opened the coffin and Rabban Yohanan stood up before him.

"Art thou Rabban Yohanan ben Zakkai?" Vespasian inquired. "Tell me, what may I give thee?"

"I ask naught of thee," Rabban Yohanan replied, "save Yavneh where I might go and teach my disciples and there establish a prayer [house] and perform all the commandments."

"Go," Vespasian said to him, " and whatever thou wishest to do, do."

Said Rabban Yohanan to him, "By thy leave, may I say something to thee?"

"Speak," Vespasian said to him.

Said Rabban Yohanan to him, "Lo, thou art about to be appointed king."

"How dost thou know this?" Vespasian asked.

Rabban Yohanan replied, "This has been handed down to us, that the Temple will not be surrendered to a commoner, but to a king; as it is said, *And he shall cut down the thickets of the forest with iron, and Lebanon shall fall by a mighty one*" (Is. 10:34).

It was said: No more than a day, or two or three days, passed before messengers reached him from his city [announcing] that the emperor was dead and that he had been elected to succeed as king.

A catapult was brought to him, drawn up against the wall of Jerusalem. Boards of cedar were brought to him which he set into the catapult, and with these he struck against the wall until he made a breach in it. A swine's head was brought and set into the catapult, and this he hurled toward the (sacrificial) limbs which were on the altar.

It was then that Jerusalem was captured.

Meanwhile Rabban Yahanan ben Zakkai sat and waited trembling, the way Eli had sat and waited; as it said, *Lo, Eli sat upon his seat by the wayside watching; for his heart trembled for the ark of God* (I Sam. 4:13).

When Rabban Yohanan ben Zakkai heard that Jerusalem was destroyed and the Temple was up in flames, he tore his clothing, and his disciples tore their clothing, and they wept, crying aloud and mourning.[1]

Yohanan's point is that the Romans ask nothing but a bow and an arrow— that is, signs of submission. But this is precisely what the rebels would not give, for control of Jerusalem meant more to them than the right to offer

---

[1] *The Fathers According to Rabbi Nathan,* trans. Judah Goldin (New Haven: Yale University Press, 1955), pp. 35–37.

sacrifices on the Temple altar. It meant that Palestine was to be the *Land of Israel,* entirely under the sovereign domination of the Jews themselves, and, among the Jews, of the Zealots.

To Yohanan, preserving the Temple was not an end in itself. As we saw (p. 98), he taught there was another means of reconciliation between God and Israel, so the Temple and its cult were not decisive. But the Temple now represented what truly mattered—the service of God through keeping the Torah, which included commandments concerning Temple sacrifice. The issue between Yohanan and the rebels was, therefore, What really counted in the life of the Jewish people? The answer for Yohanan was Torah, piety (Torah as taught by the Pharisees and, later, by the rabbis, their continuators). For the Zealots and messianists of the day, the answer was power, politics, the right to live under one's own rulers and to stand apart from, and independent of, other nations.

Why did Yohanan ben Zakkai come to such an interpretation of the meaning of the life of Israel, the Jewish people? Because he was a Pharisee, and the Pharisaic party had long ago reached that same conclusion. It had begun, as we saw, as a political party, not much different from other political groups in Maccabean times. But toward the end of the Maccabean period the party faced the choice of remaining in politics and suffering annihilation, or giving up politics and surviving in a very different form. On the surface, the Pharisees' survival, the achievement of Hillel in response to the challenge of Herod, tells us that the choice was to abandon politics. But that is not the whole answer.

The Pharisees determined to concentrate on what they believed was really important in politics, which was fulfillment of all the laws of the Torah, even ritual purity and tithing, to achieve elevation of the life of all of the people, at home and in the streets, to what the Torah had commanded: *You shall be a kingdom of priests and a holy people.* Such a community would live as if it were always in the Temple sanctuary of Jerusalem. Therefore the complicated and inconvenient purity laws were extended to the life of every Jew in his own home. The Temple altar in Jerusalem would be replicated at the tables of all Israel. At first only a small minority of the Jewish people obeyed the law as taught by the Pharisaic party, so the group had to reconsider the importance of political life, through which the law might be effected everywhere. The party which had abandoned politics for piety now had to recover access to the instruments of power for the sake of piety. It was the way toward realization of what was not an essentially political aspiration.

After 70 A.D. the Romans gave the Pharisees their opportunity to reenter the political arena. Just as Pompey had been asked to rule the country so that the Jews could truly rule themselves, the Pharisees and the Romans now came to an agreement: The Pharisaic party would keep the country peaceful, and the Romans would leave internal matters in the hands of the party.

What was the Roman plan for Jewish Palestine?

The Romans knew that they had an ethnic revolt on their hands. Anxious not to meet an underground revolution throughout the Diaspora and intervention from Parthia, they were careful not to transform the war into a religious persecution. Pursuing a policy of divide and conquer, they tried to find allies among the enemy and to discern who could be won over and neutralized. Though they considered the war an ethnic struggle, they did not stop trying to win over all Jews they could reach.

It was clear that they succeeded. Large sections of the Jewish population remained at peace throughout the war. The rebellion in no sense enlisted the support of the entire Jewish population. In fact, it progressively lost whatever support it had at the outset.

Next, the consequences of the war did not include destruction of the economy or social foundations of Jewish settlement in the land. The Jewish populations in the mixed cities were molested, but mostly survived the war intact. The Roman policy after the war was not generally to enslave or deport noncombatant, loyal civilian populations, except from the regions in revolt.

Most strikingly, there *is* evidence of Roman reconstitution of limited self-government, if not under Yohanan, then surely under Gamaliel II. If the Romans intended to destroy Jewish settlement in the land, they had sufficient information about Yavneh to know that the activity of the sages there endangered such a policy. Although they had sufficient force to destroy that work, they did not do so because they approved it and hoped to use it for their own purposes.

What then was the Roman attitude toward the Jews? It was to pacify the country, and this was effected by military action. More important, the Romans wanted to conciliate Jewish opinion in the vast Diaspora during the war, and in Palestine itself afterwards. That they succeeded in substantially retaining the loyalty of the Jewish populations in the Diaspora is proven by the absence throughout the entire course of the war of significant military or political support for the revolutionaries by Diaspora communities or Babylonian Jewry. Indeed, the one instance of exilic support, by the Jewish converts in Adiabene, demonstrates that such support was possible and yet was never rendered in a meaningful way by the other exilic settlements. Josephus wrote his *Jewish War* as a part of the Roman propaganda effort, designed to placate the Diaspora, specifically the Mesopotamian settlements, and, as Morton Smith writes:

> ...to demonstrate that the rebels had brought their ruin upon themselves by their own wickedness, that the Romans were not hostile to

Judaism, but had acted in Palestine regretfully, as agents of divine vengeance, and that therefore submission to Roman rule was justified by religion as well as common sense.[2]

If this was the purpose of the Roman propaganda, what was their postwar policy in the Land of Israel itself? It was to reconstitute limited self-government among the Jewish population through loyal and nonseditious agents. Such a policy would have two favorable consequences.

First, it would further conciliate the Diaspora communities and demonstrate in action the theory of war guilt advanced by the Roman propaganda effort. Destruction of the Temple and enslavement of thousands of Jewish soldiers and civilians certainly weakened the bonds of loyalty holding the vast Diaspora communities to the Imperial government. By genuinely constructive and conciliatory actions after the war the Romans could manifest their true policy: not persecution, but tolerance and legal scrupulousness.

Second, survival of the Jewish settlements in the Land of Israel necessitated some form of government. One means which Rome had pursued for almost a century had been the use of native, pro-Roman authorities to continue the type of religious-legal jurisdiction which was so important to the Jews themselves. Jewish law was obviously going to remain operative among the Jewries of the land and the Empire. Since the Romans made no attempt to stamp out Jewish legal autonomy at this time, the best policy was probably to continue its operation through agencies loyal to the government. The situation of the Jews in the Land of Israel made such loyalty imperative.

Why did the Romans choose the Pharisaic party, which had been one among a number of contending sects before the destruction, to be the instrument of the reconstitution of Jewish autonomy? To be sure, the influence of the Pharisees before the war had supposedly been widespread. If, as Josephus maintains, they favored peace with Rome, however, their authority was insufficient to effect that crucial policy. And they were certainly unable to force the priests and Sadducees to conduct Temple affairs according to their doctrines.

Faced with the question of which Jews among those who would work with the government could command sufficient popular support to maintain the stability of the Jewish communities in the Land of Israel, the Roman government very likely was guided by three main considerations.

First, Josephus wrote his *Antiquities* to provide the answer.

Second, the other parties, as Josephus represents them, were ineligible for serious consideration. The Essenes were a philosophical curiosity. The Zealots were, as everyone knew, anti-Roman. The Sadducees were an aristocratic

2 Morton Smith, "Palestinian Judaism in the First Century," in *Israel: Its Role in Civilization*, ed. Moshe Davis (New York: Harper & Row, Publishers, 1956), pp. 74–75.

minority. Thus Josephus himself was probably instrumental in obtaining the recognition of Pharisaic hegemony.

Third, the Pharisees actively advanced their own candidacy as Roman supporters, and possibly after Yohanan's death negotiated for it. We discern significant evidence that Yohanan ben Zakkai's policies took hold among the refugee sages at Yavneh. Above any other in his generation, he was responsible for the ultimate success of Pharisaic Judaism, made possible by Roman encouragement and, in unequal measure, by the Pharisaic policy and program. If Rome did recognize the sages of Yavneh as a legally constituted and legitimate authority in the Jewish community in the Land of Israel, we may well regard accounts of Yohanan's escape from Jerusalem as a legendary but fundamentally accurate representation of that recognition.

A final question remains. Why did the Romans burn the Temple? Was it their intention to destroy the Jewish religion? M.P. Charlesworth points out that the only exceptions that Rome made in her general rule of toleration were when a religion appeared to be so closely intertwined with the history and customs of a nation that it fomented or promoted nationalist feeling and led to revolts. "After the Jewish rebellion of 66, the Romans destroyed the Temple at Jerusalem deliberately, to cripple the religion."[3] Evidence on the burning of the Temple is equivocal. The Romans through Josephus denied responsibility and attempted to represent it as either an accident of war or the act of the Jews themselves. If the Romans bear full responsibility, however, we must take account of that additional evidence of their policy. So far, I have maintained that Roman policy after 70 did not include absolute prohibition of the free practice of Judaism, and I think the evidence supports that contention. Assertions to the contrary ignore the events at Yavneh and Rome's willingness to deal with the authority of the rabbinical court, as well as her later support for the Palestinian patriarchate. If Rome intended to destroy Judaism, she changed her mind when faced with the realities of the Roman Diaspora as well as the Babylonian Jewish community.

Destroying the Temple and disclaiming responsibility at the same time constituted a shrewd policy. To the Roman mind, the inevitable effect of the destruction may have been the eventual dissolution of Judaism. Without a Temple such as was enjoyed by all other religions, without a cult and a ritual to serve as the focus for Jewish loyalty throughout the world, the Romans quite naturally expected the Judaism they knew to die out, and with it, in time, the Jewish people as well. Whatever their ulterior motives, however, the Romans made no substantial attempt at outlawing Judaism.

[3] M.P. Charlesworth, *The Roman Empire* (New York: Oxford University Press, 1968), p. 100.

Only one religion in antiquity was persistently outlawed and at times systematically persecuted by Rome, and it was not Judaism but Christianity. For the rest, sporadic and halfhearted persecutions were occasionally provoked by sedition or war.

This, I think, was the case with Judaism, both in the aftermath of August 70 as well as in consequence of the Bar Kokhba War. By 75, as again by 145, Jewish autonomous government was functioning once more. That fact is more decisive than the burning of the Temple. Whatever their hope, the Romans behaved in such a way that destruction of the Temple posed no formidable obstacle to the survival of Judaism. But the kind of Judaism that survived was different from the forms predominant before 70, and was shaped by men who shared a community of interest with Rome. If Rome wanted to extirpate the Judaism that had caused so much trouble, she enjoyed complete success. What survived became in time a force for peace, not subversion, and its central institutions consistently and, after the Bar Kokhba War, effectively worked to secure loyalty to Rome and tranquillity in Palestine.

So much for the Romans. What did the Pharisees, led by Yohanan ben Zakkai, have to say to the surviving Jews of Palestine? Yohanan had a detailed, practical program to offer for the reconstruction of the social and political life of the Land of Israel. It was intended, first, to provide the people with a source of genuine comfort by showing them how they might extricate themselves from the consequences of their sins. Second, he placed new emphasis upon those means of serving the Creator which had survived the devastated sanctuary.

Finally, he offered a comprehensive program for the religious life, capable of meeting any vicissitude in Israel's history. By concentrating on the immediate problems of the day, Yohanan showed how to transcend history itself—not through eschatological vision, but through concrete actions in the workaday world. His message of comfort was preserved in this story:

> *Because thou didst not serve the Lord thy God with joyfulness and gladness of heart, by reason of the abundance of all things, therefore thou shalt serve thine enemies whom the Lord will send against thee in hunger and thirst, in nakedness and in want of all things . . .* (Deut. 28:47).

> Once Rabban Yohanan ben Zakkai was going up to Emmaus in Judea, and he saw a girl who was picking barley-corn out of the excrement of a horse.

> Said Rabban Yohanan ben Zakkai to his disciples, "What is this girl?"

> They said to him, "She is a Jewish girl."

> "And to whom does the horse belong?"

"To an Arabian horseman," the disciples answered him.

Then said Rabban Yohanan ben Zakkai to his disciples, "All my life I have been reading the following verse, and I have not until now realized its full meaning: *If you will not know, 0 fairest among women, follow in the tracks of the flock, and pasture your kids beside the shepherds' tents* (Song of Songs 1:8).

"You were unwilling to be subject to God, behold now you are subjected to the most inferior of nations, the Arabs. You were unwilling to pay the head-tax to God, *A beqa a head* (Ex. 38:26). Now you are paying a head-tax of fifteen *sheqels* under a government of your enemies.

"You were unwilling to repair the roads and streets leading up to the Temple. Now you have to keep in repair the posts and stations on the road to the imperial cities. And thus it says, *Because thou didst not serve....* Because you did not serve the Lord your God with love, therefore you shall serve your enemy with hatred.

"Because you did not serve the Lord your God when you had plenty, therefore you shall serve your enemy in hunger and thirst.

"Because you did not serve the Lord your God when you were well clothed, therefore you shall serve your enemy in nakedness.

"Because you did not serve the Lord your God by reason of the abundance of all things, therefore shall you serve your enemy in want of all things...."

Yohanan thereupon explained, "*Happy* are you, 0 Israel! When you obey the will of God, then no nation or race can rule over you! But when you do not obey the will of God, you are handed over into the hands of every low-born people, and not only into the hands of the people, but even into the power of the cattle of that low-born people."[4]

This incident epitomizes Yohanan's viewpoint on the disaster. He never said, "Take comfort, because in a little while, suffering will cease." Yohanan called on the people to *achieve* a better fortune through their own efforts. Like Josephus, he taught that Israel can be happy if she submits to God and to the Romans, and follows the laws laid down by both. Yohanan and Josephus conceived of the fulfillment of Jewish law as interpreted by the Pharisees to be the good life in this world and assurance of a portion in the next. Unlike Josephus, Yohanan did not go to Rome but remained at home among the suffering folk.

And what was the will of God? It was doing deeds of loving kindness, as noted earlier. *I desire mercy, not sacrifice* (Hos. 6:6) meant to Yohanan,

[4] Mekhilta Bahodesh, Jacob Z. Lauterbach, ed. and trans., *Mekilta de Rabbi Ishmael* (Philadelphia: Jewish Publication Society of America, 1949), Vol. II, pp. 193–94.

"We have a means of atonement as effective as the Temple, and it is doing deeds of loving kindness." Just as willingly as men would contribute bricks and mortar for rebuilding a sanctuary, so willingly ought they to contribute renunciation, self-sacrifice, and love for the building of a sacred community.

Earlier Pharisaism had held that the Temple should be everywhere, even in the home and hearth. Now Yohanan taught that sacrifice greater than the Temple's must characterize the life of the community. If one wants to do something for God in a time when the Temple is no more, the offering must be the gift of selfless compassion. The holy altar must be built in the streets and marketplaces of the world, as the purity of the Temple formerly had to be observed in the streets and marketplaces of Jerusalem.

The kingdom of ritually pure priests, the holy people, living in the sacred land, must perceive its vocation: to offer itself as the perfect sacrifice to God, to renounce selfishness in favor of selfless love, to bring to the altar, which is the home and street, the gift of obedience to God, which is love of neighbor. The rite of ritual purity outwardly expresses the inner right; the priestly people in its holy place offers up itself. Psalmist and prophet had said no less. Isaiah had answered those who inquired, "Why have we fasted and thou seest it not?"

> *Is not this the fast that I choose:*
> *To loose the bonds of wickedness,*
> *to undo the thongs of the yoke,*
> *to let the oppressed go free,*
> *and to break every yoke?* (Isaiah 58:6)

The Psalmist had described the sacrifices of the Lord:

> *Hear, O my people, and I will speak,*
> *O Israel, I will testify against you.*
> *I am God, your God.*
> *I do not reprove you for your sacrifices;*
> *your burnt offerings are continually before me.*
> *I will accept no bull from your house,*
> *nor he-goat from your folds.*
> *For every beast of the forest is mine,*
> *the cattle on a thousand hills.*
> *I know all the birds of the air,*
> *and all that moves in the field is mine.*
> *If I were hungry, I would not tell you;*
> *for the world and all that is in it is mine.*
> *Do I eat the flesh of bulls,*
> *or drink the blood of goats?*
> *Offer to God a sacrifice of thanksgiving,*
> *and pay your vows to the Most High;*

and call upon me in the day of trouble—
I will deliver you, and you shall glorify me....
He who brings thanksgiving as his sacrifice honors me;
to him who orders his way aright
I will show the salvation of God. (Ps. 51:7–15, 23)

Just as the prophet and psalmist had described the cult in the setting of the streets, the sacrifice in terms of men's deeds, and piety in the framework of the soul and the spirit, so, after the Temple was destroyed, the heir and continuator of the Pharisees, Yohanan ben Zakkai, saw cult, sacrifice, and piety as aspect and mode of the common life. The priestly people became the last, most perfect sacrifice.

Let us now stand back from the complex traditions we have studied, and ask what we have learned about Pharisaic Judaism.

We have seen a small group of learned men eventually become the leaders of a whole nation. The esoteric and irrelevant laws kept by those men taught lessons which would save the people and guide it past its worst catastrophe.

But the Pharisees' success must be seen in a secular as well as a religious framework. Their movement from politics to piety and back into politics represents a sage, functional, and highly adaptive policy. Clearly, the party could not take over the government from the Maccabees, and under Herod any sort of political life was impossible. Later on, under Roman rule, certain aspects of political life were closed, but others were open to sectarians. After 70, the whole situation had changed. The ideals shaped under the Roman procurators (if not earlier) proved entirely functional in the new age. The Jews were weak, could not maintain their independence against Rome, and had to accomodate themselves to a situation of powerlessness.

After 70, with the destruction of Jerusalem, the whole people faced the situation of the earlier Pharisees, who had been few in number, unable to control the course of events, and forced to accomodate themselves to a situation they could not control and probably did not like. In turning the nation into a religious community, in eschewing force, which they did not have, in favor of faith, which they might nurture, and in lending matters of faith—even humble details of keeping the law—a cosmic, transcendent importance, the Pharisees succeeded in reshaping the life of Jewry in a way appropriate to their new situation. Their success in the next four centuries in Pharisaizing, or rabbinizing, the Jewish people assured that the Jews might flourish in an age in which they would be unable to make important decisions, but could very well control homely matters.

The Pharisees helped the Jews to reconcile themselves to their new situation, to accept what could not be changed, and to see significance in what could yet be decided. They invested powerlessness with such meaning that ordinary folk, living everyday lives, might still regard themselves as a kingdom of priests and a holy people. The ideals of Hillel and Yohanan ben Zakkai for 20 centuries illuminated the humble and, from a worldly viewpoint, unimportant affairs of a homeless, often persecuted, despised, and alien nation, dwelling alone among other nations.

Suggestions
for Further Reading

Chapters One and Three: Morton Smith, "Palestinian Judaism in the First Century," in *Israel: Its Role in Civilization,* ed. Moshe Davis (New York: Harper & Row, Publishers, 1956); Saul Lieberman, *Greek in Jewish Palestine* and *Hellenism in Jewish Palestine* (New York: Jewish Theological Seminary of America, 1942, 1950); Elias J. Bickerman, *From Ezra to the Last of the Maccabees. Foundations of Postbiblical Judaism* (New York: Schocken Books, Inc., 1962); Victor Tcherikover, *Hellenistic Civilization and the Jews,* trans. S. Applebaum (Philadelphia: Jewish Publication Society of America, 1959).

Chapter Four: W.D. Davies, *The Setting of the Sermon on the Mount* (Cambridge: Cambridge University Press, 1964).

Chapters Two, Five through Eight: Jacob Neusner, *The Rabbinic Traditions about the Pharisees before 70* (Leiden: E.J. Brill, 1971), I–III; *Life of Yohanan ben Zakkai* (Leiden: E.J. Brill, 1970); *Development of a Legend: Studies on the Traditions Concerning Yohanan ben Zakkai* (Leiden: E. J. Brill, 1970).

Historical background: Palestine—Emil Schürer, *A History of the Jewish People in the Age of Jesus Christ,* trans. and rev. by Geza Vermes

and Fergus Millar (Edinburgh: T. & T. Clark, 1972 *et seq.*) ; Babylonia—
Jacob Neusner, *A History of the Jews in Babylonia, I. The Parthian Period*
(Leiden: E.J. Brill, 1970).

Studies of the state of the question and bibliographies: A brief and
comprehensive account of current scholarship on the Pharisees is A. Michel
and J. LeMoyne, "Pharisiens," in *Suppléments* to the *Dictionnaire de la
Bible,* ed. Henri Cazelles and Andre Feuillet, Fascicule 39 (Paris, 1964), pp.
1022–1024, and Fascicule 40 (Paris, 1965), pp. 1026–1115. For Josephus, a
compendious bibliography is provided by Heinz Schreckenberg, *Bibliographie
zu Flavius Josephus* (Leiden, 1968: E.J. Brill). An important commentary
on recent scholarship is Louis H. Feldman, *Scholarship on Philo and Josephus (1937–1962)* in *Yeshiva University Studies in Judaica* (New York:
Bloch Publishing Co., 1963). Bibliographical studies of critical, traditional,
and pseudocritical scholarship on the Pharisees are found in my *The Rabbinic Traditions about the Pharisees before 70 III. Conclusions. Appendix:
Bibliographical Reflections,* pp. 320–68.

Later rabbinical Judaism: Jacob Neusner, *History of the Jews in
Babylonia* (Leiden: E.J. Brill, 1966–1970)), II–V; *There We Sat Down.
The Story of Classical Judaism in the Period in Which It Was Taking
Shape* (Nashville: Abingdon Press, 1972) ; and *Way of Torah: An Introduc-
tion to Judaism* (Belmont: Dickenson Publishing Co., 1970) ; for Palestine,
George Foot Moore, *Judaism in the First Centuries of the Christian Era.
The Age of the Tannaim* (Cambridge: Harvard University Press, 1927),
I–III.

Glossary

A fortiori An argument, called in Talmudic literature *qal vehomer,* lit.: light and heavy, in which it is claimed that what is the case in a lenient situation will certainly be regarded as the case in a stringent situation.

Apocrypha A book attributed, or pertaining to, biblical times, but not accepted into the canon of the Hebrew Scriptures; rather, hidden away.

Aqiba Important rabbi of Yavneh, responsible for development of exegetical principles that greatly expanded the possibilities of applying Scripture to new legal problems.

b. ben, son of.

Baba b. Buta A contemporary of Hillel, pictured as very pious, who, while adhering to the House of Shammai, knew that the law "really" is as decided by the House of Hillel.

Bar Kokhba General who claimed to be the Messiah, led a revolt against Rome between 132 and 135 A.D.

Bene Bathyrans Babylonian Jews settled in the frontier of Palestine by Herod, the Bathyrans (after the name of their village, Bathyra) were important Temple officials before 70 A.D., and contested the authority of Yohanan b. Zakkai at Yavneh afterward.

Gamaliel II Head of the Yavneh consistory from *ca.* 80 A.D. to *ca.* 120 A.D. Loyal to Rome, he was deposed before the Bar Kokhba War.

Gezerah Shavah Logical category: an equal or identical category, an analogy between two laws established on the basis of the verbal likeness of the texts in which they occur; an argument by analogy.

Havurah Fellowship, from *haver*, fellow, member or associate of Pharisaic sect.

Heave offering The priest's share of the crop, that which is raised up (*Terumah*) from the crop for the priest.

Heqqesh The analogy between two laws which rests on a biblical intimation or on a principle common to both; a law derived by analogy.

Judah [b. Ilai] Important authority at Usha, *ca.* 150 A.D.

Judah the Patriarch Head of the Palestinian Jewish government from *ca.* 170 to *ca.* 210 A.D., promulgated the *Mishnah,* code of the Oral Law of the rabbinical schools.

Levirate Marriage If a husband dies without children, his brother marries his wife (Deut. 25:ff.). This is known as a Levirate marriage.

Mamzer Illegitimate child according to Talmudic law, e.g., the progeny of parents who may not legally marry under any circumstances.

Meir Important authority at Usha, master of Judah the Patriarch.

Mekhilta Tannaitic commentary on the Book of Exodus.

Midrash Exegesis or commentary on a biblical verse.

Mishnah Law code, in six parts, promulgated *ca.* 200 by Judah the Patriarch, dealing with agricultural, festival and Sabbath, family life, civil and criminal, Temple cult, and ritual purity laws.

Nasi Patriarch, head of the Jewish community.

Nisan Month in early spring, corresponding to April.

Peah The "corner of the field" one must leave for the poor; an agricultural tax.

Pericope A section, or completed unit, of tradition.

Pesah Paschal sacrifice, on the eve of Passover.

Prozbul A declaration made in court before the execution of a loan, to the effect that the law of limitation by the entrance of the Sabbatical Year shall not apply to the loan to be transacted.

Pseudepigrapha A book attributed by its author to an eminent ancient authority, e.g., to Adam, or Moses, or Ezra, in order to gain greater credence.

Qal vehomer   See *a fortiori.*

R.   Rabbi; master of Pharisaic-rabbinical Torah.

Rav   Third century Babylonian master, died *ca.* 250.

Red Heifer Sacrifice   The Red Heifer (*Parah Adumah*) is burned in accordance with the laws of Num. 19:1–22; the ashes are mixed with water, which is used in purification rites.

Sadoq   Jerusalemite Pharisee, active at Yavneh, died *ca.* 75 A.D.

Seder   Lit.: Order. Here: The Order of the Passover meal. Also: A section of the Mishnah.

Sifra   Tannaitic commentary on Leviticus.

Sifré   Tannaitic commentary on Numbers and Deuteronomy.

Tanna   Repeater, memorizer of traditions of the rabbis from 70 to *ca.* 200 A.D. Tannaitic: Traditions attributed to masters of that same period. A *Tannaitic midrash* is a biblical commentary produced by, or attributed to, a rabbi who flourished between the destruction of the Temple and the redaction of the Mishnah.

Terminus ante quem   The point before which a saying or story had to have received the form in which we now have it.

Tosefta   Supplement: Tannaitic traditions shaped at the same time as the Mishnah, but not included in the Mishnah, were redacted in the Tosefta, the supplement to the Mishnah, in approximately the same period. Thus: Corpus of traditions from 70 to 200 A.D., secondary and additional to the Mishnah.

Usha   Galilean town where rabbinical government was reestablished after Bar Kokha War. Adj.: Ushan.

Yavneh   South coastal town in Palestine where rabbinical movement was founded by Yohanan b. Zakkai in 70 A.D. Adj.: Yavnean.

Zuz   A small coin, penny.

Index of Biblical
and Talmudic Passages

Acts of the Apostles
    4:1–2, 72
    5:34–39, 72
    5:34, 8, 54, 81, 99
    15:5, 72
    22:3, 47
    23:6–9, 72
    26:5, 72

Deuteronomy
    4:6, 8
    6:7, 112
    15:3, 14
    15:9–10, 15
    18:4, 118
    24:1, 113–14
    25:5–10, 86
    28:47, 150
    33:3, 19

Exodus
    4:22, 39
    38:26, 151

Genesis
    49:10, 98

Hosea
    6:6, 75, 98, 151

Isaiah
    7:21, 118
    10:34, 145
    65:8–9, 127

John
    1:24, 69
    3:1, 72
    4:1, 69
    7:32, 69
    7:45, 69
    8:3, 69
    8:12–13, 69
    9:13–17, 70
    9:40, 70
    11:46–47, 69
    11:57, 69

John *(cont.)*
    12:19, 69
    12:42–43, 69
    18:3, 69
    21:1–8, 69

Leviticus
    25: 29–30, 18–19

Luke
    5:17–26, 70
    5:29–39, 74
    6:1–11, 74
    7:30, 71
    7:36–39, 69
    10:25–28, 72
    11:16, 69
    11:29–30, 69
    11:37–41, 75
    11:53–54, 69
    21:1, 71
    13:31, 72
    14:1–6, 74
    16:10–14, 71
    16:18, 69
    17:20, 69
    18:9–14, 71
    19:39, 69
    20:19–26, 69
    20:27–40, 72
    20:45–47, 76
    26:6–13, 69

Mark
    2:2–10, 113
    2:15–27, 78
    2:15–28, 74
    3:1–6, 74, 78
    3:4, 79
    7:1–13, 75
    7:1–23, 78
    7:15, 79
    8:11–12, 69
    10:2–10, 69, 115
    11:25, 71
    12:13–17, 69
    12:18–27, 72
    12:28–34, 72
    12:38–40, 76
    14:3–9, 69

Matthew
    2:15–23, 74
    3:7, 70
    5:20, 70
    6:5, 71
    6:6, 71
    7:1ff, 79
    7:15–21, 79
    8:15, 71
    9:10–17, 74
    9:11–14, 70
    9:34, 70
    12:1–14, 74–75
    12:38–40, 69
    15:1–20, 75
    16:1–4, 69
    9:3–12, 69
    19:16–30, 71
    21:45, 69
    22:15–22, 69
    22:23–33, 72
    22:34–40, 72
    23:1–36, 76, 78–79
    23:2–3, 79
    23:4, 79
    23:16–19, 79
    23:23, 79
    23:25, 79
    27:67, 69

Micah
    7:1, 127

Numbers
    9:2, 24
    9:3, 28
    28:2, 23, 28
    28:10, 33

Phillippians
    3:5, 47

Proverbs
    11:24, 22

Psalms
    68:20, 40
    119:126, 22

I Samuel
    4:13, 145
    25:18, 118

Sifra Behar
    4:8, 18

Sifra Shemini
    8:5, 120

Sifra Tazria
    1:5, 139

Sifré Deuteronomy
    113, 14
    166, 118
    269, 114

Avot
    1:12–14, 19
    2:5–7, 20
    4:5, 11

Berakhot
    1:3, 112

ʿEduyyot
    8:4, 119–20, 1

Gittin
    8:9, 140–41
    9:10, 114

Ḥagigah
    2:2, 104, 106–108, 110, 119, 121, 128,
        132
    2:3, 107–108, 110

Parah
    3:5, 132

Sotah
    9:9, 127

Terumot
    5:4, 116

ʿUqsin
    3:8, 121

Yevamot
    1:4, 125

Bava Qama
    8:13, 128

Berakhot
    1:4, 113
    2:21, 22
    6:24, 22

Gittin
    8:8, 141

Ḥagigah
    2:8, 106, 132
    2:9, 126
    2:10, 109
    2:11, 110

Pisha
    4:13, 24

Sotah
    13:3, 130
    13:7, 129

Pesaḥim
    6:1, 29

Sukkah
    2:8, 102

Taʿanit
    4:2, 35

Yevamot
    6:6, 102

'Eruvin
13b, 102

Gittin
81a, 141

Menahot
10b, 134

Pesahim
66a–b, 34

Qiddushin
66a, 60, 94–95

Shabbat
17a, 36
30b–31a, 39

General Index

Abba, R., 101
    Abba Saul, 104, 109, 120
Abbaye, 94
Abtalion
    Hillel traditions, 26–27, 29–32
    laying on of hands, 104–106
    purity laws, 82, 85
Academies
    poor students, 126–27
    Usha, 123–41
    Yavneh, 97–122
Adiabene, 147
Agent, liability for, 85
Agricultural laws, 83
    Yavnean traditions, 116–18
Alexandrian wheat, 85
Antigonus of Sokho, 82, 84
Antipater the Idumean, 59, 91
Aqiba
    divorce, 113–15
    fleece offering, 118–19
    grapeclusters, 128
    Hillel traditions, 17
    historic themes, 136–37
    purity laws, 119–20

    rabbinical traditions, 93
    Ushan traditions, 123, 125
    Yavnean traditions, 99, 102–103, 112
Archelaus, 135
Aretas the Arab, 62
Aristobulus, 50–52, 61–63, 66, 91–92

Baba b. Buta, 110–11
Bannus, 46–47, 55
Bar Kokhba, 41, 99–100, 123, 126–27, 130–31; 135, 137, 143–44
Bathyrans, 27–35
Bibi, R., 102
Bickerman, Elias, 9, 49–51, 53, 54n
Bultmann, Rudolf, 78, 115

Charlesworth, M. P., 149
Circumcision, 87, 138–40

Damages, assessment of, 87
David, descendants, 35
Davies, W. D., 79
Day of Atonement, 85
Dead Sea Scrolls, 87
Dietary laws, 90

Diogenes, 51, 62
Divorce, 69, 78
    Rabbinical traditions, 83, 85
    Yavnean traditions, 113–15
Doves, price of, 86

Eleazar b. Azariah, R., 113
Eleazar ben Poirah, 58–60
Eliehoenai b. Haqqof, 132
Eliezer b. Hyrcanus
    heave offering, 116–17
    purity laws, 119–30
    Yavnean traditions, 98, 102–103, 111
Epiphanes, 48, 58
Essenes, 4, 10
    administration of Pharisees, 53, 55–56, 64–65
    Rabbinical traditions, 90

Fasting, 73, 78
Fleece offering, 118–19
Fourth philosophy, 4, 66

Gamaliel, 8
    Christian traditions about Pharisees, 71–82, 80
    Rabbinical traditions, 81–82, 85–89
    Yavnean traditions, 99, 111
Gamaliel II, 41, 54, 93–94
    heavenly echo, 130–31
    laying on of hands, 105
    Ushan traditions, 123
    Yavnean traditions, 99–100, 103, 105
Golden rule, 19–22
Gospels and Pharisaic traditions, 67–80
Governmental administration, 45–66
Grapeclusters, 127–29, 135–36
Guryo, 129

Haggai, 129
Hanamel the Egyptian, 132
Hananiah, 137
Heavenly echo, 101–102, 129–31
Heave-offering, 85
Herod, 7–8, 27, 35, 153
    administration of Pharisees, 50, 52, 55, 60, 63–64, 66
    Christian traditions, 71–72
    Rabbinical traditions, 90–92
Hillel, 5, 9, 57, 146, 154
    ancestry, 35

Bathyrans, 27–35
Christian traditions, 67–80
circumcision, 138–40
crown sayings, 19–22
divorce, 114–15, 140–41
fleece offering, 118–19
gentleness, 37–40
golden rule, 19–22
heavenly echo, 129–31
heave offering, 116–18
historic themes, 135–36
influences, 13–44
laying on of hands, 104–11
loans, 14–17, 43
Passover and Sabbath, 23–29
purity laws, 120
property redemption, 17–19
Rabbinical traditions, 82, 85–86, 91–93, 95
Sabbath preparations, 40
Shammai disputes, 35–41
Shema, reciting, 112–13
Ushan traditions, 125–31
Yavnean traditions, 98–122
Hyrcanus, John, 43, 49–51, 57–63, 91

Ishmael, R., 113, 130
Ishmael b. Phiabi, 132

Jannaeus, Alexander, 49–52, 57, 59, 61–65, 91–95
Jesus
    divorce, 114–15
    Hillel traditions, 13–35, 44
    Pharisaism, 1–2, 5, 11
    Yavnean traditions, 98
John the Apostle, 70–72, 74
John the Baptist, 70
Josephus, 1–4, 7
    Hillel traditions, 14, 43
    Pharisees appraised, 45–66
    political policies, 143, 147–49, 151
    Rabbinical traditions, 81, 90–93, 95
    Yavnean traditions, 99
Joshua, R., 144
Joshua b. Hananiah, 137
    Yavnean traditions, 98, 102–103, 111
Joshua b. Perahiah, 82, 85, 104–105, 107
Jotapata, 45
Jubilee Year, 17–19, 85
Judah, R., 134; Ushan traditions, 131

Judah b. Baba, R., 128–29, 134–36
  heavenly echo, 129, 131
Judah b. Gedidiah, 59
Judah b. Ilai, 134
  laying on of hands, 106–107
Judah b. R. Pazzai, R., 102
Judah b. Tabbai, 82, 85, 104–106, 132, 136
Judah the Maccabee, 48–49
Judah the Patriarch, 4, 113, 132
  divorce, 114–15
  Hillel traditions, 27, 35, 41
  historic themes, 134–36
  post-Ushan circle, 138–41
  Rabbinical traditions, 92, 94
  Ushan traditions, 124
  Yavnean traditions, 97, 105, 107
Judah the Pharisee, 66
Judas, 55

Law and the Pharisees, 82–90
Laying on of hands, 85
  Yavnean tradition, 104–11
Levi, R., 35
Levirate marriage, 86–87
Leviticus, 83
Lieberman, Saul, 10
Loans, 14–17
Luke, 72, 77; traditions, 70

Maccabees, 35, 55, 153
  administration of Pharisees, 48–50, 52, 53, 57–59, 65–66
  Rabbinical traditions, 90–91
Marriage contract, 85–87
Mattathias, 48
Matthias, 45
Meal-time traditions, 73–74, 78–80
Meir, R.
  laying on of hands, 105–107
  Ushan traditions, 132–36
Menahem, 104–106
Menstruants, 85–86
Moore, George Foot, 4
Morality, 74

Nicolas of Damascus, 64
Nicodemus, 71–72, 80–81
Nittai the Arbelite, 104–105

Onias, 133–34, 137

Pascal sacrifice, 23–29, 85
Passover observance, 15, 85, 88
Passover and Sabbath, 23–29
Paul, 71–72, 81
Pheroras, 7–8, 52
Philo, 9
Philosophical schools, 52–54, 55–57
Phylacteries, 85
Ploughing in seventh year, 85
Pompey, 50, 55, 146
Poor students, 126–27
Praying, 83
Property redemption, 17–19
Prozbul, 14–17, 43
Purity laws, 36, 73–80, 83–85, 119–120

Qumranian law, 87–89, 93

Rava, 94
Ritual purity, 73–76, 78–80, 83, 85–86, 88, 91

Sabbath
  Christian traditions, 70, 73–75, 78
  preparation for, 40
  Rabbinical traditions, 85
  Yavnean traditions, 100–101
Saddok, 55
Sadducees, 4, 10
  administration of Pharisees, 53–58, 64–65
  Christian traditions, 70, 72
  Rabbinical traditions, 91
Saddoq, R., 21
Salome, Alexandra, 50–53, 57, 60–65, 91
Samuel, R., 101
Samuel the Small, 129–31, 135
Second tithe, 85
Seventh year debts, 14–17, 43, 85
Sexual relations, 85–86
Shammai, 9, 57
  circumcision, 138–40
  divorce, 114–15, 140–41
  fleece offering, 118–19
  heavenly echo, 131
  heave offering, 116–18
  Hillel disputes, 35–41
  impatience, 37–40
  laying on of hands, 104–11
  purity laws, 120

Shammai (cont.)
  Rabbinical traditions, 82, 85–86, 92–93
  Shema, recital of, 112–13
  Ushan traditions, 125–31
  Yavnean traditions, 98–122
Shema
  recital of, 87, 122
  Yavnean traditions, 111–13
Shemaiah
  Hillel traditions, 26–27, 29–32
  laying on of hands, 104–107
Shimei, 133
Simeon ben Eleazar, 140–41
Simeon b. Gamaliel, 41, 54
  administration of Pharisees, 47, 54,
    65–66
  heavenly echo, 131
  laying on of hands, 105
  Rabbinical traditions, 81–82, 86, 93, 95
  Ushan traditions, 123
  Yavnean traditions, 98–100, 103
Simeon b. Shetah, 60
  laying on of hands, 104–106
  purity laws, 82, 85, 91
  Ushan traditions, 132
  Yavnean traditions, 99
Simeon the Just, 129, 131–36
  purity laws, 82, 84
Smith, Morton, 8–9, 11, 64–65, 84, 147
Sukkot festival, 85

Tarfon, R., 102–103; Shema, recital of,
  112–13
Taxation, 68, 73–74, 78–80
Temple cult, 132–33
Tithing, 73–74, 76, 78–80, 83, 86
Titus, 46

Usha, 41–42
  Academy and traditions, 123–41
  historic themes, 134–38

Judah the Patriarch and circle, 138–41
laying on of hands, 105
Rabbinical traditions, 92, 94

Vespasian, 45–46, 144–47

War, 48–54; see also Bar Kokhba
Wolfson, Harry A., 9–10

Yavneh, 3
  academy and traditions, 92–122
  administrative influences, 54–55, 65
  Christian traditions about Pharisees,
    68, 79
  Hillel traditions, 13, 17, 22, 27, 36, 42
  historic Pharisees, 144–47, 149
  Rabbinical traditions, 92–93
Yohanan, R., 102
Yohanan b. Zakkai, 34
  Hillel traditions, 17, 27, 41
  historic themes, 137
  Shema, recital of, 111
  Vespasian, 144–47, 149
  Yavneh traditions, 97–122
Yohanan the High Priest, 131–32
Yosi b. Halafta, R., 126
Yosi b. Yoezer
  grapecluster, 127–29
  laying on of hands, 104–105, 107
  purity laws, 82, 84, 119–21
  Yavnean traditions, 99, 104–105, 107,
    120
Yosi b. Yohanan
  grapeclusters, 127–29
  laying on of hands, 104–105
  purity laws, 82, 84

Zealots, 4, 65, 146, 148
Zechariah, 129
Zeitlin, Solomon, 60